CHASING
THE
RABBIT

CHASING
THE
RABBIT

How Market Leaders
Outdistance the Competition
and How Great Companies
Can Catch Up and Win

STEVEN J. SPEAR

New York   Chicago   San Francisco   Lisbon   London
Madrid   Mexico City   Milan   New Delhi   San Juan
Seoul   Singapore   Sydney   Toronto

The **McGraw·Hill** Companies

1 2 3 4 5 6 7 8 9 0   DOC/DOC   0 1 0 9 8

ISBN: 978-0-07-149988-0
MHID: 0-07-149988-1

This publication is designed to provide accurate and authoritative information in regard to the subject matter covered. It is sold with the understanding that the publisher is not engaged in rendering legal, accounting, or other professional service. If legal advice or other expert assistance is required, the services of a competent professional person should be sought.

—From a Declaration of Principles Jointly Adopted
by a Committee of the American Bar Association
and a Committee of Publishers and Associations

McGraw-Hill books are available at special quantity discounts to use as premiums and sales promotions, or for use in corporate training programs. To contact a representative, please visit the Contact Us pages at www.mhprofessional.com.

This book is printed on acid-free paper.

Library of Congress Cataloging-in-Publication Data
Spear, Steven J.
    Chasing the rabbit / by Steven J. Spear.
        p. cm.
    Includes bibliographical references and index.
    ISBN-13: 978-0-07-149988-0 (alk. paper)
    ISBN-10: 0-07-149988-1 (alk. paper)
    1. Organizational effectiveness. 2. Management. I. Title.
    HD58.9.S676 2009
    658.4—dc22

                                                                    2008036858

In memory of
Jacob Irgang (1930–1995),
Korean War veteran, Purple Heart recipient,
Stuyvesant High School teacher extraordinaire, 1963–1995.
*He knew his students were capable of far more
than even they realized.*

CONTENTS

FOREWORD

The term *theory* gets a bum rap among most managers because managers are practical people and theory normally is associated with the word *theoretical*, which has a connotation of impracticality. However, a good theory is consummately practical because a well-researched theory is a contingent statement of what causes what and why. The law of gravity, for example, actually is a theory. It is extremely useful because it allows us to predict in advance, without having to collect experimental data, that if we step off a cliff, we will fall. Good theories allow us to predict the result of an action accurately.

Even though most managers do not think of themselves as being theory-driven, they are in reality voracious consumers of theory. Every time managers make a plan or take an action, it is based on some theory or mental model in the back of their minds that leads them to believe that the action being taken will lead to the desired result. The problem is that managers are rarely aware of the theories they are using and often use the wrong theories for the situations in which they find themselves. It is the absence of conscious, trustworthy theories of cause and effect that makes success in building successful businesses seem random.

Because of the central role good theories play in bringing predictability to management and innovation, I've spent a good portion of my academic career studying what good theories are: How can I tell a good theory from a bad one when I'm looking at it? I've tried to help researchers learn how to build valid theories that managers can rely on so that their actions have the desired effects. Unfortunately, as our understanding of the theory-building process has coalesced, the report card on most of those who research and write about management has been abysmal. The preponderance of what is written for managers about management is bad theory and should not be trusted. I'm not the only one who has reached this conclusion: Professors Jeffrey Pfeffer and Robert Sutton at Stanford and the late Professor Sumantra Ghoshal of the London Business School have written eloquently about this problem. Professor Phil Rosenzweig at the Institute for Management Development in Lausanne recently published *The Halo Effect*, a scathing, cogent, and compelling indictment of most management research.

A happy and humble young man named Steve Spear walked into this paucity of sound management theory about 12 years ago as a doctoral student at the Harvard Business School. He was fortunate to have been taken under the wing of Professor H. Kent Bowen, one of the world's foremost materials scientists, for whom the scientific method of building robust theory was second nature and whose discouragement with the state of management research mirrored my own. The puzzle Bowen and Spear decided to unravel was intriguing. Despite Toyota's openness and all that had been written about the "secrets" to its success, no other company had been able to replicate Toyota's achievements in profitably making its cars continuously better and cheaper (when adjusted for quality and performance improvements). Their hunch, which proved right, was that prior students of Toyota's methods had observed "artifacts" of the system such as lean (low-inventory) manufacturing and just-in-time "pull" scheduling of production. However, those researchers were measuring *correlations* between a factory's possession of those attributes and its performance. No scholar had unearthed the *causal* mechanism that led to what Steve ultimately termed a self-improving system.

Whereas many business researchers prefer to collect data from the Internet or from easily accessed databases so that they can analyze the data in the comfort of their offices, Steve essentially got himself employed in the factories of Toyota and its suppliers and competitors to learn from the inside out and answer the question, "How do these guys *think* when they design and improve a process?" Steve's interest wasn't just in fabrication and assembly processes. It spanned processes such as training people, designing products, building management strength, and maintaining equipment as well. Every evening, Steve returned to his room and painstakingly chronicled everything he had observed.

Out of that extraordinary detail, Steve distilled the mental models and frameworks that the people at Toyota instinctively followed when they designed, used, and improved a process of any sort. Those things weren't written down anywhere, yet people seemed instinctively to follow them as if the rules were tattooed on the backs of their hands. Nobody—not even Toyota's most senior managers—could articulate those culture-embedded instincts. Yet when Steve described them, they instantly agreed that those instincts were guiding their actions. Steve had uncovered the fundamental causal mechanisms underlying the success of the Toyota Production System. I honestly think that history will judge Steve Spear's doctoral thesis to have been the finest, most impactful thesis ever written at the Harvard Business School, and that includes my own doctoral work on the phenomenon known as "disruptive technology."

We were blessed that the Harvard Business School invited Steve to join the faculty so that Professor Bowen and I could continue working with him as a colleague.

As the great historian of science Thomas Kuhn taught, the key to developing a theory that is valid internally and externally is to seek anomalies, to find instances in which the present explanation of causality *does not* yield the results that the theory predicts. In contrast to researchers who believe that a theory is strengthened by the finding of more and more examples in which the theory *works* to get ever-higher levels of statistical significance, the scientific method requires researchers to search for instances in which the theory *does not* work. That is what Steve did next.

To this point, those who had studied the artifacts of Toyota's system had convinced us that the system was useful only in industries in which physically discrete products are manufactured. In an anomaly-seeking mode, Professor Bowen and Steve decided to see if the frameworks they had uncovered, which came to be called the "DNA of the Toyota Production System," could lead to similar results in a dangerous, complicated, capital-intensive process industry such as aluminum production, which is about as far from the assembly of transmissions as one can get. There was nothing to study passively in this stage of Steve's research, because no company besides Toyota was following those rules. Therefore, Spear and Bowen taught the rules to the executives at Alcoa and helped them teach and reteach them throughout their company. The management then applied the rules to the redesign of all sorts of processes in the company under the name of the Alcoa Business System (ABS). The results were astounding. In an industry in which nobody had thought that Toyota's methods were applicable, the company continues to report that its annual savings from applying ABS exceed $1 billion. Because Steve had gone beyond observing the statistical correlation between attributes and outcomes and had articulated the fundamental engine of causality; the rules worked like a charm in this polar-opposite industry.

To help with Steve's ongoing efforts to find a very different industry in which the Toyota DNA would prove *not* to be useful, Bowen and I next invited him to go to the other edge of the world with the following challenge: "The causal mechanism—the rules—clearly works in making cars, mattresses, and aluminum. I bet it doesn't work in managing a horrifically complicated service business such as a hospital." We then opened a few doors for him. Steve taught administrators in a small Boston-area hospital and then those in much larger ones in Pittsburgh what those rules are. He helped them teach their employees how to design processes that follow the rules and how to improve them with great haste when the initial design shows itself to be flawed. Again, the results were astounding in terms of errors avoided, costs reduced, and lives saved. Remarkably, Steve discovered that employees in those institutions were much happier working within the rules than without them because the rules made it easy for them to fix the broken processes that had made their work lives so frustrating.

Compared with the problems most people deal with, the contexts in which Steve has developed, refined, and tested his theories of continuously improving processes were bafflingly complex. Cars are made from 10,000 components, meaning that hundreds of thousands of things can go wrong. Aluminum is made with massive pieces of equipment that cost tens of millions of dollars and operate at temperatures, pressures, voltages, and speeds that aren't just dangerous but take place at the edge of what the laws of chemistry and physics define as possible. Hospitals try to coordinate the work of thousands of people to save thousands of lives from a nearly infinite variety of medical conditions. Rather than proposing complex solutions to those complex systems, Steve breaks down the complexity. All these systems, at the "atomic" level, consist of activities, connections, and pathways. You get them right, and even unfathomably complex systems become high performing and self-improving. Steve did research by teaching people to take action, and the quality of his theories was measured in the billions of dollars in additional profits that have been earned, the accidents that have been avoided, and the lives that have been saved that would not have been if his rules had not been followed.

Steve continues to improve his understanding by searching for companies and industries in which the rules do not work, but so far he has been "disappointed." The rules seem to be very broadly applicable principles of management. They are the causal mechanisms that, when followed, cause a company's processes to keep doing better and better, whether they are processes for understanding customers, designing products that address customers' needs, or making products at ever-increasing levels of quality and ever-decreasing cost.

This book is not the sort of easy, entertaining paperback you can buy in the San Francisco airport and finish by the time you land in Boston. There's no fluff here, no simple silver-bullet solutions to all your problems. But this is probably the most insightful book about quality and process that has ever been written. Steve Spear's research passes every litmus test for good management theory. It is internally valid, meaning that its conclusions derive unambiguously from its premises and that all other plausible alternative explanations have been ruled out. It is externally valid in that it is applicable to companies in a broad range of industries that are very different from one another. What's truly remarkable is that the validity of these ideas was not established by applying them to other data sets from the past. Instead, it was verified by applying these causal rules in companies that were not performing remarkably well and then seeing the quality, cost, and profitability of those companies' products and services improve continuously as they learned to follow the rules. Thus, Steve can teach us not just *what* to do but *how* to do it.

I count having been one of Steve Spear's colleagues and advisers to be one of my foremost credentials. I hope that from the pages of this book you'll be able to learn from Steve even a fraction of the valuable insights I've gotten as I've worked with him. In his field he has no peers.

Clayton M. Christensen
The Robert and Jane Cizik
Professor of Business Administration
Harvard Business School
Boston, MA
July 2008

PREFACE

Many organizations encounter ferocious competition in the marketplace. Try as they might to set themselves apart, any static, snapshot differences are fleeting and temporary. Identify and meet some unfilled customer need in an untapped market in a novel fashion and challengers will soon flood in. Find a preferred supplier and others will quickly clamor to gain access. Employ a new scientific insight or technological approach and everyone else will quickly adopt it. The result of such market fluidity is often intense, cutthroat rivalry. Yet here and there, we see companies and organizations, in and out of the private sector, that manage to stay ahead of the pack for years or even decades at a time. Displaying combinations of speed, agility, responsiveness, and endurance, they see and seize opportunities and, by the time rivals have responded, the leaders have raced on to further opportunities, leaving competitors in their wake.

Examples of these pack-leading rabbits, *high-velocity organizations*, whom everyone else chases but never catches, abound. Toyota generates remarkable profits year in and year out, decade after decade, based on its capacity to race past and stay ahead. While competitors sought to emulate the company's early success, launching their own affordable, reliable small cars, Toyota kept improving in that niche while adding trucks, SUVs, and minivans to its portfolio, building new brands like the Lexus and Scion, introducing new technology like the Prius's hybrid drive system, and "globally localizing"—transforming itself from an exporter to a company with design and production operations worldwide.

Southwest Airlines has recorded profits for more than 30 years while its competitors struggle to hang on, with other storied airlines going out of business. It has pioneered new routes while pressing ahead with service improvements, speed in basic operations, and continued increases in efficiency. Alcoa has had great economic success while making itself the safest large manufacturer in the country—cutting the risk of on-the-job injury by more than 95 percent while other manufacturers managed only a fraction of that improvement.

There are other examples, perhaps less well known but also extremely impressive. In the high-tech world of integrated-circuit manufacturing, "fabs" supply similar products to the same electronics companies and purchase equipment from the same vendors. They level their own playing field by participating in standards-setting industry consortia. Yet some fabs support far greater product variety, generate less scrap, and require less time from start to finish, so they are better able to respond to changing market needs quickly and economically. As for noncommercial examples, the U.S. Navy's Nuclear Power Propulsion Program has recorded one milestone after another since its inception in 1948. Yet despite all that was required to launch the first nuclear-powered submarine, the

USS Nautilus, in 1954, and despite the countless hours of nuclear reactor operation and the countless miles logged by nuclear-powered warships since then, there hasn't been a single injury due to reactor failure. The program's chief rival, the Soviet Navy, has a far less enviable record, littered with accidents, loss of crews and ships, and environmental damage, while NASA, also responsible for manned missions in a hostile environment, has lost the crews of *Apollo 1*, *Challenger*, and *Columbia*. In the much different world of medical care, there are hospitals that deliver far better care to many more people at far less cost than is typical, even though they are treating the same ailments, using the same medical science, employing people trained at the same institutions, and are subject to the same regulations and payment systems.

Since the examples I have mentioned so far (and the examples I will mention later in the book) are so very dissimilar in their missions and circumstances, you might think it's enough to say that there are some organizations that are just plain better than others at doing what they do. But in fact, the organizations that I will discuss in *Chasing the Rabbit* have something more in common. They face a common problem and have identified a common solution, which keeps them performing way ahead of the pack and always getting better (the two go together). The problem is common to more than the front-running rabbits. That the solution has been used successfully by such a wide variety of organizations for such a variety of purposes indicates that the general theory I am presenting is independent of any particular industry or activity, and that there is a world of excellence waiting to be achieved in any number of endeavors. I hope *Chasing the Rabbit* contributes to that.

The common problem these organizations face is that they produce complex products or provide complex services, requiring many varied forms of skill and expertise. Their operations, the "systems of work" that involve many people of many disciplines using equipment of various types, are correspondingly complex, requiring that the efforts and contributions of many specialists be integrated and coordinated in a harmonious fashion. The difficulty is that the more numerous and varied the people, machines, and materials involved, the more ways they can interact with each other, often with unanticipated results. Eventually, so much is connected to so much else that the system becomes "unknowable." No matter how much effort and brain power go into designing a complex operation, it is impossible to design it perfectly and to predict how it will behave under every circumstance. It is in designing and operating their complex work—how they deal with the problem of unknowable, unpredictable systems—that the front-running, high-velocity rabbits set themselves apart. Their approach and its results are the subjects of this book.

Many of the organizations that I have studied, and many more with which you are familiar, believe that they manage systems of work in a purposeful fashion. But in fact, they don't. Rather, they manage individual functions and specialties, with these pieces coming together through hard work, goodwill, and improvisation. Your typical hospital, for instance, will have defined hierarchies, career paths, and professional standards within departments—internal medicine, pharmacy, and nursing, for example—but will have no one trained in or responsible for the start-to-finish process of prescribing, dispensing, and administering medication, which cuts across all three of those departments. They'll have great orthopedists, anesthesiologists, and therapists, but no one will be responsible for the start-to-finish process of hip replacement or knee repair. I've worked in an auto supplier's plant in which stamping, welding, and shipping operated as individual silos with no one responsible for converting customer orders and raw materials into successful shipments. It was left to the daily production-control meetings and a fair amount of expediting to achieve the appearance of synchronization. I've been in design settings in which engineering, quality assurance, installation, and customer service are each managed as if they operated largely independently; in fact, they are quite interdependent.

This is not the way in the high-velocity organizations we will meet. As much as they strive to advance their competence within disciplines, they understand that all the work they do has to be in service to the boundary-spanning processes by which they create value for their customers.

There is also a dynamic difference beyond the structural one just discussed. Any complex system will be riddled with a stream of unavoidable nuisances and inconveniences, the inevitable consequence of imperfect people trying to design perfectly something very complex. Most of the time these nuisances and inconveniences are just coped with or worked around. Most organizations assume that even the best operations they can devise will have a certain amount of unavoidable noise or chatter and that a certain amount of effort will always be siphoned off into firefighting; that's just the way life is.

High-velocity organizations adopt the opposite attitude, and it makes all the difference. They treat each problem, each instance of something not working out the way they expected it to, as the voice of the operation itself, saying, "You may have created me, but you still don't know me as well as you should. Look harder, learn more, and we'll get along better." Operations in these organizations are designed not only to do the job that needs to be done but to continually let the organization know that it still doesn't know all there is to know. When the operations speak, these organizations listen, learn, improve, and keep a sharp eye out for the next lesson.

What's more, they make sure that the lesson learned here and now is spread throughout the organization. And they make sure that their managers know how to work this way and how to train others to work this way.

All of this will be discussed in detail in *Chasing the Rabbit*, with plenty of examples of things going right and things going wrong, lessons being learned and lessons being ignored. The failures can be heartbreaking and infuriating, but I believe you will find the successes inspiring. They are within your reach, although not without effort. The successes of high-velocity, high-performance organizations do not depend on mustering a workforce all possessed of some extraordinary talent. With hundreds, thousands, and even tens of thousands of employees, that would be quite impossible. What makes these organizations high-velocity is the way they deliberately and consistently make the best use of the ordinary distribution of human talent, while their competitors let so much of it be ground between the wheels of repetitive frustration, firefighting, and failure.

ACKNOWLEDGMENTS

With discovery as a theme of *Chasing the Rabbit*, it is appropriate that I thank those who invested so heavily in the discoveries reported in this book. First is Professor H. Kent Bowen of Harvard Business School and of MIT before that. Kent opened the door for me to pursue graduate studies at the doctoral level, and his involvement in what I was doing went far beyond what anyone could expect or deserve on the strength of his or her own merits alone.

Hajime Ohba of Toyota has also been my teacher since I began this research. Toyota is one of the most intensively studied organizations in this era, with thousands of academic researchers, journalists, and practitioners seeking the firm's time and access. Toyota did not need another person pestering it for access, but Ohba invited me in nevertheless. While I was there, he made sure I learned without hesitation, obstacle, or obstruction. Whenever we were together, and there were many times since 1995 when he allowed me to learn from his experiences and the perspectives he had developed or when he coached me toward discoveries of my own. Typically, it was both at the same time.

When I was a student and later a faculty member at Harvard Business School, Professors Carliss Baldwin and Clayton Christensen were constant with their inspiration and support. Those familiar with their work will see Carliss's influence on my treatment of the structure of complex systems and Clay's influence when I write about the dynamics of innovative competitors. Less visible but equally vital was their generosity in helping me express my ideas as they were taking shape. It is no small honor that Clay agreed to write the foreword for this book, once again contributing to the betterment of my work.

Learning is inherently collaborative, especially learning about how groups collaborate for maximum effect. I am indebted to thousands of people who have let me into their worlds and the daily work they do. They include but certainly are not limited to Tosh Akioka, Jamie Bonini, Toshi Kitamura, Olivier LaReau, Lisa Nichols, Christine Parker, Bryant Sanders, Cindy Voss, and others at Toyota and its suppliers. Keith Turnbull at Alcoa was a tireless colearner and teacher. I owe thanks to them and his many colleagues, including Arnoldo Cruz, Pat Love, John Marushin, and Stan Vishnevsky.

We did not know if lessons from great companies such as Toyota and Alcoa would apply to something as far afield from automation and heavy industrial processes as health care. The answer wasn't obvious. Jim Reinertsen and John Dalton at the Beth Israel Deaconess Medical Center created opportunities for my colleagues and me to test ideas in practice, and former Alcoa CEO Paul O'Neill made further exploration possible with the Pittsburgh Regional Healthcare Initiative, where we worked with many people, including Vickie Pisowicz, Mark

Schmidhofer, and David Sharbaugh. Paul's relentless commitment to the well-being of other people—at Alcoa, in Pittsburgh hospitals, and more generally—is inspirational.

David Champion, my editor at *Harvard Business Review* for ten years, has helped me bring into focus what was of the greatest interest and impact. John Elder has shaped the content and delivery of my work by playing the role of thoughtful lay reader and editor par excellence for papers, cases, and especially for this book. Jeanne Glasser at McGraw-Hill worked tirelessly on this project.

Thank you to former MIT Sloan School dean Lester Thurow, who made problems of competitiveness, globalization, and technological progress a priority for a generation of students, and who believed that we could be part of the solution. Thank you also to Professor Mike Cusumano for his deep insights about great companies; to Professor David Hardt, who taught me so much about complex systems; and to Dick Samuels for the MIT-Japan Program.

I would be remiss not to thank my parents, grandparents, and great-grandparents for the examples they provided and the standards they set. Although any family will endure trials across several generations, mine has always demonstrated the importance of appreciating and repaying life's triumphs through kindness and service. I hope their legacy shows in my own work, as it certainly does in my brother Jonathan's efforts to advance innovative educational programs.

Finally, I have to say thank you close to home. Writing a book is a luxury, a rare opportunity to explore a topic in its many nuances. The time to do so is a gift. For this, I owe an unpayable debt to my wife, Miriam, and our children, Hannah,

Eve, and Jesse. They endured my time in the field to learn from other people and my late nights and early mornings of writing at home.

But the debt is deeper than that, as my research is inexorably interwined with personal milestones—meeting Miriam the first week of school, courting while in the midst of field work, and celebrating the birth of our first child (nearly) at graduation. Moreover, *Chasing the Rabbit* emphasizes that great things come from sweating the details. Miriam models that as an architect, mother, and wife, and it is an example taken up by our kids. I would be immeasurably worse off without her and them.

Steve Spear
Brookline, MA
July 2008

CHAPTER 1

GETTING TO THE FRONT OF THE PACK

Each year, my wife, Miriam, our kids, Hannah, Eve, and Jesse, and I watch the Boston Marathon, which passes near our home. After the cacophony of the police escort and the press teams roaring past, there is a surreal calm as the first one or two runners fly by. Nearly two hours into the race, with just three miles to go, their form is flawless, their breathing easy, their faces calm. Then the clamor resumes.

A few dozen yards behind the leaders is a tight knot of athletes, all world-class but not looking as good. Their rhythm is a little off; their expressions are slightly pained. They are jostling and elbowing each other, but for all the effort, their only hope is to be runner-up, chasing the front-running, pacesetting rabbits who are pursued but never caught.

The Boston Marathon only happens once a year, but every day we can see the same kind of ferocious competition among companies fighting for a consolation prize while one or two firms cruise to a victory which appears to be easy. In automobile manufacturing, commercial aviation, metal processing, integrated-circuit fabrication, financial services, and health care, just to name a few, we can find "fair" contests in which opponents go head to head in the same product categories, woo the same customers, source from the same suppliers, hire from the same labor pools, struggle with the same dangerous conditions, and obey the same regulations. The playing fields are so level and there is so little differentiation among the rivals that one should expect cutthroat, tooth-and-nail, dog-eat-dog competition, fleeting profitability, and unsustainable leadership. And for many companies, that's how it is. Yet a few rabbits are way out ahead, chased but never caught, generating a greater range and a higher quality of products and services, responding more quickly to the changing market, with fewer people, fewer resources, and fewer mishaps and accidents. While everyone else struggles to keep up, these *high-velocity organizations* race from success to success with growing market share, profitability, and reputation. In the marathon, everyone starts together and everyone crosses the half-way and three-quarters marks. The critical difference, of course, is that the rabbits hit each milestone first and, by the time their challengers get there, the rabbits are well on their way to the next one. So it is among organizations, as represented in Figure 1-1. Everyone advances over time, improving performance along various metrics such as quality, efficiency, product or service variety, workplace safety, and time to market. The problem for the pack is that the rabbit achieves a certain level before everyone else and, while others close in on where the rabbit was, it has darted away, still to be chased but not captured.

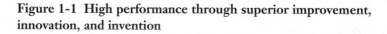

Figure 1-1 High performance through superior improvement, innovation, and invention

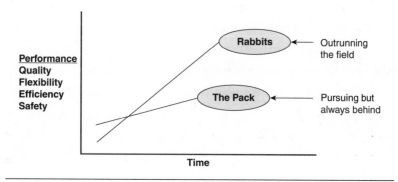

Rabbits Abound

Let me offer a few examples, beginning with the automobile industry. Every major manufacturer makes cars, trucks, SUVs, and minivans. Those vehicles come in economy, regular, and luxury versions and in small, medium, and large sizes. The manufacturers contend for customers in every major market; their dealerships are often within walking distance of each other. They have design and production facilities in every region, hire in all those places in overlapping job markets, and are subject to the same regional rules and regulations. They often buy from the same suppliers. I worked in a plant with people making parts for Toyota while many of the same people, using the same equipment, were also making parts for direct competitors.

In this highly competitive environment, while General Motors (GM) and Ford struggle from one year to the next and Daimler has shed Chrysler after destroying tens of billions of dollars in shareholder value in an ill-fated merger, Toyota roars from success to success. It raced past General Motors as the world's production leader, ran by Ford to become the second-largest seller of automobiles in North America, and passed Chrysler as the third-largest automaker in North America. While Ford shed its luxury brands, Toyota's Lexus, a relatively recent entrant, pushed ahead to become the best-selling luxury brand in the United States. The Scion, an even newer introduction, is accomplishing what has proved to be difficult for other automakers: attracting young buyers to an established maker. Despite long-standing claims by competitors that high-mileage, high-performance, low-emissions cars are a technological and financial impossibility, Toyota launched the Prius, built market share, and bested its counterparts in establishing a standard for hybrid-drive technology, which now is found across its product line. While most auto companies were shutting plants and laying off employees, Toyota expanded, creating more opportunity to widen the gap further.

All this has led to staggering profitability. Toyota crossed the $10 billion threshold in 2003. In the fiscal year ending March 2007, its net income was $13 billion, compared with losses of $2 billion and $12.6 billion at GM and Ford, respectively. Toyota's market capitalization of $187 billion was greater than that of GM, Ford, and DaimlerChrysler combined. And all this occurred despite the fact that Toyota entered the U.S. market with few products, little brand-name recognition (and even less that was positive), and no manufacturing facilities decades after its competitors were well established.

Toyota is not alone in setting itself apart in a tightly competitive market. In commercial aviation, every major airline buys equipment from the same vendors: Boeing and Airbus for large planes; Saab, Embraer, and Bombardier for regional jets; and General Electric, Rolls-Royce, and Pratt & Whitney for engines. Jet fuel is a commodity. The airlines use the same labor pool for pilots, flight attendants, gate agents, baggage handlers, and mechanics, and they compete for exactly the same customers flying between the same cities. This makes it hard for most carriers to differentiate themselves, with predictable results. Year in and year out, American, United, USAir, and the others face financial difficulties, demanding concessions from their workforces and expecting customers to put up with less comfort, worse service, and reduced reliability.

This is not so, however, with Southwest. Achieving a combination of low cost and high customer satisfaction, this airline has generated an annual profit for more than 30 years in a row, despite the spikes in fuel prices, declines in travel after 9/11, overcapacity in the industry, and price cutting by incumbents trying to fend off entrants. Whereas the industry as a whole has had a 50 percent loss in stock market value in the last decade, Southwest's valuation has doubled. Even since 9/11, Southwest has fared better than its competitors, with only a 20 percent drop in value versus 70 percent for the entire segment.

Consider another way to measure Southwest's disproportionate success in its market: In fiscal year 2006, the combined revenue for American, Continental, Delta, JetBlue, United, US Airways, and Southwest was $95.2 billion, of which Southwest accounted for 10 percent. In November 2007, the combined market capitalization of those airlines was $33 billion, of which Southwest accounted for 33 percent.

How has this been possible? According to my colleague Jody Hoffer-Gittell and others, some of the intuitively obvious answers are wrong. Southwest is as unionized as the other airlines, it has competition on all its routes, and it doesn't have the advantages of monopolistic pricing that the hub-and-spoke system gives the major carriers over some routes. So it is not succeeding thanks to some structural advantage. Rather, Southwest does the basic work of running an airline better than other airlines do—turning its planes around at the gate in less time with less effort and greater predictability and performing scheduled maintenance with greater reliability. Its crews and equipment therefore spend more time aloft with paying customers rather than sitting on the ground unprofitably and unproductively.

Manufacturing integrated circuits—microprocessors, memory chips, application-specific integrated circuits—can be brutally competitive. All "fabs," as the manufacturing facilities in this industry are called, buy equipment from the same vendors, make products that compete on the same dimensions of "device density" and speed, and sell them to the same electronics companies. Yet in this business too, some companies outrace their rivals. According to the Competitive Semiconductor Manufacturing Program at the University of California at Berkeley, there are significant disparities among competitors in terms of the performance levels they achieve for quality (e.g., defects and yields), speed (e.g., throughput and cycle time), and efficiency (e.g., labor productivity) and also, more notably, the speed with which those levels are achieved (e.g., process-development time and ramp-up time). Christensen, Verlinden, King, and Yang, in their article "The New Economics of Semiconductor Manufacturing," give an example of how this comes about. They detail how one anonymous manufacturer, through an intense focus on process excellence, cut the manufacturing time for a wafer by two-thirds and the cost per wafer by 12 percent. Effective capacity went up 10 percent and the number of products the plant could sustain increased by half. This plant became faster at meeting a broader range and volume of demand at a lower cost and with no extra capital investment.

Alcoa is in the business of mining, refining, smelting, forging, casting, rolling, and extrusion—all of which are inherently dangerous processes. Yet, during the late 1980s and early 1990s, a period of great business success for Alcoa, it established itself as the safest large manufacturing employer in the United States. According to recent Occupational Safety and Health Administration (OSHA) data, Alcoa's workplace injury rate is one-quarter the average for all manufacturers by one measure and one-twentieth by another. This wasn't accomplished by any competitive maneuvering. Something else enabled Alcoa to just say no to work-related accidents. How this has been accomplished is explored in detail in Chapter 4.

Not all rabbits are running for profit. Some measure performance in other ways. For example, nearly all leading hospitals have access to cutting-edge science, the latest technology, and intelligent, well-trained, hardworking, well-meaning employees. Yet there are large variations in safety. On the whole, hospitals are dangerous places for patients. The Institute of Medicine estimated that up to 98,000 of the 33 million Americans who are hospitalized each year die because something went wrong in the management of their care.

Other studies estimate that an equal number die as a result of an infection acquired while hospitalized and that an even greater number are nonfatally injured or infected in the course of receiving care. This puts the risk of suffering harm while being hospitalized as high as one in a few hundred and the risk of being killed as high as one in a few thousand. Yet a few hospitals have cut the risk that patients will be harmed by medical error and infections by 90 percent and more, putting themselves in a position to provide far better care to more people at less cost and with less effort than is typical elsewhere. These hospitals, like Alcoa, have that special "something else."

Being a crew member on board a nuclear-powered submarine might seem a risky proposition, as it might mean sharing space with nuclear-tipped warheads, with your ship subject to crushing pressures, while playing cat and mouse with adversaries' warships while operating blind and sometimes deaf. And we all have our impressions of nuclear energy, given the events at Chernobyl and Three Mile Island. However, nuclear-powered warships in the United States Navy have collectively accumulated over 134 million miles and over 5,700 reactor-years of nuclear reactor operation since the first nuclear-powered submarine, the *USS Nautilus*, was launched in September 1954. In all that time, with all that use, there has not been a single reactor-related casuality or fatality. In contrast, the Russian nuclear navy has been far more accident-prone. NASA, also charged with manned missions in a hostile environment, has had a tarnished record. We'll take a closer look in Chapter 3 at why NASA has been problem-plagued and, in Chapter 5, will contrast this with the Navy's approach.

High-Velocity Competitors

What is the special "something else" that separates high-velocity organizations from their rivals? There is a rich research history of attempts by practitioners and academics to answer that question. Let's look at that history to better understand what *Chasing the Rabbit* contributes.

By the 1980s, the post–World War II political and military rivalry between the United States and its allies and the Soviet Union and its allies, which had demanded so much attention for decades, was finally quieting down. However, all was not smooth sailing. An increasingly wide array of formerly stalwart American industries and corporations faced a severe competitive threat. Foreign companies, many of them Japanese, were delivering higher-quality products at lower costs than seemed possible. The implications for America's economic well-being were staggering.

Initially, this phenomenon was explained in terms of economic conflict, perhaps because the Cold War mind-set still prevailed. Books such as Chalmers Johnson's *MITI and the Japanese Miracle* (1982) and Clyde Prestowitz's *Trading Places: How We Allowed Japan to Take the Lead* (1988) attributed Japan's success to a clever trade strategy masterminded by governmental ministries and coordinated with corporate networks (*keiretsu*) that outpaced the disjointed efforts of American companies, federal agencies, and Congress. Japan rigged the game with advantageous financing structures, freedom from the pressures of what were characterized as shortsighted American financial markets, and a compliant population willing to delay gratification and suppress individual interests to achieve corporate and national interests. It was a samurai culture versus a cowboy one, and with competitiveness defined as a contest among nations, the proper response to such "cheating" was thought to be national in scope: voluntary export restraints, domestic-content requirements, and industry-wide research consortia.

Inspired by that sort of explanation, I wrote my undergraduate thesis at Princeton on the macroeconomic determinants of exchange rates with the idea that understanding why the dollar was strong and the yen was weak might offer insights into ways to reverse the flow of goods and services. After college, my work in investment banking in the mid-1980s reinforced the notion of national economic competition. My colleagues and I were attuned to "what the Japanese would do" every time a new auction of government bonds took place. Later, working in Washington, D.C., for a congressional agency, I had a close view of the debates about restoring American competitiveness, which often focused on legislative and executive branch responses to such perceived infringements as subsidization and trade dumping.

Arriving at MIT as a graduate student in the late 1980s was fortuitous for me. The prevailing view of Japanese commercial ascendancy was shifting from a Cold War-style national competition to the management practices of individual market-leading firms. Books such as *Kaisha, Made in America, Dynamic Manufacturing*, and *The Machine That Changed the World*, along with a slew of articles, detailed the differences in business practices—particularly in design and production—between the new Japanese winners and the American firms they were displacing. This shift in emphasis proved to be extraordinarily productive.

It was observed that, at winning Japanese factories, products advanced to completion along simpler process flows than they did in American factories. Production was "pulled," triggered by actual customer need, rather than "pushed" in accordance with preconceived schedules. Work sites were more orderly and were organized according to the specific task that had to be accomplished at each location. Relationships with employees and suppliers tended to be collaborative, a far cry from the antagonistic industrial relations in America.

Also observed was the relentless *kaizen* (improvement), a process of engaging those closest to the direct work of the organization in the continual improvement of that work. So it was not just the velocity of material through the factory that mattered; it was the velocity of improvement and problem solving—the speed with which these factories discovered problems and solved them.

Researchers such as David Garvin documented differences in productivity among similar plants and found discrepancies of tenfold and even a hundredfold in quality. John Krafcik documented extraordinary differences in productivity between mass manufacturers and lean manufacturers in the auto industry. Michael Cusumano provided a historical account of Toyota's rise to ascendancy. James Womack, Dan Roos, and Dan Jones illustrated some of the major differences in shop-floor management, product design, and supplier relations between the auto industry's best and the rest in their landmark book, *The Machine That Changed the World*. John Paul MacDuffie revealed some of the details of the powerful problem-solving mechanisms these manufacturers employed.

Bob Hayes and Steve Wheelwright, with coauthor Kim Clark, put aside their focus on strategic decisions as the means toward

Restoring Our Competitive Edge and later wrote glowingly about the advantages of creating "the learning organization" in order to achieve world-beating *Dynamic Manufacturing*. Collectively, these and other authors conveyed the palpable sense of urgency found throughout the market-leading organizations to identify market needs, meet those needs, and get ever better at doing so.

This new perspective was exciting. It meant that managers mattered. Even if a firm's external environment was hostile, its internal environment could be shaped to positive effect. Managers did not need government to rescue them, nor did they have to skulk around the marketplace looking for arenas bereft of competitors. They could do what the Japanese were doing and take them on in a fair fight.

Inspired by these discoveries, many people, my classmates in the MIT-Japan Program and I included, threw ourselves into understanding Japanese management so that we could do our part in helping the United States recover from its competitive malaise. Many of us joined Japanese companies for an insider's view. For me, this meant dipping my toes in the water of Japanese business at a commercial bank in the summer of 1990 through the support of the Japan Society of New York and the International House of Japan (Tokyo) and then spending more than a year as part of an international manufacturing consortium at the University of Tokyo with the support of the Japanese Ministry of Education. I worked with Japanese, Germans, French, and Canadians from construction firms, industrial equipment manufacturers, and electronics companies, all of whom were trying to understand what their firms had to do in the face of accelerated technological innovation and heightened cross-border trade and competition.

When I returned to the United States in the mid-1990s, I noticed something strange. The groundbreaking research cited above, which had shown the enormous disparities between the best in an industry and the rest, was now nearly a decade old. In that interval, Toyota, the company that epitomized the Japanese approach (which by then had come to be called "lean manufacturing"), had been studied relentlessly. Hundreds of thousands of visitors had toured its NUMMI joint venture with General Motors in Fremont, California, and its greenfield site in Georgetown, Kentucky. Countless pages had been written about Toyota specifically and lean manufacturing more generally. Hundreds of manufacturing companies had benchmarked the company and each of the American Big Three had created its own version of the Toyota Production System (TPS): the Ford Production System, the Chrysler Operating System, and the GM Global Manufacturing System. All over, people were mastering the intricacies of pull systems, work standardization, and the like, yet no American Toyota had emerged.

Here was the problem: Although Toyota's competitors had indeed improved in both initial quality and manufacturing efficiency, Toyota had not been sitting still. High-velocity organizations don't. Not only had it also improved in quality and efficiency, it had expanded the range of the competition. It had localized production, increased its product offerings, introduced new technology, and created new brands. I'm reminded of football: Everyone was trying to improve the running game, and then a few teams invented the passing game. As the other teams tried to add passing to their playbooks, the leaders put the receivers in motion and added quarterback options and calling plays at the line of scrimmage, always complicating the challenge by increasing the speed of the game and the range of plays that might occur.

When I entered Harvard Business School as a doctoral student, I set out to learn why it was so hard to overtake Toyota, and in the next four years I had extraordinary opportunities to do just that. The heart of my studies was learning by doing. For six months I was part of a Toyota team, working to develop a first-tier supplier in Kentucky (the one mentioned above that also supplied two of Toyota's competitors) and learning the Toyota Production System firsthand by solving production-related problems and working with others to do that. To appreciate the differences between what we were doing at the supplier and how more traditional manufacturers operated, I prepared by spending a week doing assembly-line work at one of Toyota's American competitors. We'll see more of that experience in Chapter 3. To appreciate the management of work systems across a broad range of products, processes, markets, and regions, I traveled to three dozen plants in North America and Japan to make observations, collect data, and interview people, from frontline workers to plant managers and corporate executives.

What I found was completely unexpected. I had already studied what had been written about Toyota, lean manufacturing, Six Sigma, and total quality management. I had a fairly good conceptual understanding of work standardization, pull versus push, the design of experiments, statistical process control, and the many other analytical and control tools that were being popularized. I thought that there must still be some tools I was missing. I couldn't have been more wrong.

The difference between Toyota and its competitors was neither more tools nor more diligent application of tools that had gained wide currency. That approach promised gains that were potentially significant but that would ultimately plateau. Michael Porter made that point in his 1996 *Harvard Business Review* article, "What Is Strategy?" If everyone benchmarks the leader by imitating how work is done at a particular time and place, no one can do any better than the leader and everyone will look and act the same, commoditizing their sector and guaranteeing that no one will enjoy an advantage.

Rather, what I was coming to appreciate was an approach to managing exceptionally complex work that mustered the hands *and* minds of hundreds of people so that improvement, innovation, and adaptation were constant. The factory was not only a place to produce physical products, it was also a place to learn *how* to produce those products and—most important of all—it was a place to *keep* learning how to produce those products. In fact, this is exactly what so much of the early research about Japanese management had revealed—that learning and discovery were intrinsic to success. But that idea had gotten lost as people focused on the particular tools and artifacts used in the workplace at the expense of understanding the principles of how those systems were managed.

The emphasis on learning and discovery went right to the heart of a fundamental managerial challenge. Complex products and services require complex design, production, and delivery operations. Organizations need to master the myriad functions that have to be brought to bear, but that alone will never be sufficient. They also need to master the countless permutations with which the various people, parts, and processes can interact within such complex product and service operations. Such mastery is never complete—it can never be designed into the operation from the start.

For example, the Toyota plants that I visited were enormous, some with hundreds of millions of dollars in equipment, dozens if not hundreds of managers, and hundreds if not thousands of hourly workers. One would expect such massive operations to have an unavoidable inertia, but my key impressions were of movement and change, much of it urgent and adrenaline-charged. This was true both for work by an individual—such as installing a seat in a car, attaching a bumper, or connecting wiring—and for complex work carried out by large groups—such as launching a new model or building a new plant. No matter what the task, Toyota had figured out how to do the work in such a way that individuals and groups kept learning how to do that work better. Good luck benchmarking that. Any snapshot would reveal where Toyota was today but not where it was headed. Later, when I began to seek out and explore other high-velocity organizations in other fields, I was to find several that had independently arrived at the same idea, strengthening my conviction that the approach described in *Chasing the Rabbit* will help any organization engaged in complex operations to improve its performance.

Though many firms had embraced various tools associated with lean manufacturing and total quality management and had gained stability and control of work sites that had been chaotic and unreliable, they still never caught up. And now I could see why. These firms had picked up the visible tools of high-velocity organizations—the value-stream maps, pull systems, production cells, statistical process control charts, and design of experiments—but they had not understood what these tools were for: managing complex work for continual improvement of that work (and therefore of the products and services that result from that work). As Kent Bowen and I pointed out in our 1999 *Harvard Business Review* article, "Decoding the DNA of the Toyota Production System," copying the tools alone did not generate the paradoxical combination of stability and flexibility that was increasingly associated with Toyota. It was Toyota's way of designing and improving processes that generated both short-term stability and longer-term agility and responsiveness.

As my research at Toyota progressed, a marvelous opportunity arose to test my findings. Alcoa had been pursuing the audacious goal of creating a perfectly safe work environment, despite the hazards that seemed inherent in its production processes, and it was coming pretty close. The key for Alcoa, as we shall see in Chapter 4, was to realize that perfect safety could not be designed into its work from the start. No brain trust could ever figure out in advance all the little things that could go wrong. Instead, the trick was to do work, take immediate notice of any risks or potential risks in the work, and make changes so that the same risks did not reappear. And finding one risk wasn't an isolated experience. Pulling on the thread revealed many other process shortcomings that had not been known. In the area of safety, Alcoa had begun developing a management system much like Toyota's, in which the creation of products and the operation of processes were coupled tightly with creating better methods for being successful. Although the perfect safety system could not be designed, it could be discovered bit by bit if enough velocity were generated and enough energy were sustained.

But could this Toyota-like approach be applied to Alcoa's business as a whole, a business very unlike Toyota's? In short, did my Toyota findings apply only to Toyota and to similar industries, or were they much more broadly applicable? In 1997, I worked with a group at Alcoa to develop and deploy the Alcoa Business System, based on the Toyota Production System. Some of the results were fantastic, as we will see in Chapter 4.

But the circle was to widen again. In early 2000, there was a knock on my door at the Harvard Business School, where I was now on the faculty. In walked a doctor named John Kenagy. "I'm a vascular surgeon," he explained, "and my colleagues and I have tried everything we can to raise the quality and efficiency of our practices and of the hospitals in which we work. Nothing has helped. I've heard about this Toyota research you've been doing. Could a similar approach work in health care?"

We didn't know. Here, indeed, was another kind of very complex service being provided by a very complex organization and, as I was vividly to learn, working in a hospital can be a stressful experience with little failures happening all the time, some of which might prove dangerous or fatal to patients in unexpected ways. Could the often-frustrating work of nurses, aides, doctors, administrators, and staff be managed in a way that was dynamic, adaptive, self-improving, and self-innovating? We gave it a try, first at Deaconess Glover Hospital in Needham, Massachusetts, and later at a number of hospitals through the auspices of the Pittsburgh Regional Healthcare Initiative. The results, some to be discussed in Chapter 11, were stupendous.

What do all these examples mean for you, the reader? I and other researchers have found—and in a few cases I myself helped create—high-velocity organizations engaged in a wide variety of missions. As different as these organizations are in many respects, they have one thing in common: They are adept at designing, developing, and operating exceptionally complex systems to achieve exemplary and constantly improving performance in the design, production, or delivery of complex goods or services. This is the "something else" that is needed when monopolistic advantage or a lower level of performance are not viable options. This is how the rabbits get ahead and stay ahead of the pack.

At this point, we have looked at the class of front-runners who are clearly doing something different than their peers and competitors, something that helps them take the lead and then keep increasing their lead. We have also asserted that it is not enough to imitate the distinctive techniques of these front-running rabbits, to mistake the means for the ends. It is necessary to understand the goal of those techniques and to dedicate the organization's efforts to that goal—the management of complex operations for high performance.

But having given examples of high performance and having used a historical survey to clarify the real goal, I would like to say some more about the means.

Structure and Dynamics of High-Velocity Organizations

At a high level, we can distinguish two characteristics that distinguish high-velocity organizations from those struggling behind them.

1. Structure: Managing the Functions as Parts of the Process

There is a structural difference between the high-velocity rabbits and those chasing them that creates potential for speed. While high-velocity organizations put great effort into developing the technical competency of various functions, they are equally and always concerned with the way the work of individuals, teams, and technologies will contribute to (or impede) the process of which they are part. The process orientation of high-velocity organizations is in contrast to the "siloization" of so many other organizations in which the departments may talk of integration but tend to operate more like sovereign states. In high-velocity organizations, functional integration is not just pretty talk, it is the nuts-and-bolts of management at all levels every day.

2. Dynamics: Continually Improving the Pieces and the Process

There is a dynamic difference between the high-velocity rabbits and those chasing them that generates speed. High-velocity organizations are constantly experimenting and learning more about all the work they do; this is how they cope successfully with the complexity which they all face in one form or another. These organizations do not encourage or admire workarounds, firefighting, and heroic measures. They want to understand and solve problems, not put up with them.

It would be impossible to exaggerate how valuable this is. How much time and effort is saved by getting rid of a problem once and for all? How much confidence is gained when people see that they don't have to keep putting up with one problem after another and that management doesn't want them to? How many *more* problems will be solved because people know they can? Then there is the paradoxical benefit that solving one problem often reveals another that had been masked by the first one. Another problem, yes, but now the organization sees it as yet another problem *that's going to be gotten rid of.*

Low-performing, low-velocity organizations are strikingly different. First, they tend to be *functionally oriented* and do not manage the relationships among all the elements adequately, as was mentioned above. Second, even if they think in terms of processes, they are not dynamic. Instead of constantly doing work, watching for problems in their approach, and modifying the way they work, they lock into an approach that seems good at the time and—even when it proves inadequate—stick with it and muddle through.

To sum up, high-velocity organizations differ from low-velocity organizations both structurally and dynamically. Structurally, they insist that each piece of work be done with an eye to the larger process of which it is a part. Dynamically, they insist that each piece of work be done in such a way as to bring problems to the attention of those who can best analyze and solve them. Low-velocity organizations, in contrast, are characterized by "siloization"—"You do your job and I'll do mine"—rather than integration and by endless workarounds and firefighting—"This'll do for now" or "Don't worry, this happens all the time"—rather than continual improvement, innovation, and invention.

The Four Capabilities of High-Velocity Organizations

The ability of high-velocity organizations to be so functionally integrated and continually self-improving, innovative, and inventive is rooted in four complementary capabilities. I will explain each of them briefly here. They will turn up again and again in Chapters 3 through 5 and they will be explored in detail in Chapters 6 through 9. Note that Capability 1 is the key to functional integration for high performance, while Capabilities 2 through 4 are the keys to managing an organization for continual self-improvement.

Capability 1: Specifying Design to Capture Existing Knowledge and Building In Tests to Reveal Problems

High-velocity organizations don't like anyone to start work, whatever its size or complexity, until the organization has (1) made explicit the most effective approach that is currently known for achieving success at that task and (2) built into that approach the capacity to detect failure when and where it occurs.

Whether the work is to be done by an individual or a group, with or without equipment, high-velocity organizations are uncomfortable with ambiguity. They specify in advance what outcomes are expected; who is responsible for what work in what order; how products, services, and information will flow from the person performing one step to the person performing the next step; and what methods will be used to accomplish each piece of work.

However, it is not that they want or need guarantees. This kind of specification is not a case of perverse Taylorism or micromanagement, with smart people telling less-intelligent people what to do. It is, in fact, an investment. Before the work starts, the high-velocity organization invests everything it knows so far into these specifications to maximize the likelihood that people will succeed. But this is the sort of investment that has a positive payout regardless of the immediate outcome. Specifying with clarity and care what actions are expected to lead to what outcomes makes it far easier to recognize when something unexpected has happened. This highlights gaps in the organization's collective knowledge about how to succeed. With pockets of ignorance identified, the high-velocity, front-running rabbit organizations know where they need to invest to get better. To increase their ability to discover what they don't know, the rabbits even go out of their way to build tests into their operations in order to detect abnormalities when and where they occur. In contrast, those laboring in the pack are less committed to up-front specification, already handicapping themselves from the start, since they are not using the best possible approach. And then they suppress their ability to see when what they are doing is not good enough. Like an athlete who uses antiquated equipment and doesn't keep on eye on the competition, they find themselves falling farther and farther behind the rabbits.

Capability 2: Swarming and Solving Problems to Build New Knowledge

High-velocity organizations are adept at detecting problems in their systems at the time and place of their occurrence. They are equally adept at (1) containing those problems before they have a chance to spread and (2) diagnosing and treating their causes so the problems cannot reoccur. In doing so, they build ever-deeper knowledge about how to manage the systems for doing their work, converting inevitable up-front ignorance into knowledge.

It all happens like this: In the rabbit organizations, problems are swarmed at the time and place where they occur and by the people who are affected. A benefit to swarming a problem immediately is that it can be contained before it can affect someone else's work. And the longer the problem remains unresolved, the more difficult and more expensive it will be to solve. In Chapter 3, we'll see examples of what happens when problems are left untreated.

Swarming a problem is not only beneficial in terms of what is prevented—an infectious spread of the problem's impact. It is beneficial in terms of what is allowed—the gathering of essential, contextual information that would otherwise be lost to fading memory and changing circumstances. Many problems occur because of some unexpected, idiosyncratic interaction of people, processes, products, places, and circumstances. As time passes, it becomes impossible to reconstruct exactly what was going on when the problem arose.

Once swarmed and investigated, problems are solved, but not in any ad hoc, willy-nilly fashion. High-velocity organizations insist that "the scientific method" be used in a disciplined fashion. This is not an esoteric, ivory tower exercise; it reflects the conviction that when something is changed, those making the alteration should have a clear idea of what actions are expected to lead to what outcomes and should then be able to see when they are right and wrong. Fixing the problem isn't good enough; they want to fix it while gaining a deeper knowledge of how their own processes work.

Before moving on to the third and fourth capabilities, let me point out that the first two alone are game-changing. Many people set out to do work and are either successful or not. If not, the effort was wasted. High-velocity organizations convert win-lose situations into win-win situations. If they succeed, they win. If they do not, they learn how to succeed next time, and that is also a win.

Capability 3: Sharing New Knowledge throughout the Organization

High-velocity organizations multiply the power of their new knowledge by making it available, not only to those who discovered it, but also throughout the organization. They do this by sharing not only the solutions that are discovered, but the processes by which they were discovered—what was learned and how it was learned. While their competitors allow problems to persist and propagate into the larger system because the solutions, if they are found at all, remain contained where they were found, the high-velocity leaders contain their problems and propagate their discoveries. This means that when people begin to do their work, they do so with the cumulative experience of everyone in the organization who has ever done the same work. We'll see several examples of that multiplier effect.

Capability 4: Leading by Developing Capabilities 1, 2, and 3

Managers in high-velocity organizations make sure that a regular part of work is both the delivery of products and services and also the continual improvement of the processes by which those products and services are delivered. They teach people how to make continual improvement part of their jobs and provide them with enough time and resources to do so. Thus, the organization's ability to be both reliable and highly adaptive becomes self-reinforcing. This is a fundamental difference from their also-ran competitors. High-velocity managers are not in place to command, control, berate, intimidate, or evaluate through a contrived set of metrics, but to ensure that their organizations become ever more self-diagnosing and self-improving, skilled at detecting problems, solving them, and multiplying the effect by making the solutions available throughout the organization.

Certainly, the idea that success comes to those who learn the most quickly and effectively has antecedents and, before we move on, let's recognize some of those. After all, the point of this book is not to refute that previous research, but to show that many of these ideas are actually part of a holistic approach to managing complex systems for great outcomes. For example, Nelson and Winter emphasize, in *An Evolutionary Theory of Economic Change*, that managers don't necessarily plan their organizations' way to greatness, but that successful organizations develop routines, test them in practice, recognize which don't work, and reinforce those that do. Eric Von Hippel and his coauthors have demonstrated the importance of learning in context. Because there are so many circumstantial factors that cannot be codified, learning must occur when and where problems are experienced. My late colleague Jai Jaikumar had "information perishability" as one of his axioms of information. Information is not only contextual, it spoils; that is why it is so important to swarm problems. More than a few writers have emphasized that self-reflective experience is critical to improvement. This point is highlighted in Chapter 4 in the Alcoa example and later in the chapters that focus on Toyota.

Chapter Overview

Chasing the Rabbit is intended to help readers understand how market leaders outdistance the competition and how great companies can catch up and win. It does so in the following fashion:

In Chapter 1, I have introduced a category of "high-velocity organizations" whose ability to consistently outperform their competitors cannot be explained well by manipulation of their external environment—competitors, suppliers, regulators, investors, and so on. It is explained largely by their mastery of their internal environments—the complex operations needed to produce or provide complex products or services. This mastery boils down to the four capabilities just described, all of which contribute to these organizations' ability to discover more quickly and to bring discoveries to bear in accomplishing the organization's mission.

Chapter 2 explores in more detail the basic challenge of complex operations which all high-velocity organizations face. The main point is that the very scientific discoveries that inspire or improve the products and services on which we depend also increase the difficulty of managing their design and delivery. We'll look more closely at how systems evolve from simple and linear to complex, highly intertwined, and strongly interconnected, and what challenges that presents. Supporting the premise that the themes of *Chasing the Rabbit* are independent of particular sectors, one example is from the design and production of a manufactured product, and the other is from medical care.

Chapter 3 is the "doom and gloom" portion of the book, in which we look at approaches to managing complex work that bring all kinds of frustration, waste, and failure, ranging from the time nurses spend looking for rubber gloves to the sudden demise of two space shuttle crews to the slow-motion failure of once-grand automotive corporations. While the contexts are different, the failure modes are nearly identical.

Things look up from there. Chapter 4 provides a detailed example (the first of several) of how exceptionally complex work can be managed for outstanding results. We'll see how Alcoa converted itself into the safest manufacturing employer in the country by shifting from an approach more typical of the organizations in Chapter 3 to a dynamic discovery approach based on seeing problems, solving problems, and sharing quickly and broadly what was learned—all this supported by senior leadership.

Chapter 5 shows how the same commitment to managing systems with a bias toward discovery led to great success for several other organizations far afield from Alcoa and from each other. These are the U.S. Navy Nuclear Power Propulsion Program, Pratt & Whitney's jet engine design group, and Avenue A, an Internet advertising agency. As pointed out earlier, the variety of examples is evidence that we are talking about general principles, not the particulars of any one industry or setting.

Chapters 1 through 5 give an overview of the main thesis of *Chasing the Rabbit*, that some organizations achieve exceptionally high velocity in self-correction, self-improvement, and internally generated innovation and invention and use this velocity to set themselves apart in situations that should otherwise be intensely competitive or constraining. In Chapters 6 through 10, we'll look in depth at how one company, Toyota, puts the principles outlined above into action.

Chapter 6, after setting up Toyota as an example of a high-velocity organization, focuses on Capability 1—the design and operation of self-diagnostic systems. A simple, robust framework for describing processes will be introduced. Then we'll walk through several examples—from simple to complicated and from tangible to less so—showing how specification is used to help work start off strongly and how tests built into systems help catch problems before they metastasize.

Chapter 7 focuses on Capability 2—swarming problems to contain them and solve them. We'll see how several Toyota teams learned how to solve problems and fix work processes so that the processes improved and, at the same time, the individual workers became more skillful and productive. We'll also see the same problem-solving discipline practiced at senior levels.

Chapter 8 is about Capability 3—how local discoveries are made useful throughout an organization. Common themes will emerge from an example of disseminating the most effective known methods of "master craftsmen," an example of capturing knowledge and using it over several product design cycles, and an example of collaborative problem solving and process improvement. The most compelling theme is that when the solution to a problem is discovered, the discovery process itself must be conveyed along with the solution.

In Chapter 9, we will turn our attention to the critical role of leaders in high-velocity organizations—their exercise of Capability 4. Like other leaders, they are responsible for setting objectives and allocating resources, but they are also the stewards of the three other capabilities by which organizational velocity is generated. They must deliver those capabilities to those for whom they are responsible.

Chapter 10 concludes our in-depth look at Toyota by showing how the four capabilities are brought to bear in crisis-recovery situations like the overnight loss of a critical supplier or the closure of an essential port of entry. Those people who hold the belief that the high-velocity approach applies only to repeatable processes and fosters only incremental improvements will see that it can produce results at a speed and on a scale that are astonishing to most.

With Chapter 11, we leave Toyota and turn to the important task of creating high-velocity organizations in the American health-care industry. Those in the health-care field will see that better care does not have to come at greater cost, nor do spending caps necessarily require denial of care. Other readers will see that the four capabilities can work wonders not only in capital-intensive, technology-driven sectors, but in knowledge-intensive, service-based, nonrepetitive situations.

Chapter 12 will tie some parting thoughts together as a conclusion.

Before Chapter 2 begins, I want to say again how privileged I have been to be exposed to the great organizations and people represented in this book and to the many others for whom there was not space. I've learned a great deal from them, enjoying the experience every step of the way. I hope that I allow you, the reader, to enjoy the journey and its discoveries as well.

CHAPTER 2

COMPLEXITY: THE GOOD
NEWS AND THE BAD NEWS

I sometimes wonder how my grandmothers, Anita and Gussie, have held it together across nearly a century of scientific advances. Not that they started with a flat Earth perspective. Yet, time and again, across every aspect of their lives, their basic assumptions of how the natural world works and what tools and machines would allow people to accomplish in that world have been shattered.

They have seen transportation progress from carriages and the most rudimentary internal combustion engines up to the most advanced automobiles. Flight, in its infancy during their infancies, is now a routine matter on jets that cruise at previously unimaginable speeds at incomprehensible altitudes over incredible distances. The moon, once merely an interesting object in the night sky, has been visited by their countrymen. Robots explore other planets or leave the solar system altogether while telescopes peer back in time to the birthing of the universe. Between their TVs, radios, computers, cell phones, and cars, they probably each have more computing power than existed on the whole planet when they were children. X-rays, CT scanners, and MRI machines let doctors peer inside their bodies with incredible clarity and safety. The wealth of scientific and technological advancement that they have had to assimilate, the changes in technology, and the resulting transformations of what is normal and possible, have been remarkable.

The perspectives of my grandmothers are on my mind in light of the question of why some organizations consistently outrace their competition and are far better at extracting extraordinary yield from their people, products, and processes than are their peers.

Simple Systems and Complex Systems

In many fields, scientific advances have a peculiar good news/bad news duality. For most of us, technological achievement is good or even great news if we are the end users. We take for granted commercial products, medical and other services, and entertainment and travel opportunities that were not even exorbitant luxuries for past generations; they were unimaginable except by the most creative futurists and science fiction writers. Could even Isaac Asimov or Gene Roddenberry have imagined logging onto Orbitz or Expedia from a mobile phone and booking a flight from the United States to India for "medical tourism"?

But for those responsible for managing the design, generation, and delivery of those products and services, continual progress means ever more headaches. In the past, simple science often meant simple systems, whether those systems were the physical products that people used or the systems of work (the organizations or the processes) that generated those products. There were few pieces; their relationships tended to be linear and predictable—one thing leading logically to the next. The key challenge was to make sure that everyone had a good command of his or her particular skill and carried out his or her responsibilities at the right time. With only a few specialties needed in any system and few interdependencies among them, managing the integration of the distinct pieces into a well-functioning whole was reasonably straightforward, accomplished in one of two ways. For small-scale systems, the "pieces" could be brought together through informal, ad hoc collaboration and problem resolution. For larger systems, bureaucratic coordination served the purpose of ensuring that the pieces acted in concert with each other. Both approaches depended on someone being able to see the system as a whole, to understand its structure, and to have a reasonable sense of how it would behave in the limited range of circumstances which might arise.

We are in a much different situation today. Scientific progress has led to products and services that have better performance but are far more complex, requiring the integration of an increasing number of specialties that are linked to each other in far more convoluted ways. This, in turn, requires the organizations responsible for their design, generation, production, and delivery to be more complicated, with more individual specialists linked to and dependent on one another in ever more convoluted ways. Even for smaller systems, it is exceptionally hard to see the whole for the parts; figuring it out as you go is inadequate. As for large systems, no one can be expected to fully understand their structure and behavior. Even bureaucratic command-and-control won't do; it is too difficult to know who should do what and who actually is doing what with enough clarity and timeliness to direct them appropriately in a top-down fashion. Yet it is more important than ever to achieve effective integration, collaboration, and coordination.

Let's move from general observations to a pair of examples illustrating how scientific and technological progress offers much greater benefits but also complicates the managerial and leadership challenge. Chapter 3 will then explore how complex systems can fall apart and Chapters 4 and 5 will show how they can be managed for great success.

Two Examples of the Dilemma of Scientific Progress

When I was growing up in New York City, our neighbors' son, Eddie, brought home a real junker—a beat-up muscle car from the late 1960s or early 1970s. Over the next few months, he and his friends pounded, banged, drilled, ground, sanded, welded, riveted, and crimped that car until it was a thing of beauty. Although it had arrived on the back of a flatbed carrier—dented, rusted, and near ruin—it roared off with a hearty rumble and a glistening shine (much to the amazement and delight of the neighbors, who hadn't thought much of this project's potential and hadn't enjoyed all the banging, pounding, and grinding).

But imagine a teenager today—Eddie's son, say—attempting to rebuild a ten-year-old wreck, this one from the late 1990s. It would be impossible, but not because the teen today is any less skilled, smart, or diligent than Eddie was. Rather, no amount of skill would be sufficient for the task.

The car Eddie refurbished was made of steel and iron from front to back and from top to bottom, so as long as he and his friends were competent at metalwork, they could do nearly anything necessary to return it to working condition. With a small set of tools and skills, they could reshape broken body panels, weld pieces, grind bumps, drill holes, and work on the power train and steering.

Doing the same would be impossible for Eddie's son. His junker would have a steel body, though perhaps with some plastic panels. But the engine might be aluminum, with multiple computer-controlled precision valves in each cylinder. The fuel-air mixture would be done by computer-controlled fuel injection, not a mechanically tunable carburetor, and he would find electronic hardware intertwined with everything else, all of which would be overlaid with software controls. The number of individual disciplines he and his friends would have to know would be great, the number of interactions among them even greater. Refurbishing the car would require far more knowledge than they would ever be able to master.

If, overwhelmed by the number of disciplines they would need to tackle the car as a whole, Eddie's son and his friends were to make a valiant attempt at just the steering wheel, they would still be stymied. Looking inside, they would find that the air bag is made of an advanced polymer material that can be folded and compressed for years on end and subjected to hot spells and cold snaps with no ill effect. When necessary, the bag will inflate and deflate in less than a moment, despite the abuse it has taken over its life. It does not inflate on its own but only when an explosive charge detonates at precisely the right moment with precisely the force needed. That right moment is determined by numerous sensors laced throughout the car that are constantly monitoring pitch, roll, yaw, and acceleration or deceleration. Of course, those signals make sense to the explosive only after they have been fed into computer chips which, through a combination of hardware and software, can distinguish between riding down a potholed street in Boston from being rear-ended or sideswiped.

To rebuild the steering wheel, Eddie's son and his pals would not only need advanced degrees in materials science, pyrotechnics, combustion engineering, dynamic controls, electrical engineering, and computer science, but would also have to understand how those fields worked together—and that would be before they tried their hands at the onboard navigation and entertainment controls on either side of the air bag, which would require expertise in an even greater number of disciplines.

The predicament of Eddie's son and his friends is emblematic of the challenge faced in the automobile manufacturing industry. Today's cars offer functionality, reliability, durability, and safety that would have been unimaginable two decades ago. However, these improvements have come at a price. The number of disciplines that have to be mastered has increased (moving from left to right in Figure 2-1), the depth of knowledge required to be an expert in each discipline has increased, and the breadth of each discipline's knowledge—certainly relative to the entire knowledge content of the product or the process that makes it—has narrowed considerably.

Figure 2-1 Advanced performance and increasing complexity: automobile manufacturing

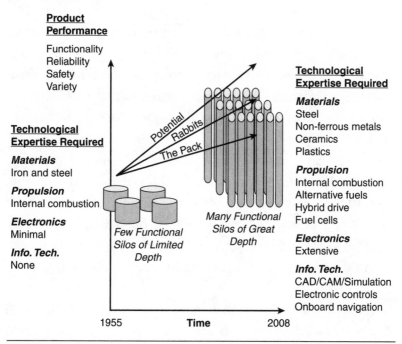

A major upgrade of a car model can require hundreds of person-years of engineering effort, while designing a new engine and the plant to build it has engineering costs of tens of millions of dollars and total costs in the hundreds of millions. No longer is it possible to focus on developing deep expertise and leave integration to informal collaboration. Today, bringing the pieces together into a coherent whole is a discipline in its own right. The better you are at it, the closer your organization's performance is to the potential of the science and technology. The worse you are it, the farther off the curve you are. We'll see later how badly organizations can stumble when they have not mastered it and how well they do when they have.

Of course, the challenge of managing ever-increasing complexity in order to achieve far better outcomes is not limited to manufacturing or even to business. The same good news/bad news paradox is certainly evident in delivering medical care. (See Figure 2-2.) Consider the awful prospects for a patient diagnosed with breast cancer in the 1950s. If the cancer was not treatable surgically, as it often was not, the patient received what today would be considered minimal palliative care. If the malignancy was operable—that is, if it hadn't metastasized and spread to other organs and regions, which it often did given the poor state of the diagnostic art and the poor odds of catching the disease early—it was removed with a painful, disfiguring, disabling radical mastectomy. Even then, survival rates were low.

Today, the likelihood of successful treatment has increased dramatically. Death rates from all cancers fell in the United States by 10 percent just between 1991 and 2002, building on improvements over the preceding decades, with similar trends in other industrialized nations. As for localized breast cancer specifically, the survival rate was 72 percent in 1940, 80 percent in the 1950s, 96 percent in 2000, and 98 percent in 2007, according to the American Cancer Society. The decrease in mortality was due to improved detection and better treatment—better science being brought to bear for better results.

However, it wasn't just a single scientific breakthrough that did the trick. Rather, it was the numerous individual advances and the increasing ability to use them in concert. There have been "substantial advances in the treatment of breast cancer,"

Figure 2-2 Advanced performance and increasing complexity: Medical care

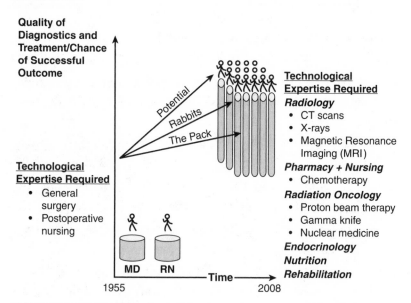

for example, "based on clinical trials which showed the benefits of using various combinations of medications in conjunction with surgery." Moving from left to right in Figure 2-2, the potential of medical science has progressed, but so has what must be mastered and coordinated to realize that potential.

With these gains for the patient came increased challenges for management. Today, *cancer* still refers to malignancy, but it no longer applies to one or even a few distinct diseases. Rather, *cancer* has become an umbrella term for hundreds of distinct illnesses, each characterized by its own genetic mutations, influenced by particular environmental triggers, identified by its own combination of diagnostic tests, and targeted with its own specialized treatment, which may be tailored specifically to the individual patient. What once would have been fatal for many people is now often curable.

And herein lies the problem. As horrible a disease as it was, cancer was not a managerially complex problem in the 1950s. Because the opportunities to intervene were relatively rare and there were only a few surgical approaches in use, roles were few—a surgical team and a postoperative recovery nursing team. This meant that each team member could focus on his or her discipline; the integration of one aspect of treatment with the others could be resolved informally and collegially, but quite satisfactorily, through personal familiarity and the repetition of a narrow range of routines (see Figure 2-3).

Today, capitalizing on the scientific gains requires that hospitals and clinics master a greatly expanded portfolio of techniques and technologies, all the while managing them in idiosyncratic combinations and permutations. While a breast cancer diagnosis in 1950 might have been based on a simple X-ray, today it can require blood work, CT scans, MRI, biopsies, and genetic testing. When a particular breast cancer is identified, many experts are needed to design an appropriate treatment. There can be several surgical options, including mastectomy or lumpectomy, with or without the removal of

Figure 2-3 Simple treatment flows, circa 1955

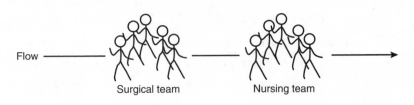

Flow ——————— Surgical team ——————— Nursing team ——————→

surrounding lymph nodes. The surgery may be followed by one of several types of radiation treatment, chosen to suit each patient's particular condition. Chemotherapy may be introduced before or after the surgery and may or may not be concurrent with radiation; again, the mix, strength, and timing of the medications will be customized to the patient. Hormone treatments and nutritional therapy may be required. Recovery and rehabilitation may involve an additional array of therapists, social workers, and visiting nurses. All told, modern cancer treatment may require choreographing the efforts of dozens of experts in order to customize care for each patient (see Figure 2-4). This, of course, is good news for the patient unfortunate enough to be stricken by the disease. The customized response may beat the illness. However, just as in the auto example above, the range of disciplines has expanded, the depth of each one has deepened, the breadth of each one has

Figure 2-4 Multiple, complex treatment flows, circa 2008

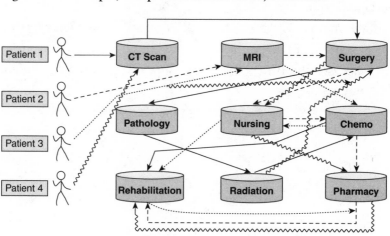

narrowed, and the number of ways in which the various, fragmented disciplines come together has exploded. Manage the integration well, and you can promise your patients that the best science will be brought to bear. Don't, and the outcomes will be needlessly disappointing.

In any hospital oncology wing and in the hypothetical driveway of Eddie's son, we see the same basic problem that affects organizations across a broad range of industries. To get the full yield from the promise of their science and the potential of their people, they have to design, operate, and continually improve exceptionally complex systems: not only the products and services they offer, but also the systems of work by which they design, produce, and deliver those products and services. When all these systems were simpler, the organization could focus formally on pushing the boundaries of functional knowledge and leave the start-to-finish process to informal guidance. That is no longer sufficient. Complex organizations delivering complex products and services must be formally dedicated to process excellence in order to be world-beaters.

Starting in Chapter 4, we'll look at how high-velocity organizations manage the challenge of work system complexity successfully. But before we do so, Chapter 3 will explain the typical failure modes.

CHAPTER 3

HOW COMPLEX SYSTEMS FAIL

High-velocity organizations, the pack-leading, front-running rabbits, are found in a wide variety of fields. Of course, we want to know how they get and stay ahead, but we'll understand the explanation much better if we look first at what keeps the others behind. This is important because the problem for them is usually not stupid blunders, but very ordinary behavior on the part of hard-working, well-meaning people.

A basic difficulty for those responsible for complex systems, in which many people (often using large and complex machines) have to work collaboratively and in concert, is that the more different disciplines and specialties that are involved, the harder it becomes to determine *a priori* exactly who should do what, when, depending on whom and responsible to whom. With all this uncertainty, it is also difficult, if not downright impossible, to predict the system's behavior under the range of circumstances in which it must perform. So many unexpected things can happen. It is how the uncertainty, the expectations, and the unexpected are managed that separates the high-velocity rabbit organizations from their pursuers and proves to be a source of sustainable competitive advantage.

Most organizations put a lot of effort, energy, enthusiasm, and creativity into designing their systems of work. But of course, once the systems go into operation, they prove to be imperfect, and people find themselves contending with a steady chatter of things not going as hoped, expected, or needed. At some point, these organizations decide to put up with a certain level of one inconvenient thing after another. The creativity and effort that were focused on developing a great system are now devoted to workarounds for the system's deficiencies. People work hard, but things do not necessarily get better.

We'll soon look in more detail at how most organizations struggle with designing and operating complex systems. First we'll examine situations in which mismanagement led to dramatic, sudden cataclysm—mismanagement of medical care leading to patient harm and insensitivity to technical faults leading to disaster in the space shuttle program. We'll also see that the same behaviors can lead to slowly unfolding catastrophes—the downward spiral of a once-proud company becoming ever less competitive. But first, let's look at the basics of how complex systems fail.

People, Processes, and "Normal Accidents"

In the wake of the Three Mile Island crisis, which involved a partial meltdown of the radioactive core of a nuclear reactor which took weeks to stabilize, the Yale professor Charles Perrow was struck by what had *not* gone wrong. No critical component had failed cataclysmically. There had been no sabotage or gross negligence on the part of an individual worker. In fact, only rather trivial things had gone wrong—a stuck valve, a balky pump, an obscured gauge, an inaccurate sensor, the misinterpretation of a reading—and these were things that went wrong all the time with no apparent ill effect. However, this time they had gone wrong in just the right (or wrong) combination and at just the right (or wrong) time to bring the plant down. Because of the resulting fear, the nuclear-power industry was brought to an extended standstill.

Instead of a single weak link, according to Perrow, the real problem was the complexity of the technical system *and* the complexity of the organization responsible for its operation. So many subsystems and components were linked to so many others—what Perrow referred to as a high degree of *interconnectedness*—that it was impossible for anyone to understand how the reactor would behave in all circumstances and how it might fail. When the reactor started to fail, operators in the control room found it impossible to interpret and act on the indications because they contradicted each other. Furthermore, the system was *tightly coupled*, meaning that a problem in one component was hard to isolate from the other components to which it was linked. Once a problem got started, it could easily flow over paths of least resistance in ways that could not be predicted. After looking at this and other examples of complex technical systems intertwined with complex social/organizational systems, Perrow reached the pessimistic conclusion that society was going to be regularly exposed to *normal accidents,* so called because of their potential prevalence and also because they seem to arise in situations that seem perfectly normal right up to the moment of failure.

Perrow is not alone in his prognosis. Jim Reason, another influential writer about human error and system failure, emphasizes the point that "organizational accidents" don't occur because of a single dramatic misstep. Rather, a number of vulnerabilities and errors line up in just the wrong way for something very bad to occur.

Perrow's and Reason's analyses warn us away from a metaphor we conventionally use to describe things going wrong—the chain with a weak link. That evocative image implies that (1) relationships, interactions, and events proceed linearly, and (2) the system as a whole is sound but for the one inadequate element. This leads to the conclusion that when systems fail, individuals can be blamed. For complex systems, none of this is so. A more appropriate image is the spider web, a complex intertwining of strands. One or another may snap, and the web may hold, but if just the right combination fails, the web collapses. No wonder then that spiders repair rips and tears as they occur, not waiting for the failures to accumulate.

Other research raises a concern beyond the interconnectedness of complex systems and the tight coupling of their components. It is that little things go wrong all the time. But rather than being recognized as indications of vulnerability, these small disturbances are typically left unresolved—like the broken threads of a spider's web—until they combine in just the right way to wreak havoc. Perrow alludes to just this behavioral failure at Three Mile Island, the consistent suppression of signals which could have been occasions for learning and improvement. According to his account, the things that went wrong at Three Mile Island had gone wrong before, but never in a combination that caused the system to fail badly.

Something had been wrong, but no harm done—that's how it always seemed.

In short, one characteristic of lower-performing organizations is that they make matters worse by suppressing their ability to learn from experience. They are responsible for systems that are impossible to understand conceptually, yet they diminish their ability to learn about them experientially. When something goes wrong—those seemingly trivial events that seem to have no immediate consequences—people discover how to contain the problem, using a variety of workarounds and firefighting techniques, often showing remarkable creativity. The problem seems to go away, but all the factors that caused it remain in place to cause reoccurrences. Eventually, enough little things occur in just the right combination to cause a disaster. In short, low-velocity organizations, unlike the high-velocity leaders, are slow learners, slow improvers, slow innovators, and ultimately sluggish competitors. Let's examine how their low-velocity approach plays out in several situations—a failure in health care delivery, two catastrophes at NASA, and the stagnation of one of Toyota's competitors.

Death of a Patient:
Functions but No Process

In America, there is a heartbreaking gap between the care we actually have and the care we should get. Conditions that previously could not be described and diagnosed now can be treated and even cured, including infertility, myriad forms of cancer, and a host of genetic diseases. Limb reattachment and reconstructive surgery are now possible, along with minimally invasive orthopedic procedures and the conversion of HIV into a chronic condition. To find a previous period when life could be improved and restored with such certainty, we would have to go back to the age of biblical miracles—fertility being granted for faithful prayer, the dead being restored to the living, ailments like blindness being cured by the laying-on of hands.

And yet modern medicine has become a terrible disappointment. There are the exorbitant costs, but even for those who can find and afford treatment, the risks are considerable. The Institute of Medicine has published studies estimating the number of patients who lose their lives to medical error—defined as the mismanagement of medical care while a person is hospitalized—to be as high as 98,000 people each year out of 33 million hospitalizations that occur annually. This does not include the equal number felled by hospital-acquired infections. This makes the risk of injury one in a few hundred, the risk of avoidable death one in a few thousand. As Dr. Lucien Leape, a pioneer in the patient-safety movement, described it at a lecture I attended, you would have to ride in motorized hang gliders or parachute off bridges to face risks similar to those of being a hospitalized patient. And that is only for acute care. There are those who succumb to illness because of failures in preventive, primary, and chronic care as well.

It shouldn't be like this. Medical science is great and the people who employ it are bright, well educated, well trained, hardworking, and altruistic. But they work in systems that compromise their best efforts. For instance, the *Annals of Internal Medicine* published a series of articles called "Quality Grand Rounds." These were detailed case studies of breakdowns in the delivery of care that led to human suffering. The variety of things that could go wrong was both shocking and fascinating. My friend and colleague, Dr. Mark Schmidhofer, and I began to wonder what these cases had in common. We found out that the answer was "plenty."

In all of the cases that we examined, there were common characteristics that led to painful results. People lacked a systems view—a full appreciation of how the work they did was affected by and affected the work of other people. Granted that, as Perrow pointed out, it was exceptionally difficult to understand all the nuances of how such a complex system worked, but the people in these cases did not advance their understanding when there were warnings that they should have. Rather than push for ever-better clarity as to how things should work, they were exceedingly tolerant of ambiguities regarding who was supposed to do what, how to convey information from one person to the next, or how to perform a particular task. And even when it was obvious that something was wrong, they worked around the problem, relying on extra vigilance and extra effort. Thus they imposed on themselves the same set of problems day after day, consistently turning down the chance to understand the complex interactions of people, technology, place, and circumstance better and thus improve the system as its flaws were discovered.

Let's look at a case in which skilled and dedicated workers in different departments failed to heed warnings that they didn't fully understand how their work affected each other. Their failure to do so killed a patient.

Mrs. Grant, a 68-year-old woman, was recovering from successful, elective cardiac surgery. At 8:15 a.m., the day nurse who was just starting her shift discovered that Mrs. Grant was having a full-body seizure. A code was called; blood was drawn and rushed to the lab. Mrs. Grant was then raced to radiology for a scan. Was there an undetected mass, blood clot, blood leak, or other neurological cause? All those tests were negative. Mrs. Grant was wheeled back to the nursing unit. Awaiting the code team were the shocking results of the blood work: an undetectably low serum-glucose level. Mrs. Grant had nearly no blood sugar. Her brain was sputtering like an engine pulling from a dry gas tank. Hurried attempts to intervene intravenously failed. Mrs. Grant's condition worsened and she went into a coma. Weeks later, her family withdrew life support. What had happened?

To the hospital's credit, an investigation was started immediately, with interviews, analyses, and a reconstruction of events. They started by talking with the day nurse. What did she know? Nothing, as it turned out. She had just started her shift; her first interaction with Mrs. Grant had occurred when she observed the seizures and alerted the code team. The night nurse had more to say, but nothing that seemed to shed any light—at first. Apparently, he was at the nursing station when an alarm sounded at 6:45 a.m. The monitor was reporting that a catheter snaked through Mrs. Grant's vein to administer medication was showing a possible occlusion, a potentially life-threatening blood clot. Understanding the severity of the situation, he hurried to Mrs. Grant's room, loaded a syringe with a dose of the anticoagulant heparin, and injected it into the line. He then checked that Mrs. Grant was resting comfortably and resumed caring for his other patients. Not until the code was sounded about an hour and a half later did he see Mrs. Grant again.

The investigation was drawing blanks until someone taking inventory of Mrs. Grant's room asked where the empty vial of heparin was. It should have been in the sharps container, the box in which used vials, needles, and other dangerous materials are disposed, but it was not. Nursing is a hectic job with constant bursts of short-duration tasks and care for one patient inextricably intertwined with that of others. The vial might have gotten swept up in the flurry of work. The investigators immediately started searching for it elsewhere. Was it on a counter or in a cabinet? Had someone carried it to another patient's room? It could not be found. Then the staffer who was inventorying asked a more ominous question: Why was there an empty multidose vial of insulin in the disposal box? No one had an answer, certainly not the night nurse. There had been no orders to give Mrs. Grant insulin. The vial did not appear to have been carried in from another patient's room. There was only one remaining explanation, and the implications were horrifying.

What started as an investigation likely turned into an interrogation, with someone demanding of the night nurse, "Where is the empty heparin vial? Why do we have an empty vial of insulin?" "I don't know!" he must have protested, asserting both ignorance and innocence. Then there was a jarring finding. Someone realized that insulin and heparin vials could not easily be distinguished from each other. By size, shape, weight, and texture, they had the same feel. They looked alike, too. A quick glance was insufficient to tell one from the other because both vials were clear glass containing a clear fluid. Yes, they were labeled differently, but the vials were small, the labels were even smaller, and the type on the labels was smaller still. Of course, a person *could* distinguish one from the other—but in a rush, responding to an alarm, in a darkened room at the end of an overnight shift? Not likely.

The team then realized what must have happened. The nurse, in his rush to help Mrs. Grant, had reached for a vial of heparin and somehow grabbed a vial of insulin instead. The vials were stored only 18 inches apart on the same nursing cart. Maybe he reached for the wrong location. Maybe an insulin vial had found its way into the heparin stock. We'll never know. Once the vial was in his hand and certainly once the medicine was in the syringe, he could not know that his best efforts to protect his patient from the ill effects of a positive blood clot were going to kill her.

Whom would you blame for Mrs. Grant's death? One could immediately blame the nurse. After all, he was the one who delivered the fatal dose. While that might be emotionally gratifying, it leaves open the question of what had he actually done wrong? He heard the alarm, interpreted it correctly, rushed to do what was correct in that situation, and reached for what he thought was heparin. You can argue that he should have checked, double-checked, and even triple-checked that he had the right medication, but there is overwhelming evidence that relying on vigilance, monitoring, and otherwise being careful is a poor defense against error. People are not wired to be reliably careful. That is why, for example, such a large investment has been made in designing aircraft cockpits so that it is difficult to do the wrong thing—mistake thrust for flaps, turn or descend too sharply—and easy to do what is right. That is why airplane crews are allowed to work only so many hours at a stretch, only so many hours in a day, and only so many days in a week. Yet here was Mrs. Grant's nurse, rushing to save a life early in the morning and at the end of his shift, hardly the sweet spot of his circadian rhythm. Do we insist that he should have interrupted his urgent response in order to examine the vials calmly and coolly—in dim light, mind you? As I mentioned above, this kind of carefulness is not really what we are wired for.

The truth is, the nurse was tricked—by packaging, presentation, lighting, and timing—into killing Mrs. Grant. But who set this booby trap? Was it the pharmacy staff? After all, it was their job to prepare, package, and present medication to the nursing staff. But the pharmacy staff might protest that they had done nothing wrong. Mrs. Grant did not die because the medication was of the wrong concentration or contaminated or mislabeled.

The nurse had done what a nurse was expected to do. The pharmacy staff had done what a pharmacy staff is expected to do. But Mrs. Grant was dead. The real problem is that the system's pieces may have worked, but their interaction failed, as the work of the pharmacy was grossly flawed from the perspective of nursing. Why?

If this hospital was like many with which I am familiar, it had a hierarchy within nursing—a charge nurse, the unit's nursing manager, and a chief of nursing—and a hierarchy in pharmacy. But what it likely lacked was someone responsible for the whole process of medication administration—all the way from the doctors who write the orders to the pharmacy where the orders are checked and filled to the nurses who give the patients their meds. In the absence of an efficient way—or perhaps any way at all—to manage the functional pieces in the service of the whole process, there turned out to be a fatal disconnect.

But if that process was booby-trapped, you might ask, wouldn't people like Mrs. Grant get killed all the time? And wouldn't that already have gotten management's attention? This brings us to workarounds, firefighting, making do, and other means of coping with system chatter as a basic pathology of complex work systems. David Bates, a physician at Brigham and Women's Hospital in Boston and the author of the case about Mrs. Grant, has done extensive research on the frequency of medication-administration errors. He and his colleagues discovered that for every patient killed by an error in medication administration, 5 to 10 are injured. (For example, Mrs. Grant might have lived but suffered harm.) For every injury, there are 5 to 10 close calls. (Mrs. Grant's nurse might have caught his mistake just as he was about to inject the insulin.) For every close call, there are 5 to 10 slips and mistakes. (Mrs. Grant's nurse might have picked up a vial of insulin, noticed that it was the wrong medication, put it back, and picked up the correct one instead.) Behind the one mistake that killed Mrs. Grant, we can imagine 5 to 10 injuries, 25 to 100 close calls, and 125 to 1,000 slips and mistakes—a total of between 155 and 1,110 chances for someone at that hospital to say, "Hey, these vials are easy to mix up! Let's do something about it before we kill someone."

That's exactly what would have happened in a high-velocity organization. But in low-velocity organizations, people suppress those indications that the work processes are inadequate and have to be modified. When they run into obstacles, they treat them as the normal noise of the process, its unavoidable perturbations, around which they must work. They get the job done, but they do not increase the chance that the next person will have a higher chance for success and a lower chance for failure.

For example, my colleague, Harvard professor Anita Tucker, made detailed minute-by-minute observations of nurses and found that they confronted some sort of operational failure—a glitch, an interruption, a misunderstanding, the absence of something needed—every few minutes. Ninety percent of the time the nurses found a way to make do, finish the task, and meet their other responsibilities. What do you think they did the remaining 10 percent of the time? Remember: Even if only 1 in 10 slips, mistakes, and close calls with insulin and heparin had been investigated, that might have saved Mrs. Grant's life. Unfortunately, at least for the nurses Tucker tracked, the other 10 percent of the time they did not draw someone's attention to the problem so its causes could be rectified and its recurrence prevented. They did show the problem to someone else, but that was only to get help working around it: a fellow nurse who could decipher a particular doctor's illegible handwriting or someone heading down the hall who could snag some gloves or gowns.

Some of the temporary fixes were creative and expressed the nurses' determination to meet the needs of their patients, but they had the inadvertent consequence of leaving in place the factors that had caused the problem in the first place. (One nurse with whom I worked, when confronted with this reality of working around problems, blurted out, "I thought I was a great problem solver, but I just realized I've been solving the same problem every day for twenty years!" We'll visit with her later and see the results of her change from persistently working around problems to seeing problems and solving them.) Applying the findings of Bates and Tucker to the situation in Mrs. Grant's hospital, it is possible that despite the hundreds if not thousands of warnings that there was something deficient in the way those medications were presented to nurses, nothing was done in an environment of workarounds and firefighting, leaving Mrs. Grant and her nurse to their fates.

What killed Mrs. Grant? The nurse? The pharmacist? No. It was an ineffective approach to managing complex interactive work that proved to be her undoing. It was not clear to people how their work fit into a larger system. The nature of the situations in which they found themselves was often ambiguous, and even when it was obvious that something was amiss, they kept plugging away, dealing as best they could with one thing after another. Diane Vaughn calls this the normalization of deviance, and we'll see it again later in this chapter when we turn to NASA.

There is a sad irony here. The hospital staff was able to determine what had killed Mrs. Grant only because they did exactly the right thing, quickly swarming the catastrophic situation once it had been discovered. If they had waited a day or even an hour, memories might have changed, the sharps container might have been emptied, and the conditions that had allowed the problem to occur might have changed enough to prevent anyone from ever figuring out what had happened. If that staff had only worked in an organization which trained and expected them to swarm small discrepancies with such velocity and determination—the slips, mistakes, and close calls—they would have seen the medication-administration system's vulnerabilities earlier on and this disaster might have been averted.

WHY HEALTH-CARE PROFESSIONALS ARE ILL PREPARED TO MANAGE SYSTEMS

When medical science was simpler, coordination was easier. A small group of people who worked together frequently could establish reliable patterns of behavior, and when those patterns failed, they could resolve the problems informally, as discussed in Chapter 2. Today, however, a patient may have several doctors, many nurses, and a dozen or more medications. A more disciplined, scientific approach to managing such complex work is necessary. Why is it not used? Health-care professionals are not trained to do that, as the following example illustrates.

My cardiologist friend, Mark Schmidhofer, was brought up short when his eight-year-old daughter asked, "Daddy, what grade did you go to?" Including primary and secondary school, premed, medical school, internship, residency, a master's in physics, and fellowships, he realized that he had gone to 27 grades. Of course, his daughter, not at all impressed, replied, "Well, I'm starting the third grade today."

Despite his daughter's condescension, my friend reflected on what had occurred during those 27 grades. As he had progressed, his expertise had become deeper in a narrower field, culminating in his cutting-edge knowledge about a particular subspecialty—not cardiology or even angioplasty, but laser angioplasty.

As a master of his subdiscipline, he faced a conundrum. When he completed his fellowship and joined the ranks of more senior physicians, he was sometimes put in charge of inpatient units, a role in which he was responsible for the care of all the patients. He realized that, although he was tremendously competent at contributing the portion of the work in which he had specialized, patient care depended on the myriad contributions of people on the other side of one boundary or another: those in disciplines such as pulmonology, endocrinology, surgery, and psychiatry; those in professions such as nursing and pharmacy; and those in his own profession but at other levels, such as residents and medical students.

When he objected to his colleagues that he had deep knowledge within his discipline's silo, the vertical element of his role, but far less expertise in creating systems of care from the disparate disciplines and managing them, he was assured: "Don't worry. You'll figure it out like the rest of us did."

Death of Two Crews: Unheeded Warnings

Chasing the Rabbit is not a book about disasters. The stakes in managing complexity are generally much lower. But disasters do focus the mind, so let's look at a pair that have much to teach us and that many of us will remember.

On January 16, 2003, the space shuttle *Columbia* rocketed off a launch pad from the Kennedy Space Center. *Columbia*, named for the first American ship to circumnavigate the globe, was historic in its own right. It had been the first shuttle to fly and had completed 27 successful missions. Its twenty-eighth was number 113 for the fleet as a whole. During two weeks in orbit, the *Columbia* crew ran a series of experiments, tests, and high-altitude observations. Aside from a few inconveniences along the way, the spacecraft and its equipment performed well. Their flight nearly over, the crew prepared for an exciting but uneventful landing. The mission for which they had spent years preparing and which they had carried out successfully was at an end. Tragically, they never celebrated a reunion with their families, friends, and colleagues.

On February 1, 2003, about two weeks after liftoff, while traveling at 17,500 miles an hour, the pilot fired retrorockets that slowed the *Columbia* just enough for it to leave orbit, lose altitude, and begin its descent. On the way home, disaster occurred. Rather than surfing down through the earth's atmosphere, losing height and speed on the way to a successful landing, *Columbia* broke up. It shed pieces of itself in the skies over California, Nevada, and New Mexico, leaving in its wake a debris field that stretched from western Texas to Louisiana. The crew of seven was killed, but not instantly; the data recordings indicate that the pilot tried vainly to regain control of his out-of-control vehicle. In addition, two members of a helicopter search crew died taking part in the recovery effort. How could such a seemingly mundane mission end with such loss? We'll see that the same organizational shortcomings that punished Mrs. Grant—not seeing the system for the pieces and suppressing evidence that the system was behaving in unexpected and undesirable ways—were endemic at NASA.

According to the board charged with investigating the accident:

> The physical cause of the loss of *Columbia* and its crew was a breach in the Thermal Protection System on the leading edge of the left wing. The breach was initiated by a piece of insulating foam that separated from the left bipod ramp of the External Tank and struck the wing in the vicinity of the lower half of Reinforced Carbon-Carbon panel 8 at 81.9 seconds after launch. During re-entry, this breach in the Thermal Protection System allowed superheated air to penetrate the leading-edge insulation and progressively melt the aluminum structure of the left wing, resulting in a weakening of the structure until increasing aerodynamic forces caused loss of control, failure of the wing, and breakup of the Orbiter.

Here is what this means: A space shuttle has a large external fuel tank, filled at launch with liquid oxygen and liquid hydrogen (see Figure 3-1). These fuels are so extremely cold that the tank would ice over if not for its distinctive orange coat of foam insulation. Icing over would be hazardous because of debris during launch, excess weight, and compromised aerodynamics, among other reasons.

According to the board that investigated the accident, what apparently happened is that during takeoff, a piece of foam insulation broke off and hit the leading edge of the left wing, cracking a "reinforced carbon-carbon" (RCC) panel.

Figure 3-1 Space shuttle *Columbia* sitting at Launch Complex 39-A.
The upper circle shows the left bipod (–Y) ramp on the forward
attach point, while the lower circle is around RCC panel 8-left.

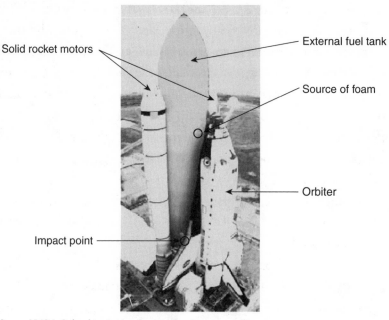

Source: NASA, Columbia *Accident Investigation Report*, page 49.

The RCC panel is a technological marvel. When space
shuttles begin their reentry, they are moving at approximately
17,500 miles per hour. Aside from a brief rocket burn to slow
slightly, they lose all their velocity through friction with the
air. As shuttles rip through the atmosphere, temperatures in
the thousands of degrees are formed on their leading edges.
Most materials would incinerate from such abuse, but not
RCC panels. Lightweight and precisely formed to the optimal
aerodynamic contours needed for flight, RCC panels are so
impervious to heat that one side would be cool to the touch

even if a blowtorch were being applied to the other side. When the RCC panels are intact, they effortlessly deflect the superheated gases up and around the wings.

The breach in the RCC panel to which the report referred, caused by impact with foam debris, had no effect on the mission; in the low-gravity, no-atmosphere environment of earth orbit, there was no need to deflect heat away from the wings. Reentry was a different matter. Superheated gases that should have been deflected away from the spacecraft roared into the wing—one estimate placed the size of the breach at 140 square inches—causing mayhem as they incinerated components and melted support structures, destroying the spacecraft's aerodynamic integrity and sabotaging the pilot's ability to control its flight. Once the crew started their reentry, their fate was sealed.

However, the board did not assign all the blame for the disaster to that technological cause. In the board's view, NASA's organizational culture and structure had as much to do with this accident as the external tank foam. The board found that:

> Cultural traits and organizational practices detrimental to safety were allowed to develop, including: reliance on past success as a substitute for sound engineering practices (such as testing to understand why systems were not performing in accordance with requirements); organizational barriers that prevented effective communication of critical safety information and stifled professional differences of opinion; lack of integrated management across program elements; and the evolution of an informal

chain of command and decision-making processes that operated outside the organization's rules.

The board went on to say the following:

> More troubling, the pressure of maintaining the flight schedule created a management atmosphere that increasingly accepted less-than-specification performance of various components and systems, on the grounds that such deviations had not interfered with the success of previous flights.

As in the case of Mrs. Grant, there was a specific technical failure to which blame could be assigned. But then there were the organizational factors that allowed the technical failure to occur. The booby-trap had been set because NASA was managing an extremely complex operation without due respect for how much it still needed to learn about that operation. NASA's fault was not that it didn't know everything about the foam insulation problem, but that it had stopped learning, as we'll see below.

The original design criteria for the space shuttle precluded foam loss from the fuel tank. It was considered an extremely dangerous problem, in large part because there was no margin for error on the RCC panels. Their original design specifications "required the RCC components to have essentially no impact resistance." Yet even on its first flight, *Columbia* had significant debris hits, with over 300 tiles needing replacement, and the problems of foam-induced damage did not end there. After every flight, there were scores of impact marks in the thermal protection tiles, with dozens of them over an inch in depth.

Here was overwhelming evidence that the system was behaving contrary to design and expectations. And no one could be sure why. Was it the material, its application method, an aging problem, contamination? Whereas the certainty of a problem and the uncertainty of its cause and its effects might have—should have—triggered greater caution, it instead became a source of confidence. Though based on no engineering analysis, shuttle managers used past success as a justification for confidence in future flights and made no change in the external tank configurations for future missions. Foam strike, once a cause for serious concern, had been diminished to "a maintenance and turnaround concern rather than a safety of flight issue." This makes about as much sense as flipping a coin twice, getting heads both times, and assuming, without any further investigation, that it will land heads, not tails, on all further flips.

Recall that high-velocity organizations recognize that the complex systems which they have designed—technical or organizational—are imperfect. Of course such organizations are delighted when their operations work as planned. But they are also respected when the systems do not perform as expected. They interpret these deviations and departures from predication as important signals—indications of a circumstance that was poorly understood initially, if it was anticipated at all, but that might lend itself to investigation, deeper understanding, and resolution. In contrast, those who are chasing the rabbits do not see departures and deviations as positive signals, opportunities for improvement and innovation. For those organizations, the deviations are noise, one thing after another, the distracting chatter with which they somehow cope.

NASA's managers fell into the latter category, dismissing evidence that they didn't fully understand the system for which they were responsible. That allowed them to launch repeatedly without resolving or even addressing the problem of foam debris—without even granting that it was a problem.

It wasn't just lessons from previous launches that went unlearned. NASA suppressed its ability to learn from the experience of *Columbia* 's own launch and mission, cutting off the possibility of determining just how bad the situation actually was. Within a day of *Columbia* 's launch, NASA managers knew there had been yet another instance of foam striking the wing. Had they at least taken that one warning seriously, they might have bought themselves time by canceling their experiments and otherwise conserving energy, air, and water. That might have given them an opportunity to conduct a midflight repair, or another shuttle might have been rushed into an orbital rendezvous. *Atlantis* was being readied for its next flight and its pilots, commanders, and space-walk-trained crew members were on hand. Technologically, both of these alternatives were possibilities, albeit risky ones. It turned out that, organizationally, they were not.

Here are the reasons why. There is a group within NASA responsible for analyzing video images immediately after launch. Within a day, it was known that a significant piece of material had struck *Columbia*. By Friday, the first full day in orbit, higher-resolution images helped nail down to a tenth of a second when the debris hit had occurred. Back in 1988, when foam loss and foam strikes were considered serious, a similar discovery had been made during the flight of the shuttle *Atlantis*, whereupon "the crew was immediately directed to inspect the vehicle." Tile damage was found, and it was only by luck that the consequences were not more serious. "More severe thermal damage—perhaps even a burn-through—may have occurred were it not for the aluminum plate at the site of the tile loss." Yet 15 years later, when concerns were raised about the consequences of a debris strike for *Columbia*, those concerns were dismissed. According the investigation board, "The history of foam-problem decisions shows how NASA first began and then continued flying with foam losses, so that flying with these deviations from design specifications was viewed as normal and acceptable."

During *Columbia*'s fatal mission, this played out in a series of missed opportunities to recognize how bad things were, so that no corrective action was ever considered, let alone tried. The Columbia Accident Investigation Board (CAIB) found that as early as Friday, the first full day in orbit, engineers who were concerned about what had happened wanted to begin a more detailed analysis. But managers, expressing less concern, decided to delay any additional analysis until Monday. Nevertheless, one engineer started using a software package to create estimates of the extent of possible damage. However, he had used this software only twice before; he was hardly an expert. The software had never been used to model the impact between the shuttle and such a large object; in fact, this was outside its design parameters. So you had an "out of spec" person using software in an "out of spec" application, trying to determine how far "out of spec" the shuttle might be, on behalf of managers who weren't seeing the big picture. On

Sunday, another engineer e-mailed a manager to request that *Columbia*'s crew make a visual inspection of the left wing. He never received an answer. This was only the first opportunity to ascertain the severity of the situation.

The board also learned that on day 1 of the mission, crew member David Brown had downlinked a 35-second clip of the external tank separation. In that segment, the bipod ramp was out of view, but the board determined that Brown had probably had a longer stretch of video than what he had downlinked, which would have included images of the bipod ramp from which foam had fallen. However, no one asked him to review his video or downlink a longer clip. That was a second missed opportunity. A third took place when the foam strike was mentioned in an unrelated meeting and the possibility of asking the Department of Defense for ground- and space-based imagery support was discussed, but without follow-up. All in all, the CAIB found three requests for imaging that went nowhere— one on day 2 and two on day 6—and eight other missed opportunities to gain more data on which to base a more informed decision. Without convincing data that something was definitely wrong and having dismissed the evidence that something might be wrong, NASA's managers proceeded as if they were certain nothing was wrong. The consequences were catastrophic. Table 3-1 shows a section from the CAIB report.

What makes the *Columbia* accident and the death of its crew even more frustrating is the fact that NASA had shown nearly identical organizational dynamics leading up to the explosion of the *Challenger* moments after launch in 1986. True, the technical details were considerably different. In that case, flames burned through the rubber gasket O-rings at the joints between

Table 3-1 Summary Table from CAIB Report

Missed Opportunities

1. Flight Day 4. Rodney Rocha [NASA's designated chief engineer for the Thermal Protection System] inquires if crew has been asked to inspect for damage. No response.

2. Flight Day 6. Mission Control fails to ask crew member David Brown to downlink video he took of External Tank separation, which may have revealed missing bipod foam.

3. Flight Day 6. NASA and National Imagery and Mapping Agency personnel discuss possible request for imagery. No action taken.

4. Flight Day 7. Wayne Hale [launch integration manager for the next shuttle mission] phones Department of Defense representative, who begins identifying imaging assets, only to be stopped per Linda Ham's orders [Ham was chair of the Mission Management Team].

5. Flight Day 7. Mike Card, a NASA Headquarters manager from the Safety and Mission Assurance Office, discusses imagery request with Mark Erminger, Johnson Space Center Safety and Mission Assurance. No action taken.

6. Flight Day 7. Mike Card discusses imagery request with Bryan O'Connor, Associate Administrator for Safety and Mission Assurance. No action taken.

7. Flight Day 8. Barbara Conte [Missions Operations Directorate representative], after discussing imagery request with Rodney Rocha, calls LeRoy Cain, the STS-107 ascent/entry Flight Director. Cain checks with Phil Engelauf [Chief of the Flight Director's Office] and then delivers a "no" answer.

8. Flight Day 14. Mike Card, from NASA's Safety and Mission Assurance Office, discusses the imaging request with William Readdy, Associate Administrator for Space Flight. Readdy directs that imagery should only be gathered on a "not-to-interfere" basis. None was forthcoming.

sections of the solid-rocket boosters, causing an explosion. But former Secretary of State William Rogers and his colleagues, who had the macabre task of investigating the loss of that shuttle, reached the conclusion that NASA had missed and/or dismissed warning signs of threats. "When the joint began behaving in unexpected ways [on previous flights], neither NASA nor the Solid Rocket Motor manufacturer Morton-Thiokol adequately tested the joint to determine the source of the deviations from specifications or developed a solution to them, even though the problems frequently recurred. Nor did they respond to internal warnings about the faulty seal. Instead, Morton-Thiokol and NASA management came to see the problems as an acceptable flight risk—a violation of a design requirement that could be tolerated." Things had gotten so bad that the Rogers Commission concluded that "a contractor [had] to prove that it was not safe to launch, rather than proving it was safe."

Nearly twenty years later, NASA still had not learned the lesson that design specifications reflect expectations and latent assumptions and that *any* deviations from specifications refute or contradict the assumptions. Once the systems assumptions are refuted, its viability should be doubted. Ignorance should be assumed to be dangerous; indications of ignorance should be seen as welcome warnings that hazards lurk ahead.

Slow Death of an Automaker: Coping but Not Improving

The argument of *Chasing the Rabbit* is that the way complex work systems are managed has direct and predictable ramifications for performance. Manage complex systems so that there is a poor view of how the pieces fit together and insist (explicitly or implicitly) that people work around problems when they are encountered, and the results will range from disappointing to catastrophic. We have now looked at several deadly catastrophes, but there are much less dramatic catastrophes, those which unfold slowly like a wasting disease rather than like a fiery crash. In the end, though, the destruction can be just as complete.

The U.S. auto industry has not exploded in flames. But the wasting away of great corporations—the loss of jobs and the consequent impact on individual families, the toll taken on long-established communities, and the diminishment in wealth of stockholders and creditors—is a tragedy of gigantic proportions. Let's look at what it means to be in an organization that is slowly wasting away.

Imagine waking up tomorrow morning for work. After the alarm goes off and as you roll out of bed, it hits you: Today you will fail. It will not be in a big, pronounced way, but fail you will. The product or service for which you are responsible is not world-class. Sure, there seems to be a demand for it, but that is largely because your company has been forced to cut the price to attract bargain hunters. Today you will struggle with various hassles, but there will be no recourse, no way to call for help, no way to contain the problem, no way to set things right. Instead, you'll have to soldier on, making do until the end of your shift. Of course, relief will be only temporary. This will be your plight the next day, and the day after that, and every day that follows until you retire or are fired. That is what it means to work in a system that is inherently sclerotic, stiff, unresponsive, and not self-correcting or self-improving. Let's take a closer look at what this means in practice.

Orientation and Seat Installation

I started my research on Toyota by learning what it meant to work in a Big Three plant, not merely observing or interviewing but actually participating. This wasn't an arbitrary decision. Throughout *Chasing the Rabbit*, we see how high-velocity organizations go out of their way to see surprises, recognizing as quickly as possible gaps between what was expected and what had actually occurred. The same commitment to creating an opportunity to be surprised motivated Toyota's insistence that I work somewhere other than Toyota first. Had I gone into Toyota without experiencing an alternative as a contrast, I would not have been nearly as attuned as I needed to be to what was unusual, different, or unique. But, by immersing myself in a different environment first, the differences would be all the more stark. This plant was not picked as an example of a low-performing organization, akin to the role of low-performing strawman that GM's Framingham plant played in *The Machine That Changed the World*. Indeed, it was chosen as one that was well run in the traditional fashion. I worked with hardworking people who struggled in an environment in which workarounds abounded because, as you will see, even problems that occurred hundreds of times a day were not flagged, investigated, and solved.

I started work on Monday with other temporary hires. It was not obvious at first, but we were in for a healthy dose of dissonance. We were told during orientation that our job, as frontline operators, was to see problems and draw attention to them. That seemed fairly straightforward except for two difficulties: How was one to see a problem? And how was one to call attention to it? It turned out that we often could do neither.

My first assignment was with Bill and Jim in seat installation. Seats arrived by conveyor at the preceding workstation, where a worker took them off the conveyor and placed them in the car. Bill and Jim attached the seat by driving four bolts with an air-powered torque wrench (see Figure 3-2).

Bill showed me how he did the job. First, he took four bolts out of a cardboard carton that was on a workbench a few feet from the line. He then walked to his left, placed two bolts in the rear foot well, and then drove the two front bolts through the carpet and into the frame. Then he slid the seat forward to give himself room to maneuver the air gun while driving the rear bolts. With the four bolts attached, Bill placed the air-powered torque wrench back on the workbench, punched a code into the computer indicating whether or not a problem had occurred with this particular car at his station, and waited for the next car to arrive.

After watching Bill perform this sequence several times, I tried to do the same thing but immediately discovered that

---

Figure 3-2 Workflow at seat installation

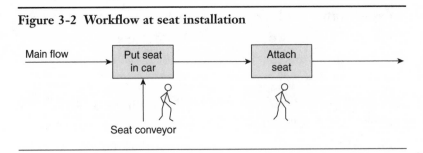

74

what Bill did effortlessly was extremely difficult for me. I fumbled while trying to grab the correct number of bolts, had problems getting the bolts seated straight, and had trouble aligning the torque wrench so that the bolt would thread properly into the frame. Each of these microtasks had its own subtleties, none of which I had absorbed. On my first try, Bill had to complete the sequence. On my second try, too. After many tries I gradually began to feel a bit more fluid. However, while concentrating on getting the bolts in the right holes within the cycle time, I continually forgot to enter in the computer console that the job had been done.

Even after several hours, I rarely was able to do a complete sequence. For the seat to be fastened correctly, the two front bolts had go through a slot in the frame and pick up the threads of a J-clip nut on the other side. The problem was that occasionally the J-clip was slightly out of line (see Figures 3-3 and 3-4). Then the bolt would not find the center of the clip but would push it aside. Not having threaded itself into the J-clip, the bolt would spin freely, with the seat not attached to the frame. When that happened, Bill would remove the bolt manually, take an awl from his workbench (or retrieve the awl

Figure 3-3 Correct: Bolt through J-clip

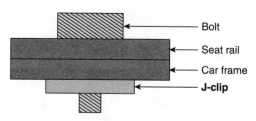

Figure 3-4 Incorrect: Bolt missing J-clip

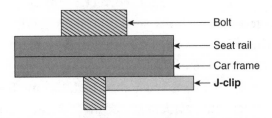

from Jim, who also needed it occasionally), use it to align the J-clip, and redrive the bolt. Finally, he taught me how to perform this workaround so that he would not have to do it. This was almost always effective, though many times I had to ask Bill to complete the sequence for me. Once, neither of us was able to get the bolt aligned in the J-clip, so Bill punched a problem code into the computer console.

This J-clip problem was just a microcosm of the general failure of organizations to manage complexity well. Presumably, the people who designed the J-clip and those who installed it didn't mean to make our work hard. But not knowing the consequence of their actions—like the pharmacy in Mrs. Grant's case—they laid booby traps for us. Managing the pieces—attaching J-clips here, attaching car seats there—without an eye toward the whole process—delivering a defect-free car to the customer—led to repeated difficulty. So too did the reliance on working around problems rather than dealing with them head on.

Not every car had this problem of out-of-line J-clips, but it occurred often enough that I took to carrying the awl in my back pocket so that I would not have to look for it each time. I gradually found it easier to use the awl for each car as insurance before driving the bolts. Thus, the workaround became part of my normal work routine because I was too slow to risk misfiring with a bolt and then having to reset it. (This strategy was not without some problems, though. One time I did okay with the awl, but when I finished, I forgot to remove it from the car. I then had to run down the assembly line and find it.)

By the end of the morning portion of the shift, I was better able to get all four bolts installed (even when a J-clip problem occurred) and enter the computer console code, all within the cycle and before the next car arrived. Although I was more or less able to do what was required, I certainly was not skillful, and I was drenched in sweat from my exertions. Yet on my subsequent visits to Toyota plants, I noticed that a single operator easily did twice the work I had done with such difficulty. In our Big Three facility, one person loaded the seats into the car while another tightened them. But the Toyota line operator's work was so well choreographed that he put the seat in the car, bolted it tight, and even added some trim to other parts. Here were the two-to-one differences in labor productivity that Mike Cusumano and others at MIT's International Motor Vehicle Program had documented a decade earlier. Here was a powerful company, not crashing or blowing up, but letting itself be overtaken and subdued one J-clip at a time.

Remember that I and the other new workers had been enjoined to see problems and draw attention to them. I was seeing problems, all right, but to whose attention was I to draw them? True, I had Bill and Jim to help me, but that wouldn't have been the case for a real worker. Our zone supervisor, a great guy, showed patience and hospitality to me during my visit and expressed concern about his crew, and when he was out of earshot, they spoke well of him. But he was responsible for 50 people in final assembly. That's a huge swath of real estate he had to cover. How did he stay in touch? With a combination of walkie-talkie and overhead page, racing from problem to problem in a golf cart. Therefore, the only resort was to punch an error code into a computer console that was yards away from my workstation. Of course, like everything else, that had a clumsy design, requiring the operator to remember a nonintuitive set of codes for which car, which location, and what sort of problem. To make matters worse, if you had a problem, you probably were running out of time as the next car was arriving in the station. Without the ability to call for help, there was no possibility of bringing a problem that had arisen to the attention of someone with more ability to do something about it. The line controlled the pace of people's work, not the reverse. When you were short on time, what was the first thing you sacrificed? That's right: entering the error code in the computer. You just had to hope someone else would catch the problem at inspection.

That was seat installation, but everywhere else I rotated, it was one workaround layered upon another layered upon yet another.

Body Shop

This problem of individual tasks not being managed as part of the integrated whole—with workarounds filling the gap when things didn't mesh—was hardly limited to final assembly. In the body shop, I attached rear-quarter and roof panels to cars as they passed between welding stations. Here again, you had

Figure 3-5 Workflow between robotic welders

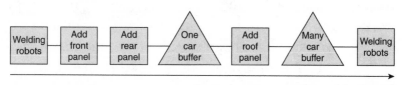

to do work that was not conducive to success. You had to try your best, compensate for system shortcomings, and labor on without a chance to fix what was wrong.

As for the rear-quarter panel, my job was to remove the parts from an overhead conveyor, place them on the car, bend a few tabs to hold them in place, and then release them to the next step, in which robots would weld them into place. Figure 3-5 shows the basic process flow and Figure 3-6 shows the part-attachment station.

Figure 3-6 Body shop part-attachment station

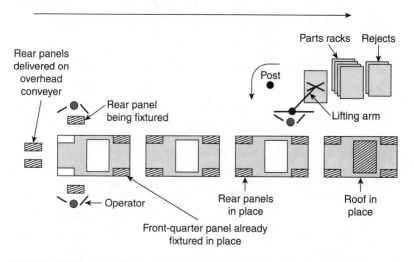

As with seat installation, training for this assignment was conducted entirely on the job. The person who normally worked in that job showed me the entire sequence for several cycles, coached me through the sequence for the next several cycles, and then left me on my own until the break (about an hour). My situation was not artificial. While I was banging away on one side of the line, one of the guys who had started on Monday morning with me was banging away on the other side. Table 3-2 shows the steps in the process.

In the brief period that I worked in the body shop, the equipment I used to lower the quarter panel off the overhead conveyer failed twice, dropping the metal piece about 10 feet and right past my face. Both times, the person working next to me and I were able to pick up the piece, visually confirm that it was not damaged (though, in hindsight, I realize that I wasn't really knowledgeable enough to distinguish good pieces from bad), and put it on the car body within the cycle time of 100 seconds. After the second failure, the area team captain came over and fiddled with the equipment, explaining that this was a recurring problem.

The adjustment he made solved the immediate problem but not the underlying problem. The equipment would fail again—it always did—and I feared that eventually it would drop a quarter panel on someone's head, maybe mine. Something else occurred to me later: I had not called the area team captain for help. Either someone else had called him or he had observed the difficulty I was having and had come to my assistance—after the *second* failure, that is. To be precise, I was not doing, nor was I able to do, the job I had been assigned during orientation. We had been told that when problems

Table 3-2 Body-shop Processes

Rear-Panel Placement

Raise a small hydraulic parts carrier up to the part (at a height of approximately 12 feet).

Press buttons to "grab" the work piece with suction cups and a clamp.

Lower the piece to waist height.

Use an air gun to apply a bead of sealant.

Release the clamp so that the panel is held only by suction cups.

Push the panel onto the waiting car.

Hold the panel in place with the left hand and release the suction cups with the right hand by pressing a button.

Push the conveyor away and make sure the panel is well seated.

Bend two metal flanges by hand to hold the panel to the car.

Walk five steps to a parts bin to get a 3-foot horizontal crosspiece.

Attach this piece to the rear panel and the car body with a thumb-push plastic "rivet."

Place a bead of sealant where the roof panel is to be placed.

Take the next panel from the overhead conveyer.

Press an "all-clear" button that releases the car to the next station.

Roof Placement

Using a mechanical parts carrier with suction cup attachments, lift the roof from a parts bin.

Turn to the left (counterclockwise) to face the car body and align the roof (this requires clearing the light post shown in Figure 3-8).

Lower the roof panel onto the car body.

Press a button to release the part from the carrier.

Bend a metal flange to hold the panel in place.

Turn clockwise to take the next piece from the parts bin.

Periodically, when the parts bin is empty, push a button to remove the empty bin and replace it with a full bin.

Use a separate bin in which I can place roof panels I judged to be defective.

occurred, we should notify the area team captain or the area supervisor. But we were never told who those people were or how to notify them.

As for the roof panel, that job was somewhat different from installing the quarter panel. First, the roof panel came out of a carrier and did not have to be lowered from a moving conveyor. Second, I had fewer and less time-consuming steps to perform with the roof panel. Therefore, even when the line was running without pause, I had a fair amount of waiting time. In contrast, although I was able to work at a comfortable rhythm when attaching the rear panel, it took nearly the full cycle to complete the work.

Although the roof-placement job was one of the least rushed ones I performed at that plant, it did have its frustrations. Moving the roof from the parts rack to the car body meant clearing a light post, as diagrammed in Figure 3-7. But I had no way of removing the obstacle. I had no idea about whom to tell about the difficulty. Judging by the banged and cracked lens on this light, it was obvious that the work piece often hit it, potentially causing damage to the product and to the light, and that the regular worker also lacked the authority or responsibility to do anything about it. Therefore, every

Figure 3-7 Avoiding the light-post obstacle

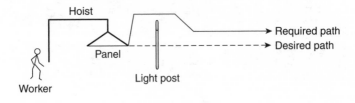

car required that the operator not only do his job but also make an extra effort not to damage the light or the roof piece.

There was another problem which I recognized only in hindsight. There was a place to put defective roof panels. It was not empty when I began working at that station, indicating that panels were occasionally defective. However, I did not know how to determine whether a panel was defective. And even if I were to identify a defective panel, it was not clear how putting that panel in the defective-panel rack would have generated information useful for process improvement.

The Three-Wheeled Car

While back-of-the-pack organizations may not be good at seeing myriad small problems, containing them, solving them, and building deeper process knowledge, they sometimes display remarkable creativity and urgency in trying to contain the bigger challenges.

For example, vehicles arrived at the wheel-installation station hanging from a fixture and left the station standing on their new wheels, bearing their own weight for the first time. It was important to attach the wheels successfully while the cars were at the workstation. If a car left the station unable to support itself, it might topple, stopping the line and perhaps causing damage or injury.

While I was with a zone supervisor, he was called on the walkie-talkie. His help was needed urgently at wheel-install. A car had arrived, but the brake was hanging loose, preventing the wheel from being attached. In a high-velocity organization, this defect would have been spotted at the station where the brakes were attached and the problem would not have traveled this far. But in this plant, several workers and two zone supervisors were called by walkie-talkie and raced over. The car would be in wheel-install for only a few minutes. The clock was ticking. While both supervisors watched, some workers came up with a clever improvisation. They grabbed the jack from the trunk, using it to brace the right front axle in the absence of a wheel (see Figure 3-8).

The brace supported the car as it was transferred automatically from the conveyor fixture to the conveyor belt. Then, as the car went through the remaining stations (fluid fill and the electronics test), other workers stayed with it, trying to attach a temporary wheel so that the car could roll off the end of the assembly line 10 minutes later (see Figure 3-9).

In this case, help was summoned, but in an ad hoc fashion. The immediate problem was solved, but only through a temporary impromptu response. In addition to the haphazard way in which a multitude of people were drawn into addressing the immediate problem, there was something else in this incident that was characteristic of low-velocity organizations. I spent

Figure 3-8 Temporary brace

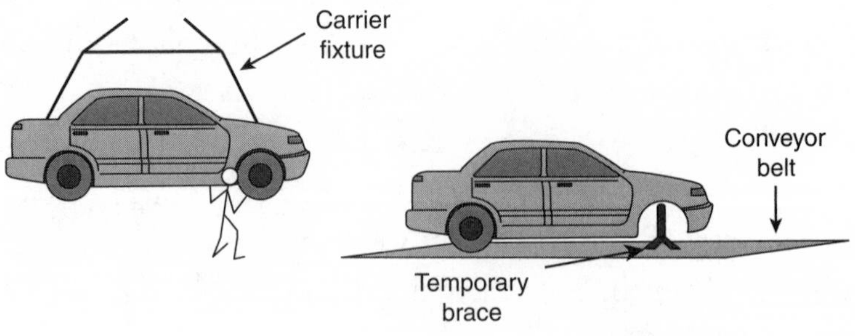

Carrier fixture

Conveyor belt

Temporary brace

Figure 3-9 Temporary wheel

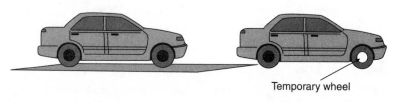

Temporary wheel

hours that day with several of the zone supervisors, yet I saw no attempts to change the work methods, train the workers, adapt the equipment at brake installation, or otherwise change the process to prevent the problem from recurring.

Despite the admonition that operators had both the authority and the responsibility to see problems and call attention to them, if not be part of their solution, the reality was nothing like that. What was the real quality control in the plant? It gets back to what we were told during orientation. Quality was inspected in. Periodically, cars were checked to see that various standards had been met; for instance, that particular bolts had been tightened to the correct torque. If a car was found not to spec, as at "check 3" in Figure 3-10, that triggered a sweep and

Figure 3-10 Quality checks and system sweeps

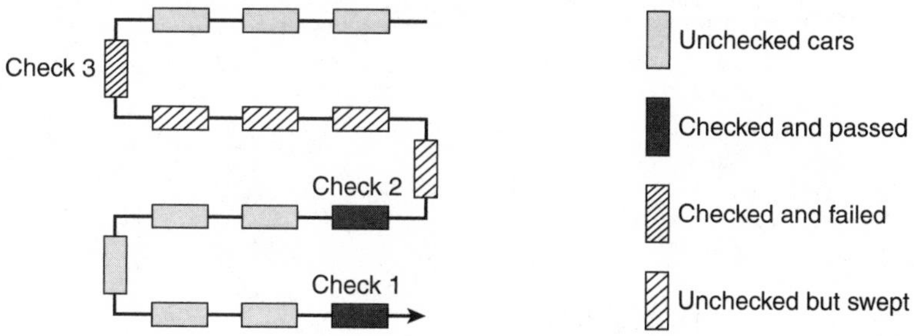

Check 3

Check 2

Check 1

☐ Unchecked cars

■ Checked and passed

▨ Checked and failed

▨ Unchecked but swept

reinspection of the several cars made immediately before it, all the way back to "check 2," looking for the same problem.

If we stopped here, it might be appropriate to be depressed and disappointed about people and organizations that have such great potential but which fail to capitalize on it. Inside them, the sense of stagnation can be palpable, particularly when you realize that as these organizations plod along, squandering the time and talent of countless people, the rabbits are racing ahead. As we will see though, it is possible to accomplish much more with far less headache. People don't have to get up each morning knowing they are doomed to fail. Rather, they can rest easy each night knowing that the next day they will succeed in doing something valued by someone else and that, by the end of the next day, they will be even better at it.

CHAPTER 4

HOW COMPLEX SYSTEMS SUCCEED

We now leave the failures behind to look at the successes. In a broad variety of sectors there are organizations with a much more productive approach to managing the complex operations on which they depend. Unlike their counterparts, who manage functional specialties in isolation from each other, without a view of the pieces in relation to a larger whole, the leaders invest continually in the integration of specialties into a process. Unlike their counterparts who dismiss the regular chatter of imperfect processes (and products) as unavoidable noise, they continually advance their expertise. When their operations speak up—in the language of problems or unexpected outcomes— these organizations stop, listen, learn, improve, and innovate, propagating what is learned in one situation to have maximum impact throughout the organization.

Alcoa: Safety In Unsafe Situations

Producing aluminum products—soda cans, window and door frames, automobile wheel rims, and aircraft landing gear—requires that Alcoa use processes that would appear to be people-eating. Work begins in the bauxite mines with huge digging machines. Then the bauxite has to be refined into an intermediate product, alumina. This compound of aluminum and oxygen is not a usable commodity. It becomes valuable when it is dumped into containers called pots that are the volume of a railway car. Electrodes as big as telephone poles are jammed into the pots, delivering current that strips off the oxygen and leaves behind molten aluminum. With many scores of pots in a facility, the electricity used is enough to power a small city. But no one is in the market for liquid aluminum, so it has to be tapped and run into molds. Then it is reheated and stamped, forged, molded, rolled, or extruded under great pressure.

This combination of volume, mass, velocity, temperature, pressure, voltage, and current, with some caustic chemicals thrown into the mix, sounds dangerous. And at most companies engaged in such lines of work, it would be. Yet, Alcoa somehow defies those conditions. It is the safest large manufacturing employer in the United States, with a risk of an on-the-job injury that is one-twentieth of the national rate.

The graph in Figure 4-1 top shows the rate of lost workdays for Alcoa and for the overall U.S. manufacturing economy. This is the measure of a worker's chance in a particular year of getting hurt on the job seriously enough that he or she has to miss a day or more of work as a result. Even in the late 1980s, Alcoa already had an enviable safety record compared to the

Figure 4-1 Workplace safety at Alcoa: From safe to safest

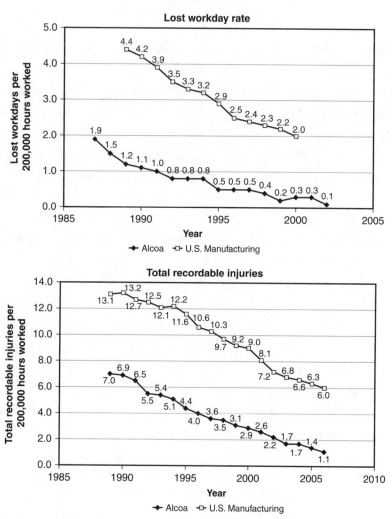

nation as a whole. But what is astounding is how much it out-paced the pack in the ensuing 20 years. Whereas the United States overall had a 60 percent cut in risk from 4.4 percent to

2 percent, Alcoa's reduction in risk was more than 95 percent, from 1.9 percent to less than 0.1 percent.

On the more comprehensive measure of total recordable injuries, which includes less severe events that do not cause the loss of a day of work, Alcoa reduced risk by more than 80 percent, in comparison to a cut of 50 percent for manufacturing overall, as can be seen in Figure 4-1 bottom. And there is something else to keep in mind. Alcoa's progress during this period was not a trade-off, optimizing workplace safety at the expense of other measures. During the same period, Alcoa handily outpaced the Dow Jones Industrial Average (DJIA), with a stock price appreciation of nearly 700 percent, compared to approximately 470 percent for the Dow. (That Alcoa is a component of the DJIA, and so pulled up the average, indicates an even wider gap between itself and its large-market-cap peers). Alcoa did equally well when compared to a broader market index, the Standard and Poor's 500. Let's take a closer look at how Alcoa managed to tie exceptional improvements in workplace safety with outstanding economic performance leading to great market returns.

Back in 1987, the odds of getting hurt seriously enough to miss work at Alcoa were 2 percent per year. How bad was that? That meant that the odds of getting hurt in a decade were nearly 20 percent and that if you were going to make a career at Alcoa, the risk of getting hurt at least once would have been 40 percent over 25 years. With 90,000 workers at Alcoa at the time, it meant that seven or more workers were getting hurt on the job every day, approximately one per business unit. That was a hard responsibility to bear, particularly in a company in which it was not uncommon for neighbors and family members to work together.

Historically, there had been a view within the company that processes involving such complex chemistry and physics are inherently unstable and unavoidably dangerous. Certainly, you've encountered versions of this attitude in many other sectors, where the particular product, process, markets, and people—including employees, customers, and patients—are blamed for compromises in quality, safety, effectiveness, efficiency, and responsiveness that actually result from the failure of leaders to manage complex work systems for high performance.

All the same, there was a growing discomfort with the rate at which colleagues, friends, neighbors, and family members were being hurt. Alcoans began to reexamine their assumptions. Perhaps harm was not inevitable. But in that case, what were the causes?

The idea that the processes were basically safe but that workers were deliberately self-destructive was rejected. So was the hypothesis that the workers were not smart enough to work safely. The record suggested that people got hurt not because they were stupid but because they found themselves in circumstances in which it was easy to get hurt and hard to be safe. (Remember Mrs. Grant's nurse in Chapter 3?) If the workers were not at fault, perhaps it was the research scientists and design engineers. Could they have designed safer processes? But no one believed they had deliberately failed to do so. The only explanation left was that Alcoa's processes and work sites presented unacceptable levels of risk because the company's scientists and engineers did not know how to design processes and workplaces correctly and its supervisors and operators did not know how to run them well enough.

This was a huge mind-shift. Like AT&T with Bell Labs, Xerox with its Palo Alto Research Center (Xerox PARC), and IBM with its research center, Alcoa was an industrial giant with a deep commitment to cutting-edge research and development. For years, Alcoa had been hiring top doctoral candidates in materials science, engineering, and industrial engineering from top universities and training them at Alcoa's Technical Center. If those geniuses did not know how to design a safe system, who did?

Alcoa was now on the verge of understanding one of the cornerstones of managing complex operations for high performance: No team can *design* a perfect system in advance, planning for every contingency and nuance. However, as Alcoa realized, people can *discover* great systems and keep discovering how to make them better.

When Alcoans got hurt or had close calls, leaping away to dodge a splatter of molten metal in a smelting plant or ducking at the last moment to avoid being hit by a swinging boom, they did so because they found themselves in situations no one had anticipated during design, which had been done at a time and place far from the actual work. Idiosyncratic confluences and coincidences of people, processes, products, places, and circumstances could create a hazardous situation where none had been known to exist. This was a seminal insight.

The problem was not bad motives, incompetence, or anything of that sort. Rather, it was a lack of foresight rooted in the inherent impossibility of anticipating the myriad interactions among the components that make up complex systems of work. Despite all the effort put into up-front design, something will always be overlooked. If it is impossible to be completely knowledgeable, ignorance is inevitable. However, it is not irreversible. At Alcoa, people came to realize that behind ignorance lay opportunity. If Alcoans could spot unanticipated situations when and where they occurred, they could bring to bear the same disciplined knowledge-building behavior they exhibited in the R&D labs and get better processes as a result. The key was to identify problems as they occurred—the more, the better—and solve them when they were seen. If you had to depend on a single explanation for Alcoa's success, it would be that Alcoa gave up depending on *designing* perfect processes and committed itself to *discovering* them instead.

The Four Capabilities at Alcoa

This idea of seeing problems and then solving them was operationalized in myriad ways, none of which should be held out as a universally correct or comprehensive method. From what I've written earlier in this book, you know that I'm critical of those who try to achieve great outcomes by copying the specific solutions other people have developed for their own idiosyncratic problems. Look instead at the reasons why these solutions were successful where and when they were used. A good way to do that is to see how Alcoa's policies and actions helped it to develop and use the four capabilities necessary for high-velocity management of complex organizations.

Capability 1: Seeing Problems as They Occur

In 1987, Alcoa announced the hiring of a new CEO, Paul O'Neill. From the start, his approach was unusual. One might expect a new

CEO to establish corporate goals involving stock price, market share, return on assets, or return on investment—financial measures of success. Not O'Neill. As he announced in his first public appearance to the media and "the Street," his primary concern at Alcoa would be safety. What might be a reasonable safety goal for a company engaged in so many perilous processes? How about reducing injuries by half? How about moving Alcoa into the top quartile, decile, or percentile compared with its peers? O'Neill ignored such relative measures. The goal was to be zero injuries to employees, contractors, and visitors. Why zero? Zero injuries meant perfect processes based on perfect knowledge of how to do work. Anything less than zero meant imperfect processes, and imperfect processes implied imperfect knowledge or ignorance. Therefore, when ignorance was found, it had to be rectified.

O'Neill and his colleagues built their strategy from this fundamental realization that things go wrong because there is insufficient understanding of how to make them right. As one way of acting on this belief, they insisted that within 24 hours of someone getting hurt in an Alcoa facility, something that was happening up to seven times a day, O'Neill had to be notified. (Over time, the reporting threshold became lower, including not only injuries but close calls or any unexplained worsening of someone's condition that caused him or her to miss work.) However, it was not just that O'Neill was a data geek eager to track trends and tendencies or a megalomaniacal control freak dying to look over everyone else's shoulder. He wanted to know within 24 hours because of the dynamic it would establish within the organization.

The kicker was that the reports had to come directly from the business-unit presidents. Why? After all, Alcoa had operations around the world; O'Neill might be anywhere at any given moment. This was a deliberate effort to create urgency around seeing and solving problems. For a business-unit president to inform O'Neill within 24 hours, he or she had to know about the problem well in advance of that deadline. This meant that the president had to hear from the vice president within an even shorter time frame, and the VPs had to know about injuries from their direct reports quickly enough to reach their unit presidents. When you consider the number of layers in the Alcoa hierarchy, this means that the first-level supervisors had to turn to the frontline employees and insist, figuratively if not literally: "If news of your injury is to make it to O'Neill in a day, you had better start yelling the moment you get hurt, before the pain sets in, maybe even before you are sure you have been injured."

What was this all about? O'Neill's 24-hour policy not only conveyed urgency but also encouraged accuracy. The sooner a problem is flagged, the more "perishable" information can be collected about it. Remember our reflection in Chapter 3 that if the staff at Mrs. Grant's hospital had waited to take stock of what had happened, empty vials would have been disposed of, memories would have faded, and they might never have reconstructed what had doomed the patient? In an industrial process, there is also the issue of information perishability. Temperature may change, pressure may drift, voltage or current may ebb or flow, and speeds may pick up or slow down. Enough drift and change, and the situation may be so different at the time of investigation that it is impossible to re-create the conditions associated with the failure and thus impossible to determine the cause. Without a known cause, treatments will be arbitrary at best and recurrences will be likely. Even if machine conditions remain unchanged, people's memories are faulty and fade rapidly. In other words, if you do not see a problem when and where it occurs and swarm it to investigate it, much of the information needed to understand it will perish, spoil, fade, and dissipate. Once that happens, it becomes impossible to re-create the problem, nail down what caused it, and take corrective measures that will prevent its recurrence.

Capability 2: Swarming and Solving Problems As They Are Seen

For the reasons just stated, there was a second rule: Not only were the business-unit presidents required to inform the CEO of an injury or near miss within a day, but within two days they had to report what the initial investigation had revealed about its causes and what was being done to prevent the problem from recurring. When a code team in a hospital races to an ill patient, they quickly size up the symptoms, immediately begin a diagnosis to determine what caused the symptoms, begin a treatment based on the diagnosis, and begin monitoring its effectiveness. To wait would risk misunderstanding the situation and leaving it uncorrected for too long. Alcoans learned to go through a similar, disciplined cycle of real-time problem recognition, diagnosis (*root-cause analysis* in industrial parlance), and treatment (*countermeasures* or *corrective measures* in manufacturing vernacular). It was the discipline of the Shewhart cycle—plan, do, check, act—popularized by Edwards Deming, but accelerated to warp speed.

This emphasis on rapid identification and swift investigation of safety-related problems was backed up with a commitment of skilled resources. For all the technical expertise Alcoans had in the processes they designed and operated, many lacked the complementary knowledge of how to develop a safe work environment and foster safe work behaviors. Therefore, Alcoa invested in developing multiple layers of environmental, health, and safety (EHS) expertise that would be available when and where they were needed. If there was an injury or a near-miss in a facility, the shop floor workers and production engineers could get assistance from on-site experts. If that expertise proved insufficient, there was a pool of experts at the facility and business-unit levels who could pitch in. If they could not crack the case, Alcoa's corporate staff would dispatch additional support, and if that proved insufficient, outside experts would be contracted to the team, as we see diagrammed in Figure 4-2. The key was to main-

Figure 4-2 Environment, health, and safety expertise in support of "see every problem, solve every problem"

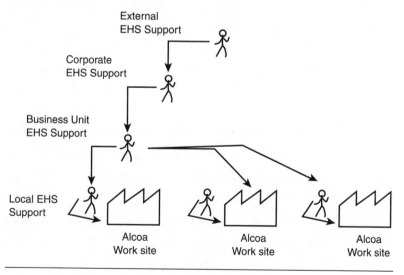

tain the urgency to see problems, swarm them when seen, solve them when swarmed, and—as we will see with Capability 3— quickly spread the new knowledge throughout the organization.

Capability 3: Spreading New Knowledge

This high-velocity approach of seeing problems and solving them when and where they occur proved pivotal for Alcoa. No longer burdened by the attitude that things inevitably go wrong when people work with large-scale industrial processes, Alcoans gradually stopped working around the difficulties, inconveniences, and impediments they experienced. Coping, firefighting, and making do were gradually replaced through-out the organization by a dynamic of identifying opportunities for process and product improvement. As those opportunities were identified and the problems were investigated, the pock-ets of ignorance that they reflected were converted into nuggets of knowledge. That knowledge had a special quality that was of great competitive significance.

Alcoa was hard-pressed to distinguish itself from its competi-tors by positioning itself uniquely relative to its external envi-ronment. Exclusionary contracts for bauxite were not an option. Electrical power and the chemicals used in refining and smelting were commoditized and the basic processes of making aluminum had been known for decades. Alcoa was subject to the same regulations as its competitors. Certainly, customers did not want to be drawn into a monopolistic dependency on Alcoa.

However, by seeing problems and solving them in an accel-erated fashion, Alcoa was building process knowledge that was not only hard won, but also scarce and proprietary—unavailable to outsiders who did not make the same efforts. Since the more use Alcoa could make of these discoveries, the more valuable it would be, Alcoa made sure that what was discovered locally was shared organizationally.

There were many mechanisms for this. First, of course, were the many cross-fertilizing "honeybees" Alcoa created by emphasizing the rapid identification, reporting, investigation, and resolution of safety-related problems. As new problems were sped up the managerial ranks, they came to the awareness of people who might have seen something similar in another part of the company for which they were responsible. Therefore, they could lend help, assistance, and insight, spreading knowledge from one area to another. Certainly the environment, health, and safety experts helped this pollination process, carrying the lessons they learned in one area to another.

Then there were the deliberate attempts to ensure that what was learned locally had benefit systemically. Just as Alcoa defied convention when it established safety, rather than a more traditional financial measure, as its top priority, it did so again when it instituted its first corporate-wide information technology system. Unlike companies that might have made accounting, payroll, taxes, benefits, or another financial function the first corporate problem to be solved with IT, Alcoa tackled safety first. The idea was that no matter where you were in Alcoa, if you had an incident, you could make it visible to anyone else in the company and if you had a problem, you could investigate what others who had had a similar experience had learned. When people did their work at Alcoa, they were drawing on much more than their individual expertise.

Individual performance could reflect the collective experience of the organization.

Capability 4: Leading by Developing Capabilities 1, 2, and 3

In most organizations, middle managers play an essential but bureaucratic role. They convey high-level goals that are set at more senior ranks, restating them as objectives relevant to the part of the firm for which they are responsible. From the lower ranks they convey information upward, taking specific data and reformulating those data so that they can be used by corporate decision makers. These middle-management roles make it possible for sprawling organizations to allocate resources and coordinate activities, as has been documented by Alfred Chandler and other business historians. However, Alcoa was not content to let middle managers be information conduits and coordinators, nor was it content with the model of scientific management championed by Frederick Winslow Taylor in which the "brains" of the organization developed optimal procedures for the "brawns" to employ.

Instead, Alcoa expected its leaders at all levels to develop the organization's ability to manage work in such a way as to see problems, solve problems where they were seen in order to build new knowledge, and spread that knowledge so it would be useful throughout the organization. Leaders not only had to have detailed process knowledge in their own right, in order to understand what was occurring and why, but they also had to coach and train others to be able to see deficiencies in how work was conducted and then develop and validate corrective measures. In this formulation, managers not only over-saw the production of physical goods with capital equipment, without doubt an essential role, but they were also responsible for cultivating the skills of inquiry and invention necessary for generating intangible assets—the process knowledge that would set Alcoa apart.

This approach was not merely preached; it was practiced. Careers rose and fell in accordance with how well the more senior managers could develop the capabilities of their direct reports and deploy those capabilities to increase safety and efficiency and reduce environmental impacts. In one dramatic case, a business-unit president was dismissed over safety-related issues.

That unit had been very successful by most measures. Revenue had grown dramatically and customers were delighted. What cost this otherwise successful leader his job was that, on his watch, a worker in an assembly plant had gone home early, feeling nauseated. The cause of the nausea was unexplained and the man returned to work the next day, apparently unaffected. Two weeks later, several more workers went home early suffering from nausea. The investigation that followed revealed that an idiosyncratic set of circumstances had resulted in indoor air pollution that, in turn, had caused the workers' symptoms.

The business-unit president lost his job because when the first incident went unexplained, it went unreported, insufficiently investigated, and unresolved. Help was not pulled in to bolster the investigation. Other people at the same site could have been exposed to the same unknown risk; in fact, they were. The new business-unit president was chosen precisely because he was deemed able to reinvigorate the "see a problem, solve a problem, share what you have learned" dynamic. Sure enough, when the dynamic was restarted, people began to discover latent problems.

Sustaining and Expanding the Results

Alcoa moved from an approach in which problems are accepted as unavoidable—the "one thing after another" we expect with complex operations—to an approach in which problems are clear signals, beneficent warnings, the system saying, "There's something important you don't know about me, but if you listen, I'll tell you."

Over the course of 20 years, Alcoa cut its rate of on-the-job injuries leading to a lost work day from 2 percent to 0.07 percent. Whereas the 2 percent rate meant that senior managers learned every day that someone had been hurt, now it was days and weeks between reports. For the shop floor worker, a risk of 0.07 percent translated into a chance of injury of less than 1 percent in a decade and meant that over the course of a 25-year career, the chance of getting seriously hurt on the job was less than 2 percent. In contrast, for a non-Alcoa employee, the risk of a lost workday fell from 36 percent in a decade and 68 percent in a career to 18 percent in a decade and 40 percent in a career.

It might be easy to attribute Alcoa's success in improving workplace safety during the stewardship of Paul O'Neill to a singular focus by a charismatic leader. However, that interpretation requires dismissing several factors. First, improvements in safety as measured by total reportable incidents and incidents leading to lost workdays continued to decline after O'Neill's departure. Second, Alcoa's intense focus on workplace safety did not mean that organizational improvement was measured by safety metrics alone. Improvement in safety did not come at the expense of improvements in quality, yield, efficiency, and cost, all of which contributed to improved profitability and market capitalization.

This ability to improve across the board, rather than improving safety at the expense of something else important, depended on the fact that focusing on workplace safety had both moral and practical motivations. The moral rationale, as described above, grew from a basic discomfort with putting people in harm's way. The practical rationale was that if people lacked sufficient knowledge to design and operate processes perfectly from a safety perspective, they probably lacked the knowledge to design and operate them perfectly in terms of quality, efficiency, yield, and timeliness. Thus, safety (or lack of safety) opened a window into all the underlying factors that compromised Alcoa's performance in terms of the measures more typically of concern to large industrial companies. During the period when Alcoa focused on safety, it improved other dimensions of performance as well. Earlier we discussed stock market returns. Now let's look more closely at specific examples.

Alcoa's engineered-products plant in Cressona, Pennsylvania, increased productivity on two lines by 87 percent by redesigning work flows, improving equipment, and developing better work methods. Packing costs were reduced, delivery performance was increased, and injury risk was cut. It was not that this plant specifically "managed safety" or that it specifically managed quality, on-time performance, or efficiency. It managed the processes it was using and thereby improved their performance by numerous measures simultaneously.

In a similar fashion, Alcoa's Davenport, Iowa, plant addressed increased demand through better process design. As with Cressona, the plant didn't make a trade-off between one good thing and another; rather, it learned to extract more yield from all its efforts. Ten extra hours of rolling time per month were freed, which had $500,000 in value; inventory was reduced by $1 million; and 19 improvements in environment, health, and safety were carried out.

Alcoa's continued focus on improving its processes, wherever and whenever the opportunity arose (that is, whenever a problem or unexpected outcome occurred), made it high-performing across the board. Safety measures continued to improve even as 2005 was marked by record revenue levels and improvements in return on capital and by recognition as one of "the best-practice leaders in cutting their greenhouse gas emissions." The year 2006 brought even better results: revenues up 19 percent to a record $30.4 billion, income from continuing operations up 72 percent, and return on capital up to 13.2 percent. It was also the twentieth consecutive year of improvement in safety measures, with a 96 percent reduction in the lost workday rate since 1987 and an 88 percent reduction in total recordable incidents.

All this resulted from deciding that problems were not a never-ending plague to be endured but a never-ending guide to improvement. In the next chapter, we'll see how a similar approach to high-velocity management led to great results in a complex, hazardous military situation.

REFLECTIONS ON MANAGEMENT
AND LEADERSHIP

When I first met Paul O'Neill, I had what I have come to recognize as a naive view. As the CEO of an enormous company, O'Neill must have extraordinary power, I thought, along with an extraordinary ability to shape events and direct people. The bases for that expectation were several. There is the business media's celebration of the individual "captain of industry" and "titan of commerce," the singular hero who introduces products, resuscitates companies, and otherwise has a profound impact. In this view, Chrysler was "saved" by Lee Iacocca, Jack Welch single-handedly drove General Electric to new heights, and so forth. One would think that Bill Gates single-handedly wrote all the code at Microsoft and designed and carried out all its strategic maneuvers. (I remember people saying that at the very least he reviewed every line of code.) Or perhaps that every element, feature, and nuance of the Apple iPhone and iPod was put in place by Steve Jobs. We celebrate celebrity and fuel the myth of the leader as supreme architect, engineer, and pilot. These notions are strengthened in business school courses that posit management as a set of chesslike strategic transactions and discuss complex systems as being amenable to sophisticated mathematical modeling and control.

That is not at all what leadership is like in a process/systems-intensive organization operating over the long haul. I came to appreciate that the leader of a large organization does have tremendous power, but much of it is of a destructive nature. He or she can fire people, shut down facilities, divest product lines, and disengage with difficult customers and suppliers. However, constructive power is harder to muster because creation ultimately is a collaborative and coordinated effort. Collaboration and coordination are tricky because they require that those who participate have at least some degree of agreement about what they are trying to achieve, what approaches are acceptable and preferable, and what is off-limits. Short of that, as Howard Stevenson pointed out, you are depending on despotism to get things done. Clear definitions of desired outcomes and clarity of roles and methods are needed even in fairly small organizations such as orchestras, dance companies, and bands. How much more so in organizations that have hundreds if not thousands of people contributing to the achievement of a larger whole?

For someone in Paul O'Neill's position, anything he or she says will be repeated, but with imperfect duplication. By the time an executive pronouncement is repeated and relayed, it will be distorted and misframed. If the leader is trying to achieve something significant, the countermeasure to distortion is to "broadcast" the key message consistently and repeatedly so the "signal" will emerge from the static and noise that develop with each successive round of transmission. In Paul O'Neill's case, this meant that his consistent message, which was not going to compete with many others, had to be that safety was a primary concern, zero injuries was the goal, and the identification of and adherence to safe practice had to be exceptionally rigorous, with immediate identification and resolution of threats to safety as the means to better outcomes.

Two images come to mind. The first is attending a kickoff meeting in Alcoa's former corporate headquarters for the Pittsburgh Regional Healthcare Initiative, of which O'Neill was a founder. Before starting the meeting, O'Neill stated that he saw many people in the room who had not been in the building before and he wanted them to be assured of their safety. Thus, to an assembly of 40 to 50 people, the chairman of one of the world's most prominent companies explained where the exits were, what to do in case of an emergency, and how to leave the room, the floor, and the building safely.

The other image gets to leadership's impact on culture. I was in a large Alcoa extrusion plant in Brazil in which aluminum logs are forced under great pressure through a series of dies to create window and door frames. There is heavy material, heavy equipment, and loud machinery. In the middle of the tour with a number of senior-level executives, I had trouble hearing the guide's explanation. I pressed closer, but when that did not help, I pulled my earplugs out so that I could hear better. In only a few moments, one of the operators came over and in a combination of Portuguese, English, and creative pantomime, indicated that I had to wear hearing protection or leave the production area. I was struck by the cultural chutzpah that was necessary for that to occur.

If I ended the characterization of leadership at this point, it might seem that an effective leader is one who "manages by objectives," with a few other platitudes thrown in. However, that is an overly reductionist view, making it sound as if the right set of objectives, repeated ad nauseam, will lead to great outcomes.

There is another piece to my picture of leadership: energetic attention to detail, grounded in the belief that leaders have to have a deep understanding of how things work if they are to develop people, guide people, and make decisions. For instance, in a talk before his retirement, O'Neill discussed the thermal inefficiencies of producing aluminum using current processes, the impact on cost, and the ability to sell aluminum for applications beyond those for which it currently is used. There was a logical thread between British thermal unit efficiency, the costs of production, industry capacity, and the effects on supply and demand.

We'll see in the next chapter how this commitment to managing from a few simple but robust principles, coupled with tremendous attention to detail and the development of people, is played out in other high-performing organizations.

CHAPTER 5

HIGH VELOCITY UNDER THE SEA, IN THE AIR, AND ON THE WEB

In Chapter 4, we looked at how one company, Alcoa, managed its complex systems of work to see problems, solve problems, and share what was learned, all the while insisting that leaders cultivate these capabilities. In this way, Alcoa accelerated the rate at which it learned how to design and operate its technical processes and systems of work, thereby achieving exceptional performance. And though it started by focusing on problems related to workplace safety, it soon found that safety problems reflected process ignorance and that this ignorance would also manifest itself in other problems such as quality, timeliness, and yield versus scrap.

In this chapter, we'll look at three other organizations that used the velocity with which they created and employed useful knowledge as the basis for achieving exceptional performance. The first case is the U.S. Navy's Nuclear Power Propulsion Program, which invented, introduced, and operated an exceptionally challenging technology with greater speed and reliability than organizations charged with comparable challenges. In the second case, Pratt & Whitney vastly improved its process for bringing new jet engine designs to market. The third case concerns a pioneer dot-com company which survived the 2000 market shake-up, established itself as a profitable enterprise, and wound up converting a small initial investment into a fortune. As widely as these examples differ in their missions and circumstances, they all illustrate how complex systems of work can be managed for superlative outcomes by applying the principles delineated in this book.

U.S. Navy Nuclear Power Propulsion Program

The U.S. Navy has launched more than 200 atomic-powered ships—using up to 30 different power plant designs, with 500 reactor cores brought into operation—since the start of the nuclear power propulsion program in 1948. As of 2006, those ships collectively have had more than 5,700 reactor-years of operation and have "steamed" well over 134 million miles.

This in and of itself is a technological and managerial marvel considering what came before. In World Wars I and II, submarines were a strategic threat, sinking substantial merchant marine traffic and, by the fear they aroused, forcing military and commercial convoys to take extraordinary precautions on open-water voyages. Watching Hollywood renditions, one might conclude that those subs were lethal because they could remain hidden for extended periods, sneak up on their prey undetected, and attack with devastating force.

That was not the case; the Hollywood image overplays the capabilities of submarines and downplays their vulnerability.

In truth, the performance of submarines was limited by the batteries that powered them when they were submerged. The batteries held charges only for short periods, so underwater range was no more than 20 miles. Most of the time, the subs were forced to operate on the surface, where they had air to run their diesel engines but were exposed to detection and destruction by larger warships and aircraft. In real life, success often meant sneaking in close, remaining submerged only briefly, then compensating for the ineffectiveness of the torpedoes by fighting a close-in battle with small mortars and machine guns mounted on the decks.

Under fire or not, life for submariners was difficult, even by the Spartan standards of military craft, which are largely designed to move weapons systems with maximum effectiveness, only accommodating the crew as best as they can. Submarines, being smaller than other ships and designed for underwater operation, ran rough on the surface. Once they were under way, the demands of power conservation meant poor ventilation and often moldy food. Their cruising range was limited by the amount of fuel they could carry; before it was gone, they had to stop to refuel at sea or in port.

Nuclear-power propulsion erased those limitations. Nuclear-powered submarines have scored repeated milestones: submerging below the polar ice cap, traveling beneath it from the Pacific to the Atlantic, rendezvousing with other submarines underneath it, surfacing through it, and circumnavigating the Earth completely submerged. Whether used for intelligence gathering during the Cold War, deployment of special forces, tracking of Warsaw Pact warships, controlling sea-traffic choke points during a conflict, or carrying intercontinental ballistic missiles and thus guaranteeing a retaliatory strike capability, nuclear-powered submarines changed the fundamentals of naval doctrine in the post–World War II era thanks to their ability to remain submerged almost indefinitely.

Nuclear power also revolutionized aircraft carriers, which had earlier revolutionized ocean warfare during World War II. The dreadnought battleships of all navies fell before the onslaught of seaborne air forces, which could project force farther and faster. In the battle of Midway, one of the decisive sea battles of the Pacific, the opposing fleets never fired on each other directly; instead, the aircraft of each one attacked the ships of the other. Carriers could also provide air cover to soldiers and marines "storming the beach" before airfields could be secured that were within flying range of the conflict's leading edge. This helped offset the advantages land-based defenders gained with artillery and their own air power.

Putting nuclear power aboard aircraft carriers was another order-of-magnitude change in the strategic balance. It provided the additional advantages of range, speed, time on station, and ability to conduct unlimited launchings and landings. The U.S. Navy's ability to police sea-lanes, keeping them open for commerce, and to project military power when and where necessary was greatly enhanced.

If we stopped here, the introduction of reliable nuclear propulsion onboard warships would be a remarkable accomplishment in its own right. Yet there are other considerations that should draw our attention. The first is the extraordinary velocity with which this technology was introduced. The first nuclear-powered submarine, the *Nautilus*, entered the fleet in 1954, a mere blink of the technological eye when one considers that it was not known how to harness the atom only a decade previously and that the program to develop nuclear propulsion did not take form until 1949. It is all the more remarkable when one considers that launching this brand-new technology required the discovery of new science, the invention of new materials for shielding and reaction control, the creation of new manufacturing systems, the design of novel devices and power plants, and the training of thousands of engineers, craftspersons, and operators. The technological and organizational accomplishments were fantastic.

And yet there is an added wrinkle. Since the launch of the *Nautilus*, the Navy hasn't suffered a single reactor-related casualty or escape of radiation—a far cry from what comparable programs have experienced. Before the dissolution of the USSR, the Soviet fleet suffered a number of nuclear calamities in its 50-year history, with substantial injury, death, environmental pollution, and destruction of equipment (see Table 5-1 for examples through the 1980s). NASA, undertaking a comparably difficult and dangerous mission, has lost one Apollo crew and two shuttle crews in a little under 50 years of manned space flight. As we saw in Chapter 3, the civilian nuclear-power industry has hardly been trouble-free.

How can this extraordinary performance be explained? Attention naturally turns to the demanding and monomaniacal commitment of the founder and longtime leader of the Navy's Nuclear Power Propulsion Program (often referred to as "NR" for *Naval Reactors*). Hyman Rickover, a 1922 gradu-

Table 5-1 Partial List of Calamities in the Soviet Nuclear Navy

Ship	Date	Problem	Consequence
K-8	Oct. 13, 1960	A leak developed in the steam generators and in a pipe. Equipment for blocking leaks was damaged. The crew began the work of stopping the leak.	Large amounts of radioactive gases leaked out, contaminating the entire vessel. Three of the crew suffered visible radiation injuries.
K-19	July 4, 1961	A leak developed in the primary cooling circuit, causing a drop in pressure and setting off the reactor emergency system.	The crew worked long periods in radioactive areas of reactor compartment. All were exposed to substantial radiation. Eight died.
K-11	Feb. 1965	While the submarine lay in dock, the reactor lid was lifted without control rods being secured. While the problem was being investigated, it happened again.	There were releases of steam, and a fire broke out. The reactor was retired and replaced.
K-27	May 24, 1968	Power inexplicably dropped suddenly during sea trials.	Radioactive gases were released, and radiation onboard increased. The reactor was shut down and approximately 20 percent of the fuel assemblies were damaged. The ship was scuttled in 1981.
K-140	Aug. 1968	Wrong installation of the control rod cables and error.	Unplanned automatic reactor start-up while in shipyard.

Name	Date	Description	Consequence
K-429	1970	Uncontrolled start-up of ship's reactor while submarine was at shipbuilding yard.	Fire and release of radioactivity.
Echo-I sub.	Aug. 21, 1980	Vessel suffered a radioactivity leak following a fire.	Nine crew members died and three others were injured.
K-222	Sept. 30, 1980	Breach in procedure let power through safety-rod mechanism without the controls being engaged. Automatic-equipment failure caused uncontrolled raising of control rods and uncontrolled reactor start.	The reactor core was damaged.
K-123	Aug. 8, 1982	Leak in steam generator caused release of liquid-metal coolant into reactor compartment.	Reactor had to be replaced. It took nine years to repair the submarine.
K-314	Aug. 10, 1985	Control rods incorrectly removed when the reactor lid was raised. Reactor went critical during refueling.	Explosion released large amounts of radioactivity. Ten people were killed.
K-431	Dec. 1985	The reactor overheated while the vessel was returning to base outside Vladivostok.	Submarine is now laid up at the naval base in Pavlovsk.
K-192	June 25, 1989	A leak was discovered in the primary circuit; the submarine surfaced. Botched attempts to fix the leak and cool the reactor led to a cascade of misfortunes.	Releases of radioactive iodine were detected in the areas surrounding the submarine and later on land.

ate of the Naval Academy, did not retire from the Navy until 1982, making him the longest-serving officer in the Navy's history. He created for himself an exceptional position of autonomy and power with two appointments: a civilian one from the Atomic Energy Commission (AEC), which was responsible for the design, development, and deployment of nuclear power generally; and a military one within the Navy, which was responsible for the contracting, design, construction, and operation of warships. In effect, he put himself in a position to make demands on the Navy from his AEC perch and on the AEC from his Navy perch. He cultivated relationships with members of Congress responsible for allocations and promotions and had influence on the budgetary process that often outweighed that of his civilian and uniformed superiors. He had influence over defense contractors as well, given his administrative power over major research, design, construction, and maintenance programs.

Furthermore, Rickover was intimidating. His interviews with prospective members of the reactor program and potential officers on nuclear-powered ships were legendary. One story is that he cut an inch from the front legs of the chair in which interviewees sat to make them feel uncomfortable without knowing why. He was known to berate and insult candidates for the program. Theodore Rockwell, who was part of the initial group that started the nuclear-propulsion program with Rickover, wrote in his memoirs about a call between the two of them, conducted over the single undersea phone cable. Rickover grew increasingly frustrated with the poor sound quality, screaming at Rockwell until the operator finally cut in, "Sir, if you would just speak in your normal voice. . . ."

"Goddammit, this is my normal voice!" screeched Rickover. To which Rockwell added: "That's true, operator, it is."

Finally, there are any number of accounts (some of which we will encounter later in this chapter) of Rickover's determination to know every detail of the technology for which he was responsible, including whatever mishaps befell it. He certainly can be perceived as an archetypical unpleasant, condescending, micromanaging boss.

But however hard-driving, cantankerous, or brilliant Rickover might have been, he cannot be the entire explanation for NR's success, simply because he could not have solved every problem—at least not every technical problem—on his own. Furthermore, in the 26 years since his retirement, there have been several successors and countless civilians and sailors have served in NR without having known him firsthand—a good number wouldn't even have been born before he left—yet the program's perfect safety record has been maintained.

It can't just be Rickover; there has to be something about the way in which the nuclear program's complex work was and still is managed. And so there is. In response to the outrageous challenge it faced, NR developed what one of its chroniclers, Francis Duncan, called "the discipline of engineering." This discipline was required because, whatever knowledge the group had, it was inadequate. Therefore, there was no room for guessing; learning had to be constant and fast, not only experiential but experimental. To accomplish this, NR had to make explicit its best understanding and expectation of what actions would lead to what outcomes. Ensuring that people started with the best possible knowledge built into their approach increased their likelihood of being successful. It also increased their opportunity to learn. With expectations clear, it would be obvious when something happened that didn't conform to those expectations. As a result, even if you didn't succeed, you created an opportunity to learn to succeed. Stating clear expectations was a given, with no exceptions; that's what made it part of the *discipline* of engineering.

With expectations clear, NR had to identify immediately when its best understanding was faulty—another discipline. And with equal discipline, each clearly identified pocket of ignorance was to be converted into usable knowledge. Finally, that knowledge had to be incorporated into updated designs for machines and procedures throughout the fleet; this, too, had to be done with rigor and discipline. All the while, this discipline of engineering was to be modeled, taught, encouraged, and harnessed by both junior and senior leaders.

When all this happens consistently, it changes the basic dynamics of an organization. Rather than letting each experience be either a success or a failure—but in neither case improving anyone's chance of success on the next try (see Figure 5-1)—every experience is *designed* to increase the likelihood of success on the next try as knowledge and know-how accumulate (see Figure 5-2). This was Alcoa's approach, it was NR's approach, and, as we'll see later, it is the consistent approach of high-velocity organizations more generally.

In Chapter 4, we saw how Alcoa's practices mapped onto the four capabilities first mentioned in Chapter 1. We'll now see how the practices Rickover instilled in the Naval Reactor program also did.

Figure 5-1 Succeed or fail

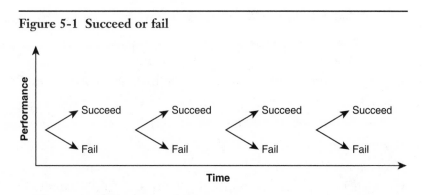

Figure 5-2 Succeed or learn to succeed

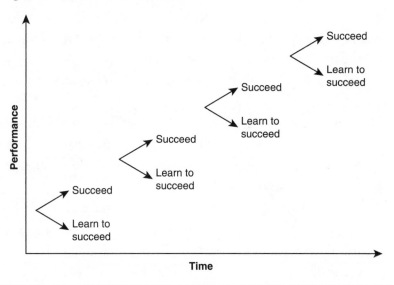

Capability 1: Capturing the Best Collective Knowledge and Making Problems Visible

What do the terms *incident* and *incident report* bring to mind? An accident, an injury, a fatality, or damage to property? Now ask yourself, why would an organization insist on incident reports? Accountability, reprimand, punishment? If your answers were any of the above, you are far from the Naval Reactor program's approach. It has a much lower threshold of what it deems an "incident" and a much higher threshold of what must be done when an incident occurs.

Let's start with a simple example: people working in a system that had already been designed and built and was now in service. Those who operated reactors onboard a ship and those who conducted maintenance and refueling onshore were expected to follow scripted procedures with exacting accuracy. There were clear expectations about what each person and each piece of technology would do, in what order, and with what effects on each other. Incidents were strictly defined as departures from procedure. If they occurred, they had to be reported. For example, if someone were to start step 3 before receiving the agreed signal that step 2 is done, that would be an incident. And however inconsequential the outcome, an incident had to be reported.

This wasn't simply bureaucratic housekeeping. Just as close calls at Alcoa were indications that something about a manufacturing process was not completely understood, an incident in the nuclear navy meant that something about the way work was done was incompletely or inaccurately understood. This ignorance could not be tolerated. That part of the system could be connected to other pieces in ways that were not well understood; an incident that seemed inconsequential in isolation might be disastrous in just the right combination with other incidents.

This discipline of specifying expectations was not just for the frontline work of operating the submarines. It applied to everything and Rickover himself modeled this way of life.

Rockwell recalls preparing for a meeting and being challenged by Rickover to describe how the meeting would conclude—before it had even started. Rickover was not hazing him and did not expect him to be clairvoyant. Rather, he wanted Rockwell to predict in advance what a successful outcome would look like and how he expected to get there so he could determine whether something was amiss as the meeting proceeded. What was there about the situation, the discussion, the technical content, or the discussants that he had misunderstood? What were the consequences of that misunderstanding? What had to be done to address those misunderstandings? Those were all critical concerns, which otherwise might have been missed had Rockwell not been prepared to be surprised by events unfolding contrary to what he had anticipated.

Even—and especially—in upfront design and development work, where there were obviously great gaps in what was known about a particularly complex situation, this discipline was required. Rockwell describes designing the radiation shielding for reactors (a topic on which he became expert enough to author several books). No one knew how neutron bombardment would fatigue the metal and how the piping's welds, joints, and bends would affect radiation patterns. Therefore, when it was time to test the shielding, a grid was laid over the surface, with sensors distributed all across it. But the evaluation didn't rest at that.

Before any measurements were taken, Rockwell insisted that predictions be made about what the measurements at each point would be. It was not sufficient to find out if the various sections passed or failed in terms of emitted radiation. Rockwell and his colleagues already knew that they would be wrong at many points since the science and technology were still in early stages. Therefore, they wanted to know for certain—sooner rather than later—exactly where and when they were wrong and what they misunderstood. The sensors were not just there to mark safe and unsafe situations. They were there to identify pockets of ignorance on the part of the shielding designers.

That is why, rather than just recording readings and noting where the exposure was too high, they first predicted what the readings would be and then compared those predictions to the actual readings to discover where their understanding was confirmed and where it was refuted. If the shielding worked less well than needed or expected, that certainly warranted investigation and additional engineering. We would all recognize that. However, if the shielding worked better than needed or expected, that, too, revealed a gap in their knowledge which could prove costly or dangerous and which needed to be plugged. It is not clear we would all see that as a learning necessity as well. The difference? Many tests are meant to distinguish good from bad. In this case, Rockwell structured the test to distinguish *understood* from *not understood*.

Similarly, when it was unclear whether hafnium or a silver-cadmium alloy would be preferable for controlling the rate of chain reactions, the choice was driven by comparative trials. But those trials were not simply tests to see which material was better than the other. Before the trials were started, the engineers predicted how each would perform, explaining why they thought so. The point was not just to make a choice between one material and the other, but to identify things still not understood about both along the way. (In Chapter 7, we will see the same point made.)

From its very beginning, the Naval Reactor program was committed to following the script it had created without exception because making an exception would be to knowingly back away from the best understanding that had so far been acquired and would needlessly confound any analysis of future experiences. Consider what happened in September 1954, when *Nautilus* was being tested only a few months before its launch date. A steam pipe burst. The investigation showed that the wrong kind of piping had been installed. The NR program had all of that type of pipe ripped out and replaced with what had been specified. There was no thought of testing to see if some of the "wrong" pipe might pass some arbitrary performance test anyway. Until there was further disciplined study, NR couldn't be confident that the other pipe was adequate to the demands that would be placed on it. NR's reaction did not stop with containment—replacing the wrong pipe with the specified pipe. That would have been a workaround that would not have targeted the underlying factors that were at the root of the problem. How had this mistake been made? What was to stop it from happening again? What was to stop it from happening with some other material or component? The progression of whys and hows traveled back through the value stream and supply chain. Until NR could answer all these questions, there was a deadly booby trap somewhere in its operations.

Not only did NR demand a high degree of specification of what was thought to lead to success, it wanted to be sure that when something was amiss, that too was clear. High-velocity organizations are not in denial about human imperfection.

What they want is operations that will snitch shamelessly—not only loudly, but accurately and quickly.

We see this in a report prepared by NASA, the background of which has a certain painful irony. More than 15 years after the 1986 *Challenger* disaster, NASA embarked on a series of benchmarking studies to understand how other organizations had achieved extraordinary levels of safety despite the hazards of their work. Subjects included Alcoa and Bath Iron Works, on the topic of workplace safety, and the Navy's nuclear-power propulsion program, its software-integration program, and the SUBSAFE program referred to later in this chapter. Between the first few studies and the last, there is a several-year gap when the *Columbia* tragedy interrupted the bench-marking effort. One cannot help but wonder if that disaster would have been averted had NASA started its studies earlier.

This is what NASA observed when comparing the Navy's design of nuclear reactors with the civilian approach at Three Mile Island:

> In the case of Three Mile Island (TMI) commercial reactor, over 50 alarms or warnings were active prior to the mishap. At the onset of the TMI event, 100 more alarms were activated (a total of 150 of about 800 alarms active). In contrast, the total number of alarms and warnings in an NR reactor system is strictly limited to those needing an operator response. The Commanding Officer must be informed of unanticipated alarms that cannot be cleared. Naval nuclear power plants do not routinely operate with uncorrected alarms or warnings.

At Three Mile Island, the system spoke up, but the staff had learned to work around chatter which could not be understood. NASA found that within the Navy, alarms are simplified, so they don't sound so often. But when they do sound, or when other things go wrong, they are taken seriously. The NASA benchmarking team observed the sheer frequency with which NR spotted and reported on problems as follows:

> This system is thorough, requiring deviations from normal operating conditions to be reported, including any deviation from expected performance of systems, equipment, or personnel. Even administrative or training problems can result in a report and provide learning opportunities for those in the program.

NASA noted that NR had established an exceptionally low threshold for what counted as a problem or incident, as was mentioned before:

> During a General Accounting Office (GAO) review of the NR program in 1991, the GAO team reviewed over 1,700 of these reports out of a total of 12,000 generated from the beginning of operation of the nine land-based prototype reactors that NR has operated.

And that 12,000 doesn't even include the far more numerous ship-based reactors. The NASA report continues:

> The GAO found that *the events were typically insignificant* [emphasis added], thoroughly reviewed, and

critiqued. For example, several reports noted blown electrical fuses, personnel errors, and loose wire connections. Several reports consisted of personnel procedural mistakes that occurred during training activities. . . .

Capability 2: Building Knowledge by Swarming and Solving Problems

In high-velocity organizations, the response to problems is frequent, serious, and disciplined.

In many organizations, such emphasis on reports and written documentation as described above might be dismissed as bureaucratic obsessive-compulsive command and control, particularly if reports were required but simply filed and ignored. This is not the case in the Naval Reactor program. NASA observed not only the frequency but the seriousness of these reports.

NR requires that events of even lower significance be evaluated. Thus, many occurrences that do not merit a formal report to headquarters are still critiqued and result in identification of corrective action. These critiques are reviewed subsequently by the Nuclear Propulsion Examining Board and by NR during examinations and audits. This is part of a key process to determine the health of the program's self-assessment capability.

This was not just paperwork and it was not delegated as grunt work to junior officers and enlisted personnel; it was treated as an essential part of leading others. When a ship was being evaluated and had done well in some but not all categories, it was the responsibility of the commanding officer to explain why in a special letter that listed the failures and detailed the corrective actions. Promises to do better or try harder were never enough. The NASA benchmarking team pointed out that during Rickover's tenure and that of his several successors, each report "identifies the necessary action to prevent a recurrence." But such actions could not be precipitous. Solutions at NR had to be found through a process of disciplined discovery so that they could be trusted and safely propagated throughout the organization.

(Imagine a nurse in the hospital where Mrs. Grant died filing a report that he had *almost* mistaken a vial of insulin for a vial of heparin—no harm done, just a close call—then the hospital's chief of nursing reporting that incident to the hospital's CEO, along with her explanation of how such a thing could happen, where else such a thing could happen, and what had been done to make sure that these things did not happen again.)

Leaders in charge of the Navy's nuclear-reactor program, like their counterparts at Alcoa, discerned that the only way to understand and improve what was poorly understood and in need of improvement was to create ample learning experiences—the more the better, the sooner the better, the faster the better, the cheaper the better, and the greater the clarity of cause and effect the better. This, too, was done with great discipline. A fundamental aspect of the approach was not to take the obvious for granted but instead to make latent assumptions explicit and then test them. The opposite approach was used at NASA: The original assumption that foam shedding from the external fuel tank posed a threat to the heat shields was gradually replaced by an assumption that it did not. The second assumption may have been *buttressed* by the fact that nothing terrible had happened so far, but it had never been rigorously *tested*. Francis Duncan, the Rickover biographer cited earlier, made a point of how reality, not human assumptions, was always to be given the final word (since reality will always have the final word whether we listen or not):

> The discipline of technology means that the organization must adapt to the technology, and not the technology to the organization. For advanced development, data are never complete, particularly if the product of a complex technology is to operate at high standards for years. The discipline of technology requires exhaustive testing of materials and components to *determine the laws of nature* [emphasis added]. If these are not absolute in the sequestered atmosphere of scientific laboratories or research centers, there is no reason to expect they are better known on the shop floor. The discipline of technology requires thorough and deep consideration of the match between the product and its use, and intense analysis of the present and anticipated future conditions of operation.

This discipline of testing and learning sooner, faster, and cheaper was carried out in many ways. Here is one example: For every version of a shipboard reactor, there was a land-based version on which people could train and on which design problems could be worked out in a safer, cheaper, more controlled environment. For each such land-based model, there were full-scale wooden and cardboard mock-ups to preview how people and machines would interact in practice. Another example was the testing to see how equipment would handle the shocks of military use. Scaled-down components were mounted in scaled-down submarine hulls with an array of sophisticated gadgetry. Where and how to affix radiation shielding was always a challenging problem. For instance, it might have been easy to calculate the exposure on one side of a smooth rounded surface, but what about convoluted surfaces? When calculation failed, experimentation was the answer; for instance, building a prototype inside a water tank to see what would happen when radiation was emitted out the bottom of the boat but was reflected back into the vessel by the water. (In later chapters we'll see how Toyota makes just such a commitment to use high-speed, low-cost pilots and trials.)

Problem solving within NR has not only been disciplined in terms of the detail, but disciplined in terms of inviting all relevant data and multiple perspectives to a problem. Duncan notes that when shipyard representatives would raise problems with NR headquarters, they would sometimes illustrate the problem with a diagram or a mock-up of a component. A few of [Rickover's] engineers would take over the conference room just outside his office, and when all was ready, he would come in. At the slightest indication of vagueness or ambiguity, he would interrupt, demanding clarity and facts. The point was not that Rickover always knew better—quite the opposite. The purpose of having detailed write-ups, diagrams, and models was to ensure that competing and complementary views were well represented. Rank, personality, and assertiveness were not going to determine a decision. The data, coupled with the best collective understanding of a situation, would do that. The NASA benchmarking study stated this as follows:

> Recommendations are prepared independently by the prime contractors and undergo extensive internal reviews by experts in all related technical disciplines. The management and personnel at the two NR laboratories are required to provide their technical recommendations independently without soliciting Headquarters' advance agreement. This ensures that each laboratory retains its responsibility for providing its own technical assessment. Any dissenting/alternate opinions are required to be documented in the recommendation with a discussion of the logic for not implementing them.

The NASA study also noted that NR didn't only want to know what people thought was the right answer. It wanted to be very clear where they were uncertain. Therefore, reports from the laboratories had to include, along with their assessments, a clear discussion of alternate or dissenting assessments. As Rickover had explained years earlier:

> One must create the ability in his staff to generate clear, forceful arguments for opposing viewpoints as well as their own. Open discussions and disagreements must be encouraged, so that all sides of an issue will be fully explored. Further, important issues

should be presented in writing. Nothing so sharpens the thought process as writing down one's arguments. Weaknesses overlooked in oral discussion rapidly become painfully obvious on the written page.

Capability 3: Spreading Lessons Learned to the Whole Organization

In high-velocity organizations, people do not learn only for themselves. They learn for their colleagues as well. The experiences of an individual contribute to the expertise of the many. Whatever is learned when a problem is seen, swarmed, and solved right where and when it occurs is incorporated into the scripts and specifications to which it applies. Of course, this can only be done if all the assumptions, expectations, and procedures are explicit and available. It would never work if the new knowledge had to be diffused by word of mouth through a complex workplace, never mind a complex constellation of workplaces that might well be scattered over several continents and oceans. In the U.S. nuclear navy, when a new crew assumes responsibility for a new ship, everything it encounters—the design of the ship, the design of its procedures, the design of problem-identification and problem-solving routines, the training—is derived from the Navy's entire cumulative experience.

John Crawford, who rose to be deputy director of the nuclear propulsion program, and Steven Krahn, who spent 10 years in the program working on maintenance and repair, described the organization-wide benefits of turning local discovery into systemic discovery:

This disciplined, formal engineering approach is pervasive in every phase of activities at Naval Reactors: development of codes and standards where none exist, the availability of formalized design manuals and engineered test procedures. . . . [O]ver the years, a comprehensive set of standards and procedures has been developed that has contributed importantly to the safety and reliability of the reactor plants that Naval Reactors builds. This set of standards and procedures permits innovation to be applied in a controlled manner and allows focus to be placed on truly important areas, while ensuring that routine work gets done competently.

The NASA benchmarking team likewise noted that when reports are completed, they are "also provided to other organizations in the program so that they may also learn and take preventive action. This tool has contributed to a program philosophy that underscores the smaller problems in an effort to prevent significant ones."

Figure 5-3, taken from the NASA benchmarking study, diagrams this constant building of knowledge out of experience, leading to better experiences going forward.

Capability 4: Leading by Developing Capabilities 1, 2, and 3 in Others

What is a leader's job? It's common to say that the leader sets goals by dint of his or her greater authority and wider per-

Figure 5-3 Technical requirements, implementation experience, and lessons learned closed loop

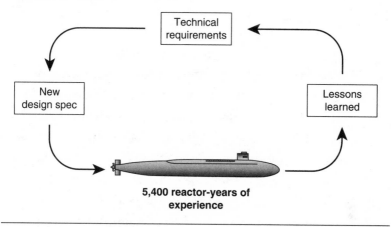

5,400 reactor-years of
experience

spective, decides how scarce resources will be allocated among competing priorities, and sets the emotional tone of a particular situation. Certainly Rickover was in the position and of the temperament to do all these.

But in high-performing organizations, the leader has two other critical roles. He or she is responsible for determining not only *what* gets done, by setting goals and allocating resources, but also *how* things get done, by shaping the company's processes and systems. Of course this isn't a one-man or one-woman job, and no one can be leader forever, so he or she must also develop in others the skills needed to lead complex operations.

Rickover modeled both roles. For one thing, he conspicuously modeled the role of leader as learner-in-chief. Ted Rockwell recalls meeting Rickover, soon after World War II, in Oak Ridge, Tennessee, where Rickover had come to learn about nuclear technology on behalf of the Navy. At that time,

Rickover was a captain, a senior officer—the equivalent of a full colonel in the other military services—but Rockwell recalls him as:

> . . . this one silver-haired guy who kept asking simple, basic questions, making himself look pretty stupid and getting a lot of knowing chuckles from the wiseacres. That course was pretty tough, even for me, and when one student asked timidly, "Please, Professor, could you tell us, at what level will this course be given?" the prof answered genially, "Let us say at a popular, postdoctoral level."
>
> At this point, the silver-haired Captain said, "I'm not getting this. Would you please go over it again?" . . . The rest of the class was getting a little restless and wondering why the Navy would send somebody down who was incapable of getting the material. The prof then asked condescendingly, "Would you perhaps like to have us provide you with some tutoring in the evenings?" Not taking this as a put-down, the Captain said merely, "I would appreciate that very much, sir."
>
> When the remedial session was arranged, it was attended not just by Rickover and the few other Navy personnel but also by the other students, including those who had mocked Rickover's questions. Upon arriving, he commented: "I guess I'm not the only dummy in the class."

Rickover was committed not only to his own learning but to others' learning. Early in his career, while serving as an engineering officer on the battleship *New Mexico*, Rickover demanded that his officers show detailed knowledge of the equipment and machinery for which they were responsible, "calmly accepting mistakes and errors when honestly acknowledged, and giving each man as much responsibility as he could handle." Three of his ensigns (the lowest rank for a naval officer) went on to become admirals.

Rickover's commitment to developing his people became institutionalized in the NR program. He personally interviewed every officer candidate for an engineering, construction, or maintenance role or for a position onboard a ship. As notorious as those interviews were for the stress and strain they produced, the objective was not sadism, hazing, or harassment. Rickover wanted to see how people handled pressure, responded to unfamiliar situations, and thought through problems—all of which would determine how well the candidate could manage NR's complex operations for very high performance. He didn't necessarily expect a "right" answer, but there were definitely "wrong" answers. "No excuse, sir" for bad grades was worse than a forthright "I was lazy." A candidate was better off acknowledging that he had reached an illogical or false position than trying to demonstrate conviction by "sticking to his guns." One candidate's interview consisted largely of the accusation that he was fat, with the challenge of what he was going to do about it. He responded by detailing changes in his food intake and activity level, with predications of how the change in calories in/calories out would affect his weight. Over the next several weeks, Rickover followed up with the candidate, who both slimmed down and was accepted into the program.

Selection into the NR program triggered an extended, intense learning process. There was the initial six months of on-the-job training in Washington, with an assignment to the office of a more experienced project officer because "new engineers lacked the background to contribute anything." But it was not enough for the new engineer to learn a particular perspective, role, and skill set in the project office; he was also being introduced to the entire system of nuclear propulsion as well, so he could understand how the piece with which he was becoming familiar fit into the whole. This was accomplished with instruction in "nuclear fission and reactor physics, reactor-plant operations, reactor-core materials, reactor-core design and construction, electrical power systems and instrumentation systems, primary and secondary fluid systems, water chemistry control, radiological control and reactor protection and safety."

Additional training followed, with the curriculum divided into intense compressed increments. Again, there was the combination of hands-on experience—operating the land-based versions of shipboard reactors—and additional classes in reactor theory and design that laid out not only how these devices were built and operated, but also the reasons why. After running a prototype reactor, officers and crew requalified onboard their ship before beginning two to three years of sea duty. This approach was repeated again for additional progressions in rank and responsibility.

Ultimately, Rickover was driving toward developing a cadre who understood "the discipline of engineering," the approaches necessary for managing the design, operation, and improvement of systems of great complexity, of great benefit when run well, and of great consequence were they to fail.

Rockwell reflected on his own relationship with Rickover, which extended beyond Rockwell's service in the nuclear-reactor program and many years into his private practice as an engineer. He wrote:

> To be categorized as "close" to Rickover needs explanation. It means that he would continue to treat me as his pupil, one still worthy of placing demands on his time and energy to help improve me professionally. This never-ending process of educating and training prospective leaders for the Navy was a driving passion of Rickover's life.

Rickover's leadership, imperious as it may sometimes have been, was a constant refutation of the view that leadership means "to command—someone else would take care of the ship." By embodying Capability 4, developing highly disciplined problem-identification and problem-solving skills throughout his organization, he ensured that NR would remain a high-velocity organization even without him.

LOSS OF THE *THRESHER*

The nuclear navy's record in submarine safety is not perfect. For example, on April 10, 1963, the *USS Thresher* was lost 200 miles off the coast of the United States, killing the 129 people onboard. Although it may never be possible to know exactly what happened to the *Thresher*, underwater communication, other sensing data, and examination of the wreckage led to the conclusion that it was felled by flooding. Although the technical details differ from the NASA cases, the same organizational faults that plagued NASA—tolerance for ambiguity in expectations and procedures coupled with willingness to work around obvious problems and to normalize deviance—plagued the branch of the Navy responsible for designing, constructing, and maintaining the nonnuclear portions of its nuclear submarines. In other words, the loss of the *USS Thresher* for non-reactor reasons makes for a striking contrast between high-velocity and low-velocity organizations and illustrates how both approaches can exist in the same parent organization if great care is not exercised by leadership.

Let's take a closer look at what happened. On a submarine, a leak in a pipe can be catastrophic. Because of the intense pressure in the lines when the ship is submerged, even a small leak that would be an annoying drip-drip on the surface can create a blinding spray, incapacitating the crew and shorting out electrical equipment. A large leak can flood a vessel, making resurfacing impossible. Therefore, when it comes to running pipes through submarines, the quality of the welds is paramount. In the late 1950s and early 1960s, there were two ways of joining pipes: welding and silver brazing. Although silver brazing was perceived to have advantages when done properly, it was technically more difficult and experience suggested that it was not reliable enough.

For example, in November 1960, the submarine *USS Barbel* left Norfolk to participate in an exercise with other ships. Its captain began a series of test dives, leveling off every 100 feet to check that nothing was amiss. At test depth, there was a report of flooding in the engine room. The crew sealed the flooded compartment, the ballast was blown, and the engines were set to full speed ahead as the captain successfully drove the ship to the surface. A pipe carrying salt water had given way at a silver-brazed joint. Other silver-brazed joints later failed on the submarine USS *Abraham Lincoln*. Inspections on yet another submarine revealed poorly brazed joints. Nevertheless, the Navy proceeded to build and operate submarines with those joints in critical lines. On another test dive a small saltwater line failed, and other pipe failures were documented.

As for the *Thresher*, it had 3,000 silver-brazed joints that were subject to full pressure. During a maintenance inspection, 145 of them were inspected, with 14 percent showing irregularities. That rate across all the joints would have meant over 400 joints with possible defects, yet the ship was put out to sea. It shouldn't have. As an accompanying surface ship listened through underwater devices, the *Thresher*'s crew encountered some difficulty, tried to surface, couldn't, and sank. Based on the sound recordings that were made at the time, the accident investigation report surmised that a pipe had burst, the crew had been unable to stop the flooding, and spray had short-circuited equipment, causing a loss of power. The ballast tanks did not operate properly, so the submarine continued to sink and finally was crushed by the pressure.

Prompted by that catastrophe, the Navy created its SUBSAFE program, an approach to designing, constructing, and maintaining the nonnuclear portions of the submarine (responsible for submergence, flood prevention, control, and recovery) as disciplined and rigorous as the NR approach.

Let's look at two other organizations that made the transition to high velocity. One, Avenue A (later known as aQuantive), was a pioneer in managing online advertising campaigns. The other, Pratt & Whitney, designs and builds commercial and military jet engines. These two organizations could hardly differ more in their markets, customers, suppliers, and technology, but both offer complex products developed in competitive industries that depend on the most advanced science and engineering. And both dramatically increased their performance by deciding to manage the functional pieces of their enterprises holistically as parts of a well-integrated whole and by recognizing that achieving high performance depended on building deeper system knowledge and could never be accomplished through workarounds and firefighting.

Pratt & Whitney: Higher-Speed, Lower-Cost New Product Development

The jet engine is a technological marvel, a vast improvement over the piston-driven propeller engines that dominated aviation through the end of the 1940s. Able to generate far more power than previously possible, jet engines have revolutionized air travel and have found use as power plants on land as well. The mechanics of a jet engine are conceptually simple—a basic application of the principle that for every action, there is an equal and opposite reaction. Throw a medicine ball in one direction while wearing roller skates and you are bound to roll away in the other direction.

In the case of the jet engine, this is what happens. A mixture of fuel and air are ignited in a combustion chamber to generate thrust, as shown in Figure 5-4. Part of the thrust drives the engine (and the plane to which it is attached) forward. Part of the thrust is captured by the turbine fan blades behind the engine. These turbines are connected by a drive shaft and spin the compressor blades at the front of the engine, which drive more air, under high pressure, into the combustion chamber to feed the process. The turbofan variation on this approach is to have two sets of turbines on the back of the engine, as shown in Figure 5-5. One drives the high-pressure compressor blades, pumping air into the com-

Figure 5-4 Jet engine basics

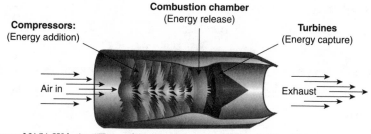

Source: NASA Web site, "Types of Gas Turbines, Glenn Research Center," at http://www.grc.nasa.gov/WWW/K-12/airplane/trbtyp.html.

Figure 5-5 Turbofan jet engine

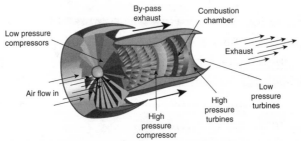

Source: NASA Web site, "Types of Gas Turbines, Glenn Research Center," at http://www.grc.nasa.gov/WWW/K-12/airplane/trbtyp.html.

bustion chamber. The other is connected to low-pressure compressor blades which move massive volumes of air past the combustion chamber and directly out the back of the engine to produce thrust. The advantages of this approach include fuel efficiency and quieter operation.

All this required extraordinary advances in materials science, combustion dynamics, aerodynamics, and control systems. Each of these is an extremely complex discipline in its own right; getting them to work together is no trifle. As a result, jet-engine compressors, combustion chambers, turbines, and other components—many of which have to work extremely reliably in conditions of extreme heat, pressure, and stress—are the products of intense research and development efforts. To ensure that they all work in concert, there have been advances in aerodynamics and fluid dynamics within the various parts of the engine and advances in the electronic controls, gearing, bearings, and virtually every other part of the engine.

In its early years, Pratt had enough time and money to figure all this out as it went along, taking a "think tank" approach to technology development. Defense contracts were rich sources of revenue and commercial contracts, once won, were a predicable income stream. After an engine manufacturer won the rights to supply the engine for a particular model of commercial aircraft, every plane of that type would be delivered with that engine. This, in turn, guaranteed the engine manufacturer a steady annuity for spare parts and other maintenance services. In those days, a young engineer joined what was essentially an apprenticeship. One engineer explained that when he first started at Pratt, his boss would give him instructions, which he would carry out. Then his boss would check his work, have him fix the problems, and check his work again. When it was deemed acceptable, it went to the next boss for checking. Quality came from hard work, inspection, and rework. If a problem couldn't be resolved on paper, engineers could build a prototype, run it until it broke down—a method that came to be known as "build and bust"—and put whatever knowledge was discovered to use in the next iteration.

But as times changed, this approach became untenable. Not only did military spending decrease with the end of the Cold War, but the commercial market changed as well. Airline deregulation increased the price-sensitivity of airlines and new entrants to the market increased the competition. Airplane makers began to certify more than one engine per airliner model. An engine maker now had to woo not only Boeing and Airbus, but each of the airlines as well. Of course, more competition and less customer lock-up made for unprecedented cost pressures on the design and development, manufacturing, and spare-parts support of jet engines.

Pratt could not afford its think-tank approach any longer. Developing a new engine had been up to a $1 billion investment, requiring nearly four years of work, but the new market dynamics convinced management that development costs had to be cut to $300 million per platform and that development time had to be cut down to 30 months.

To achieve these goals, Pratt created integrated program-management teams in the early 1990s. The rationale was that creating cross-functional teams, with representatives from different disciplines and different components working together, would reduce the rework and expense that came from developing complex jet-engine components in isolation from each other. That was an improvement, inasmuch as it addressed a key structural shortcoming of low-velocity organizations—managing the pieces of their systems without an eye to how the pieces need to come together. But it was not good enough. Pratt was still missing the dynamic component of high-velocity management—generating useful knowledge and building on it rather than having to keep acquiring the same knowledge over and over. A 50 percent downsizing only made matters worse as Pratt lost some of its most experienced engineers and managers, who not only had deep technical knowledge in their own realms but also had acquired knowledge about ways to navigate and coordinate the work system to achieve good outcomes.

Pratt now needed a better way to ensure that (a) when people started their work, they could bring to bear the cumulative experience of the whole organization, and (b) when the cumulative expertise of the organization was found to be missing something, insights from new experiences could quickly become part of that available cumulative experience. Pratt's attempt to do this was called "engineering standard work" (ESW), making a true discipline of its engineering efforts much as the Navy's nuclear reactor program had done.

First, Pratt engineers laid out everything that was already known about the design process. Extensive *workflow maps* made clear what design steps normally occurred in what sequence and with what interdependence. Understanding what step was dependent on what other steps set the stage for establishing *design criteria* to clarify what each step had to accomplish to satisfy the needs of those who depended on it. To increase the chance that each stage would be successful in meeting those criteria, *activity pages* were created, representing the best method for achieving success known at the time, with tools and methods instructions explaining how, when, and why various analytical and other design tools should be used. Then, to determine who was capable of being responsible for what stage, with what degree of support and supervision, Pratt created *practitioner proficiency assessments* to determine how much support someone needed in a role or how much he or she could provide. Readiness reviews determined if a new technology could be mainstreamed into a program or if it was still developmental.

These were all mechanisms for capturing and sharing knowledge. There was also a mechanism for building knowledge. When someone encountered a problem while using some element of ESW—a workflow map, design criteria, or an activity page—there was an owner of that element who could be called in to investigate. When the root cause was discovered, the ESW was modified, increasing the likelihood that the next person to depend on that element of ESW would succeed.

Paul Adams, a longtime engineer at Pratt, explained to me the effect of making sure that local learning became organizational learning:

> First, we had to make sure we had the handoffs down, controlling how you work in a dispersed organization. The workflow maps, design criteria, and all of that picked up that piece. We also had to get a handle on how to use the new computational tools. They are very useful, but only within boundaries that have been proven. Outside those boundaries, you're taking some real risks. We had to give people clarity as to the situations in which those tools worked and the situations in which they didn't.

(In contrast, NASA hadn't done such a good job of that, leaving it to an inexperienced engineer to use an unfamiliar software package outside its design specs to estimate the impact damage on the wing of the *Columbia*.)

> Another concern that led us to standard work was: How quickly could somebody be effective? Work flow maps, design criteria, proficiency tests—those are about execution of standard work. If we can teach and test skills, [it creates] a very substantial decrease in the time it would take people to get proficient.

The first thing people say, before they are really exposed to ESW, is that this takes away my ability to innovate. But that is wrong. It gives you a chance to innovate in a controlled manner, so you won't introduce additional risk into the product. With standards, we can distinguish where we don't need you to innovate from where you need to innovate. It helps you see where innovation is needed and helps you determine what innovation is useful. When we do need to innovate more quickly, standard work helps with our technology readiness process, because better clarity about what we have and how it fits into the entirety of the program helps us understand where we have a high and low risk tolerance.

The results of always using the best approach that had been found so far, of making sure that the people given responsibility for a task were actually capable of it, and of making sure that local improvements became organizational improvements were quite good. The commercial and military projects on which ESW was piloted came in on time and on budget—hardly a familiar experience. Engineering change orders, those late-stage design changes that are costly to implement because so much is already set in place, were down by half in the first year of using ESW and down another 15 percent in the second year. That alone saved an estimated $50 million on rework. All told, Pratt estimated that every dollar spent on ESW yielded a four-dollar payback.

Avenue A: From Chaotic Mess to Lean and Mean

Avenue A was a pioneer in creating Web-based marketing. The advantages it offered its clients were immense. Advertisers could target their audiences with far greater precision than they could with television, radio, telephone, or direct mail. They could get immediate feedback, finding out who was responding in what fashion to what ad on what page with what frequency, and modify their advertising quickly for maximum impact. In 1999, after only three years of operation, business was booming, with revenue growth of 50 percent *per month*, but the firm's poor work processes were getting in the way of its success. Head count kept increasing, but with no appreciable increase in efficiency. Employees were putting more and more effort into scheduling, coordinating, clarifying, and redoing their work and less into designing, implementing, and optimizing marketing campaigns. More success actually meant bigger losses.

Eight years and one disastrous dot-com bubble burst later, Avenue A not only had survived, but was flourishing. Now known as aQuantive, it had grown from three employees to over 2,000. In mid-2007, Microsoft bought aQuantive for $6 billion, quite a return on the early investment of $20.5 million.

How did Avenue A pull this off? There was no way for it to control an external environment as fluid as the Web, so it had to shape the fluidity of its internal environment with great sophistication, improving and innovating more quickly, for longer durations, and with greater breadth, in order to set itself apart. Let's take a close look at how this was accomplished.

Avenue A grew out of Nick Hanauer's efforts to advertise his family's business, Pacific Coast Feather Company. To reach a wider customer base, he built an online catalog, but soon found that if people didn't know about the site, they didn't visit it. He then had the idea of buying advertising space on other Web sites, paying a commission for every click-through. As his experience grew, Hanauer had the idea of brokering extra space that he didn't need. Then, as his expertise grew in designing marketing campaigns that could be managed in real time for Pacific Coast Feather, he realized that there was a business in helping others do the same. Avenue A was created as a stand-alone business offering three services:

1. *Design*. Planning an Internet-based media campaign and buying ad space (which included negotiating the rates).
2. *Implementation*. Providing the technical support for an advertising campaign: housing the ads on Avenue A's own servers and placing them according to the campaign's plan.
3. *Optimization*. Gathering data about which ads on which sites led to reader click-throughs and using those data to modify the advertising campaign.

As straightforward as that seems, there were many steps within each stage and, as Avenue A grew, an increasing number of people responsible for each step. For instance, within the design phase, an Avenue A representative had to work with the client to develop the themes and approaches of the campaign. Someone else, with expertise in various types of publishers, had to identify what type of Web sites would be most promising for a particular type of ad. These suggestions would have to be run past the client for approval before Avenue A could go back to the publishers to negotiate rates. This never got easier as the number of publishers increased and advertising options multiplied. What began as a fairly simple system— a few people doing a few things—grew in complexity, with many activities dependent on each other in often surprising ways. The results were predictable—delays, defects that had to be caught on the fly, missed handoffs, and a general demand that people go above and beyond, all the time, to succeed.

Avenue A's initial efforts to offset these problems were understandable, if not effective. Where there were bottlenecks, work was shifted from one group of specialists to another. If that didn't do it, more people were added. But that never solved the basic problem: The pieces didn't come together well without heroic efforts on everyone's part. Projects ricocheted around the organization, repeatedly ping-ponging between someone who needed something and the person who had worked hard, but not successfully, to provide it. For example, someone might have designed a marketing campaign—what ads would go on what publisher pages. Those specs would be passed to someone else who would then discover that some of those publishers couldn't support the types of ads that had been specified. Once that problem had been resolved—after several rounds of ping-ponging e-mails and phone calls—instructions would go to the engineer responsible for implementing the campaign on Avenue A's servers. He would discover that the computer codes and protocols he had been given didn't work. Once again, the work ricocheted from one person to another for clarification, modification, and renovation.

When the unmanageability reached a tipping point, Avenue A divided itself into eight teams, each a stand-alone microcosm of the larger organization with the full complement of specialties needed to pull off a campaign. That didn't eliminate the problems, it just cloned them.

Finally, Avenue A stepped back from the madness and began to work out a system for building knowledge as it solved problems rather than working around the same problems day in and day out. First, it mapped out all the work that had to be done to move a campaign from concept to completion. Then, it determined what each step had to accomplish for its work to be usable by the next step. For example, if computer codes were provided, what did it mean for them to be correct from the user's perspective? Avenue A's improvisational ways of converting a concept into reality were standardized and automated. This meant that innovative energy could be directed to devising better approaches, not to coping with flawed ones. For example, Avenue A's collective knowledge about publishers was extensive, but split up among individual media buyers who each had his or her personal expertise. The whole was much less than the sum of the parts because so much effort had to be wasted in finding out who knew the important fact of the moment. An investment was made to collect all that information so that when someone learned something new about a particular publisher, it quickly became part of everyone's expertise.

With this accumulation of expertise came the profitable opportunity to break the business into distinct modules rather than having everything tied to everything else through the tangle of requests and responses. For example, one group was expert at working with clients on campaign design. Another specialized in publisher relations, building a knowledge base about which sites were appropriate for which target audiences, how the sites had performed on previous campaigns, what was available, and what the rates would be. A third built technical expertise for campaign implementation and optimization. The services of the three distinct modules could be sold individually or in combination. A technically savvy organization could pay for design consultation. A traditional marketing firm could do its own design and receive media-buying services and technical support. All three services were now effective and reliable, both individually and collectively. Avenue A had become a high-velocity organization, managing its complex operations to deliver a complex service with a high and always-increasing level of performance.

And Now for Toyota...

In the next section, we are going to take a closer look at the four capabilities we have been discussing all along. Chapters 6 through 10 are based on my opportunity to observe and experience what form these four capabilities take and how they are managed and perpetuated at one of the all-time rabbit organizations, Toyota. Chapter 6 will show how Toyota's work systems are designed not only to capture the best currently known approaches to lead to success but also to reveal deficiencies in systems design when and where they occur. Chapter 7 will show how problem solving is practiced by people at various levels of responsibility and how these skills are inculcated. Chapter 8 will show how learning acquired locally by individuals and small groups is converted into collective knowledge for the entire organization. Chapter 9 will reveal what kind of leadership is required in a high-velocity organization. Chapter 10 will present several cases showing how Toyota engages these four capabilities not just for routine repeatable work but for large-scale, one-off recoveries from crises. Any reader who still thinks the approaches described in this book are for incremental change only will have his or her perception changed by the end of Chapter 10. Then, before concluding, Chapter 11 will look at health-care delivery organizations that have used lessons from Toyota to help more people and harm fewer, all the while working less hard and at reduced cost.

CHAPTER 6

CAPABILITY 1: SYSTEM DESIGN AND OPERATION

How Toyota Raced from Behind to Win

We have looked at instances in which several organizations do the same or very similar work under the same or very similar external conditions, but somehow one races ahead of the pack. Southwest beats the other airlines. The U.S. Navy runs a nuclear reactor program with a safety record which neither NASA nor the Soviet Navy can match. Alcoa generates great economic returns while creating a remarkably safe work environment. Then there are the companies that manage to accelerate themselves out of their troubles, such as Pratt & Whitney and Avenue A.

Toyota is undoubtedly one of these high-velocity organizations, starting off far behind the American Big Three when it first entered the U.S. market and racing ahead to become the world's most successful automaker, with "the healthiest profits in the industry." As *Fortune* wrote when putting Toyota on its 2007 list of the most admired companies:

You may recall that 25 years ago, it was just one of a herd of Asian interlopers selling fuel-efficient econoboxes, and Detroit snickered at the notion that Americans would ever want to buy many of them. As everyone now knows, that crystal ball was cloudy: Toyota's Camry has been the bestselling car in the U.S. since 2002, and the Lexus LS 430 has been the leading luxury-car brand for seven straight years. The company's long-term strategy is as green as anyone's. Sales of the Prius, which runs on a gas-electric hybrid engine, passed 100,000 units in 2006. The Prius is today as de rigueur in Hollywood as the hydrocarbon-swilling Hummer used to be.

And there's no doubt that Toyota's success is largely attributable to its "velocity of discovery"—the speed with which the company improves, innovates, and invents. Marvin Lieberman and his coauthors compared changes in productivity at the large automakers from the 1950s to 1987. They found that Toyota outstripped its competitors on improvements in manufacturing labor productivity. But it wasn't the usual matter of investing more heavily in plant and equipment—replacing human labor with mechanical labor. Rather, Toyota's capital productivity also outpaced the sector. In short, Toyota was discovering how to do ever more work, more quickly and more reliably, without using more labor or more machinery—and this process of discovery kept going decade after decade. In a separate study, Lieberman and Dhawan pointed to the durability of competitive advantage rooted in the way an organization conducts its work, even if the work it chooses to do is similar to that of others in the marketplace. Those authors found that the traditional sources of competitive advantage—differentiation and protected market niches—are not effective in the auto industry. Furthermore, when Lieberman and Dhawan compared the leading U.S. and Japanese automakers, they found that, in terms of operational effectiveness, "lagging firms have converged only slowly to industry best practices (if at all), while stronger firms like Toyota have made continual advances, thereby maintaining or expanding their lead."

Toyota's advances, which Lieberman measured at an aggregated level, come from a myriad of specific improvements that are across the board. For instance, in the 1940s, Taichi Ohno, one of the seminal contributors to the development of the Toyota Production System, became frustrated that it took stamping press operators two to three hours for a setup; that is, to shift from making one kind of part to making another kind. By the 1950s, setups consistently took less than an hour; and in the 1960s, they were often down to three minutes. Workers were not simply doing the same thing more quickly, like galley slaves responding to a quickening drumbeat; they were continually discovering better ways to perform the setup.

Charles Fishman, writing in the magazine *Fast Company*, reports on a process of incessant discovery in Toyota's paint shops. Painting cars had been a well-studied challenge ever since Henry Ford's day, yet Toyota pushed to discover new ways to lower cost, improve quality, respond more quickly to customers' wishes, and reduce risk to its employees and damage to the environment. In the initiative about which Fishman writes, the shops switched from feeding paint through hoses, which needed flushing with every color, to using refillable cartridges that could be interchanged from one car to the next. Of course, switching a cartridge was much faster than flushing a hose, but that wasn't all. When a hose was flushed, there was a lot of paint still in it; it turned out that as much as 30 percent of the paint which the shop bought had been going to waste. In addition, the shops no longer needed the solvent used to flush the lines; this not only saved money but eliminated a safety and environmental risk. As the plant could paint any color in any order, it no longer had to batch cars to reduce paint waste; this allowed a smoother flow of production from the body and weld shop through the paint shop and on to final assembly. Paint booths that had previously painted 33 cars per hour could now paint 50. One of the three booths was shut down and dismantled because it was no longer needed, which in turn freed up space in the shop.

We have already seen that not all high-velocity organizations are involved in manufacturing. But even within a manufacturing company, the practice of continual, disciplined, accelerated discovery applies to everything the company does, not just to its manufacturing operations. At Toyota, for example, we can see high velocity in the firm's creation of new brands as well as in its manufacturing. In the 1980s, Toyota was already looking beyond the success of its small and midsized cars, setting the stage for a luxury brand. Introduced in the 1989 model year, Lexus was dubbed "the imported car of the year" in 1990 by the Motoring Press Association. By 1991, Lexus was introducing new models to round out its offerings, and by 1992, it was outselling Mercedes and BMW in the United States. On the other end of the brand spectrum, Toyota, like many automakers, had been having trouble in younger market segments. But the company overcame that obstacle by inventing the successful Scion brand, with its funky styling and hip customization options.

Though many automakers have complained about the impossibility of dramatically increasing fuel efficiency, promising "silver bullet" solutions such as fuel cells and electronic propulsion that always seemed just a few more years away, Toyota launched the Prius with its hybrid-drive system, establishing the company as the leader in fuel efficiency without compromising performance or reliability. The hybrid-drive technology that Prius pioneered is now available across much of Toyota's product line and has had more than 1 million units sold.

Generating High Velocity: The Legacies of Taiichi Ohno and Sakichi Toyoda

Toyota's long history of success is founded on a commitment to seeing each piece of work as part of a whole process and by an equal commitment to discovering better ways to do work rather than succumbing to acceptance of the unsatisfactory or complacency with the successful. This is precisely what high-velocity organizations do and what those who chase them don't do. In Toyota's case, these two commitments have their roots in two corporate luminaries, Taiichi Ohno and Sakichi Toyoda.

Ohno is rightly famous for developing and deploying just-in-time "pull" production. In creating this system, which has since been surrounded (and often obscured) by a fascination with particular shop-floor control tools, Ohno was tackling a basic problem in modern enterprises: ensuring that the pieces of a larger whole are harmoniously synchronized rather than discordant.

After World War II, American automakers were eager to reenter the Japanese market. Only a slight twitch of their enormous productive capacity would have proven overwhelming. Japanese automakers were hardly in a position to fend off such competition; everything they needed—labor, equipment, and materials—was in short supply in postwar Japan. Ohno was managing in a Toyota engine plant, trying to make a go of it, but frustrated. As he looked around the plant, there was a worker diligently manufacturing parts, which just sat there waiting to be used. And there was another worker and his machine, doing nothing because he didn't have the parts he needed. Finally, more or less out of the blue, the parts he needed would turn up and he would get to work. Meanwhile that first worker, having built up an enormous pile of parts, had nothing to do.

How could an operation this wasteful of its men, machines, and supplies ever fend off Ford and GM? Ohno developed a simple rule to make sure that the pieces acted together in a self-regulating synchronization: If someone—the "customer"—needed something, he had to go ask for it, and the "supplier" was not allowed to produce and deliver something until asked. The objective was to ensure that those upstream did what those downstream needed and *only* what those downstream needed—no stockpiling on one end and no waiting around on the other end.

Of course, adherence to this rule in its most absolute form would be too much. To accommodate process times, people might keep a small store of material which gets replenished or produce in batches of a few rather than one. To accommodate the distance between a customer and supplier, requests might be conveyed by cards or electronically rather than in person. An intermediary might have the job of moving requests from customers and carrying the responses back from the suppliers. But the basic algorithm holds. Needs downstream pace work upstream so individual work is *in service to the larger process and ultimately all are linked in service to the end customer, none acting in isolation.*

Sakichi Toyoda, founder of the Toyoda Automatic Loom Works from which the Toyota Motor Company sprang, began his career during the years after Japan opened to Western trade and commerce after centuries of isolation. The way I have heard the story repeated within Toyota, women in his village, including his own mother and grandmother, wove fabric for clothing on hand-powered looms, which was hard labor. Toyoda observed that they faced a heartbreaking predicament. If one of the hundreds of threads on the loom snapped, it created a run in the material. Most of the time, the weaver wouldn't know this had happened and would continue to weave, inadvertently creating material more appropriate for rags than clothing.

To solve this problem, Toyoda committed himself to inventing a loom that would automatically stop the moment a strand broke. He dubbed the idea that work should stop when and where a problem occurred *jidoka* (which was translated into English as *autonomation*, meaning "self-regulation"). The loom was a success, and the *jidoka* concept was so compelling—building in the assurance that all work is the work that is intended and won't produce scrap—that he eventually sold rights to the patents to the British textile industry. With this revenue, he started the automotive company. Just as Ohno's innovation led to the insistence that the parts of a system always be seen as part of a whole, Toyoda's *jidoka* concept became embodied in the idea that work should be designed so problems are evident when and where they occur. Seeing problems was the prerequisite for the high-speed *kaizen* ("continuous improvement") for which Toyota came to be so highly regarded.

A Framework for Designing Systems

With Toyota's record of success in mind, let's take a look at how the company achieves it. I will repeat my key point: High-velocity organizations can sustain their high performance—staying ahead of competitors or beating seemingly impossible odds—because they achieve that high performance in a particular way, using the four capabilities necessary for managing complex operations. We have already observed these capabilities in some detail at Alcoa and in the U.S. Navy. Now we'll look at the first of these—how systems are designed and operated—at Toyota.

To do so, we first will look at a simple but exceptionally resilient framework for process design. With that under our belts, we'll look at some examples, beginning with the application of that framework to the work of one individual doing one job on a Toyota assembly line and to the on-the-job training he or she receives for that specific job. Then we'll expand our view to the process by which new hires at a Toyota plant in the United States are prepared for assembly-line work prior to their specific on-the-job training for a specific line job. Then we'll take an even wider view, applying our framework for process design to an entire manufacturing system. Finally, we'll see how this framework applies not only to the design of an operation, but also to the design of the process of designing an operation. Put another way, the approach which is used by managers at Toyota to design a line worker's work is the very same approach used to design an entire system of work.

In 1995, I was visiting a computer-equipment plant. Among the other visitors was Hajime Ohba, general manager of Toyota's Supplier Support Center. Our tour hosts proceeded logically (so I thought) from receiving to shipping, allowing us to see a variety of whiz-bang technologies along the way. Tellingly, the executives from corporate who were along for the walk could not have been less interested. It seemed as though they had seen it all before and that they spent more time talking about their latest fishing trip than paying attention to what was being said. At each stop, Mr. Ohba would ask the shop-floor employees a series of questions that seemed rather bland but, as I discovered later, were of great substance. When we returned to the conference room, our hosts, almost as a courtesy, asked him for his thoughts on what he had seen.

In what seemed an instant, Mr. Ohba sketched a schematic of the plant's production system—its key process steps and flows of material—along with his observations about work methods. Then, without hesitation, he presented a long list of things that inevitably had to go wrong: scrap here, bottlenecks there, missed defects, lags, delays. Not that he had actually seen any of these problems, mind you; he just knew they had to be happening. His analysis was so on target that the executives, who previously had not been paying attention, took out paper, pens, and reading glasses and began taking copious notes.

A fluke, I thought. But the next day we visited another plant, and the same thing happened. During the next several months, Mr. Ohba and I kept meeting each other in different facilities. It was the same story every time.

At first, I attributed Mr. Ohba's ability to characterize and diagnose complex work systems to his decades of experience running production facilities, supporting start-ups, and working with suppliers. With so much exposure to best practices, he could easily spot how other plants fell short. But that didn't explain how he could appraise any production process so quickly and astutely, even when product, process, or market was unfamiliar to him.

It took time, but I came to realize that he was not simply benchmarking against the hundreds if not thousands of analogies and cases he had seen. Burrowing through my research notes, I discovered a consistent pattern. Wherever we were, whatever we were observing, Mr. Ohba asked the same questions. His wide experience had helped him develop a robust framework for understanding and diagnosing the design of any complex work system. It was this framework, not necessarily benchmarking against particular situations, that he was calling on to perform his magic. It was this framework that gave him this ability to characterize and diagnosis complex systems, even those of which so much was unfamiliar. As my research continued, I had another realization: His most experienced colleagues at Toyota were all working from the same framework. It did not matter if they came from human resources, production, engineering, logistics, or administration; they had a shared way of thinking about system design and improvement—a real advantage, I learned, when it came to working on problems together.

What were those questions, and what was their purpose? No matter where we were, Mr. Ohba always started by asking if he could start his investigation in shipping, normally the last (and seemingly least interesting) stop on the guided tour. There he found the person responsible for loading trucks that day—not the person who managed shipping but the guy or gal who did the hands-on lifting and loading—and asked that person how much of which products was being shipped to whom and at what time. He was eager to know what it meant for the plant to be successful on that day and how one could tell if success had been achieved or not. Having learned that, he asked where the boxes that had to be shipped were and then walked to the last packing station. There he asked that worker where the materials he or she needed came from. Continually asking that set of questions—What are you doing? From where did you get what you needed?—he made his way "back" through the plant. This helped him establish what steps were necessary and who was responsible for performing them in order to ship products successfully.

In fact, at each stop he asked another layer of questions: What signals you to begin your work—a production instruction, a supervisor's instruction? How to you respond to that signal? What is the mix, volume, container, and timing of your response? Similarly, how do you signal that you need something? What happens when you do?

Having established precisely when and how material, information, or assistance is handed off from one step to the next—the linkages—he typically would ask one or two workers if he could observe how they did the work for which they were responsible. He wanted to know not only how things were done successfully, but how people knew when things were *not* working well.

I realized that Mr. Ohba had a simple, hierarchical, very robust way of thinking about the design of complex work systems, as I summarize and illustrate, below. (Figures 6-1 through 6-4 show very simple linear flows and handoffs from one person to the next with no intermediaries and no manufacturing resource planning, enterprise resource planning, or other centralized information flow system. This is deliberate, but it does not mean that Mr. Ohba's questions do not apply to more complex situations. In fact, asking these questions in this order helps reveal the complexity of a system with great clarity.)

1. *System output.* First, he had to know the objective of the system overall. What does it have to deliver, to whom, and by when to be successful? That was why he wanted to start in shipping. It was as close to the actual customer as he could get, the place where it was most clear what had to happen to be successful and whether or not it had happened. (See Figure 6-1.)

Figure 6-1 Design levels: System

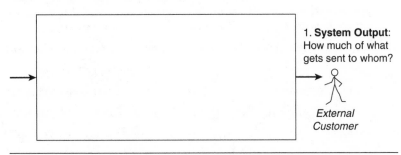

2. *Pathway design: flow of materials, information, and services.*
Second, he wanted to know the architecture of the system. Who has to be responsible and perform what steps in what sequence in order to achieve the system's overall output? By knowing this, he would know the pathways over which materials, services, and information flowed from start to finish. (See Figure 6-2.)

Figure 6-2 Design levels: Pathway

3. *Connection design: linkages between adjacent process steps.*
Third, he wanted to know how steps on a pathway were connected by handoffs or exchanges of information, material, and services, with particular attention to infor-

mation that triggered people to do what they had to. What are the form and the source of the information that signals someone to start and stop his or her work? Conversely, how does someone indicate what he or she needs in order to proceed? In reaction to those requests, what form do products, services, or information take as they are handed off from the pathway steps at which they are created to the steps at which they are used? (See Figure 6-3.)

Figure 6-3 Design levels: Connections

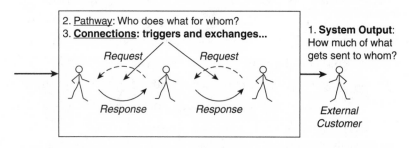

4. *Methods for individual task activities.* Fourth, he wanted to know how people actually did the work for which they were responsible. For each particular task, what steps

Figure 6-4 Design levels: Methods

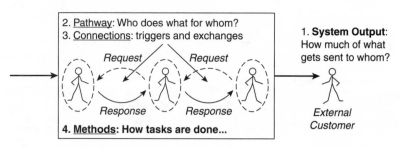

must the worker perform, in what order, at what time and location, and with what results, in order to do that task successfully? (See Figure 6-4.)

HOW THE CAPABILITIES CORRESPOND TO RULES IN USE

Some readers may be familiar with a 1999 *Harvard Business Review* article I coauthored with Kent Bowen, "Decoding the DNA of the Toyota Production System," in which we described the four "rules in use" fundamental to the Toyota Production System. Here is how those four rules map onto the four capabilities presented in *Chasing the Rabbit*. The first three rules concerned process design and operation: how to design and operate a pathway (simple and specified), a connection (direct between immediate customers and suppliers and with unambiguous, binary mechanisms for sending requests and responses), and work activities (specified in terms of work content, sequence, location, timing, and outcome). These are embodied in *Chasing the Rabbit*'s Capability 1. Since that time I have come to understand the necessity of specifying the expected output of an operation with an embedded test to indicate whether you are ahead of or behind that expectation. Hence the need for a fourth level of design. The fourth of our rules in use—that problem-solving should occur in the smallest possible group, using the scientific method with the support of a leader—is the core of *Chasing the Rabbit*'s Capability 2— swarming, containing, and solving problems when and where they occurred with those who were affected. Capability 3—sharing knowledge—was touched on in the 1999 article, and Capability 4 (developing Capabilities 1, 2, and 3) was only alluded to.

It was not enough that the design of outputs, pathways, connections, and activities be well specified. Recall Sakichi Toyoda's principle that if a thread on a mechanical loom broke, the loom should stop immediately so the operator wouldn't waste time and effort weaving material that had a run in it. His approach is embodied throughout Toyota in the principle that work cannot be performed unless a built-in test is incorporated that will immediately signal when something has gone wrong and where it has gone wrong. There are tests appropriate to each level of the four levels of system design:

1. *Outputs.* How do you know if your shipments are running ahead or behind?
2. *Pathways.* How do you know if all the process steps have been completed, each by the person who was responsible?
3. *Connections.* How do you know if you are ahead or behind in fulfilling requests from immediate "customers" and getting what you need from immediate "suppliers"?
4. *Activities.* How do you know if the method you are using to complete this task is working?

Table 6-1 summarizes this framework.

Table 6-1 Summary of System Design and Operation Framework

	Specified in Terms of	Built-in Test Indicates
System output: Matching supply with demand	• How much of what has to be delivered to whom by when for success?	• If the system is running behind, there is more demand than capacity. • If the system is running ahead, there is more capacity than demand.
Pathway: Assigning responsibility for work in sequence	• What tasks have to be completed by whom in what order to achieve the target output?	• If someone needs to do something unexpectedly, the system is underdesigned or underresourced. • If someone is idle contrary to expectations, the system is overdesigned or overresourced.
	• Is the flow simple and linear (good) or does it loop back on itself (bad)?	• If the flow loops back on itself, problems at one step may flow downstream and then be reinjected in a disruptive, amplifying fashion upstream.

(continued on next page)

Table 6-1 (continued)

	Specified in Terms of	Built-in Test Indicates
Connection: Conveying material, information, and services between process steps	• What is someone's trigger to start and stop the work for which he or she is responsible, and what is the format of his or her response? • Are requests and responses conveyed directly between immediate customers and suppliers?	• A request for which there is no response means that a customer's need is going unsatisfied. • A response for which there was no request means that a supplier is working ahead of need. • If they are, upstream and downstream process steps will be working in synchronization, with the needs of the downstream step triggering the work of the steps on which it depends. If they are not, dyssynchronization will occur.
Method: Accomplishing work for which one is responsible	• What is each step's work—content, sequence, timing, location, and expected outcome?	• If the work design is not being followed, is there something wrong with it or with the training for it? • If it is being followed but is not achieving its intended objectives, is there something wrong with it or is it being used in the wrong circumstances?

Specifying Work Designs and Building In Tests

We'll now look at several examples of what it means for a process to be highly specified in terms of what is expected to lead to success, with tests built in to indicate when and where the process is not successful. We'll start by looking at a relatively simple example, the work of a single worker and the on-the-job training for that job. The contrasts with my experiences at the Big Three plant, described in Chapter 3, will be abundant. Then, we'll look at the process by which someone is trained before he or she even starts to work on the line. Even though training is less tangible than manufacturing and much more affected by the particular skills, background, and capabilities of each individual, we'll see the same discipline of specification and self-corrective testing being applied. From there, we'll move on to an example of an entire production system and then to two examples of the design of the complex task of designing (or redesigning) an entire production system. I deliberately chose a series of examples that increases in scale and complexity in order to emphasize the fact that the same principles of specifying and building in tests for success are always at work.

Example: Assembly-Line Work

When I worked on the line at a Big Three plant, I was supposed to install right front seats, but it was very hard to know how to do that successfully. I later discovered that I had been working very hard in that plant to accomplish half the work done with far less effort in a Toyota plant.

At Toyota's Kentucky plant (Toyota Motor Manufacturing, Kentucky—TMMK), for example, installing the right front seat had seven distinct prespecified steps. Each step was expected to take a specific amount of time; intermediate tests indicated when the work was not being performed as designed or when the actual outcome failed to match the expected outcome. These are summarized in Table 6-2 and are illustrated in Figure 6-5. They required 46 seconds of work and 5 seconds of walking, thus occupying 51 seconds of the allowed 55-second cycle.

Figure 6-5 Standardized work chart for seat installation at Toyota Kentucky. Hashmarks indicate car position for each second it is in work area.

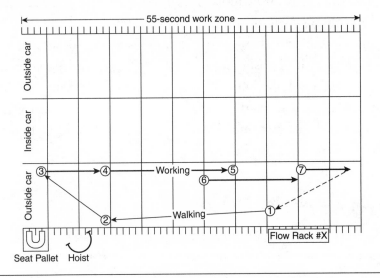

Table 6-2 Standardized Work: Right Front Seat Installation at TMMK

Step	Description	Time (Work/Walk), Seconds		Quality Check	Safety
1	Check manifest	2			
2	Set hoist to seat	3			
3	Set seat to door area	6	2	Gun torques out (to prespecified torque) to confirm tightening. Bolt head flat to seat rail.	Team member must be trained to use equipment for safe ergonomics.
	Place rear bolt covers on rear floor and return hoist	4			
4	Install two front seat bolts	14			
5	Adjust seat forward	4	3		
6	Install rear seat bolts	11		Gun torques out (to prespecified torque) to confirm tightening. Bolt head flat to seat rail.	Shoot outside rear bolt with left hand to reduce strain on right hand and elbow.
7	Install bolt covers	7			
	Total	**46**	**5**		

Example: Training Assembly-Line Workers

It wasn't just the shop-floor work which was designed and done differently from the work I had done in the Big Three shop. A new hire's preparation for that work was also worlds apart from my Big Three experience. There, I had been thrown into the thick of things with merely a cursory demonstration offered to the whole group of new hires. At TMMK and other Toyota plants where I observed the training process, new hires were shown each of the steps and then were allowed to perform the first step, with the trainer completing the sequence. This continued until the new hire could consistently perform the first step correctly and in the time indicated. Only after the new hire had passed this test did he or she move on to the second step, with the trainer completing the remaining five. This process continued until the new hire had mastered the entire sequence.

Consider the implications of teaching in a step-by-step fashion, with the worker not advancing until the preceding step has been mastered. Whereas my problems were spread out over a 57-second interval, the problems of a trainee at TMMK are confined to the few seconds needed to complete the one step which he or she is learning. Because the training process is designed, performed, and controlled with finer granularity, responses to problems have greater resolution and control. When teaching me, Bill had to be able to detect and respond to problems at any point in the work cycle. If he had been training me in a step-by-step fashion, he would have been able to concentrate his attention and his efforts more precisely.

The differences did not end (or start) there. Even before the step-by-step on-the-job training, new hires at Toyota go through an equally well-scripted onboarding process to prepare them for their on-the-job training on the assembly line. I investigated this myself at Toyota's Indiana truck and van assembly plant. Each step was designed with the needs of the next step in mind. Just as the overall objective (output) of the on-the-job training is to prepare a new hire for a particular line job, the overall objective (output) of the onboarding process is to prepare new hires to learn on the line. How this was to be accomplished was scripted and specified in detail, with tests indicating if someone had successfully completed one stage and was ready to progress to the next. It was the same principles yet again.

How was the output of the onboarding process defined? The process should deliver a person who wants to do the line work; who is physically capable of doing it—with the strength for the job, the endurance to keep it up for an entire shift, and the muscular flexibility needed to avoid repetitive stress problems; who has sufficient technical skill to handle materials and use tools safely and effectively; and who has a knowledge of basic shop-floor tools such as just-in-time pull systems to replenish material, andon cords to call for help, and standardized work to complete tasks. If a new hire emerges from the onboarding process without all these characteristics (that is, if the output is not what has been specified), he or she will be unprepared for the on-the-job training and for the actual work that will follow.

To make it easier for the new hire to master his or her new job on the line, and to make it easier for the team leader to train that new hire, human resources makes sure that many skills and attitudes are already in place. For example, even before new hires begin training for their production jobs, Toyota makes sure that they know what they are getting into. To accomplish this, an old gym was converted into a mock assembly line (1 in Figure 6-6). Job applicants spend several hours doing assembly work on mock-ups. In the spirit of continuous improvement, the original day-long mock-up session was extended to two days when Toyota discovered that it was important to find out how a new hire reacted to putting in a hard day on the line and then coming back the next day to do it again. Not everyone found that tolerable, and Toyota did not want to assign a new hire to a job in which he or she was likely to fail.

After the mock-up comes classroom orientation, with a curriculum specific to the job for which the new hires were preparing and with written and practical tests to ensure that the various teaching points had been learned (2 in Figure 6-6). There was nothing like this for new hires at the Big Three plant.

With this portion of the onboard training confirmed, it was on to the next phase—basic-shop floor production-control tools such as standard work and pull systems (3 in Figure 6-6). HR had no intention of leaving new hires to learn these things on the job, consuming the attention of a team leader and perhaps a group leader who was also responsible for other people doing actual production. (This would be a bit like giving kids their driver's licenses and then letting the cops give them driver's ed along with their speeding tickets.) Instead, Toyota created a scaled-down, tabletop model assembly line, on which the product would be miniature trucks made from Legos.

There were many skills to learn, including reading manifests to know what work must be done, using standardized work procedures to accomplish that work, using kanban cards to request parts and materials, detecting errors, using andon cords to call for assistance, and takt-time production to keep up with the rate of customer demand. But the process was brilliantly designed. The complexity of real products, real production demands, and a real production pace was removed so that only one skill had to be mastered at a time. The "student" was always focused on the teaching point at hand, while cumulatively building expertise. (In Chapter 11, we'll see the stark contrast between this approach to training and the approach typical in medical education.)

But still there was more. Assembly line work is *hard* work. It requires strength, endurance, and a good amount of dexterity. So the Toyota Indiana plant had its own aerobics studio (4 in Figure 6-6). The people in the group of new hires whom I met came in quite a variety of sizes, shapes, and conditions, all of them huffing and puffing their way to fitness on exercise bikes, treadmills, and stair-climbing machines.

Finally, there were specific technical skills that had to be mastered (5 in Figure 6-6). In a screened area of the production floor, new hires had a chance to practice shooting bolts, handling parts, and using paint sprayers, becoming competent with the physical tools of their work before they began working on real cars and trucks for which customers were going to pay real money.

Once a new hire had passed all of the tests, he or she would be eligible and *ready* for on-the-job training for an assembly-line job, like the one described just before. There was no pre-

Figure 6-6 Training pathway for new hires at Toyota Kentucky

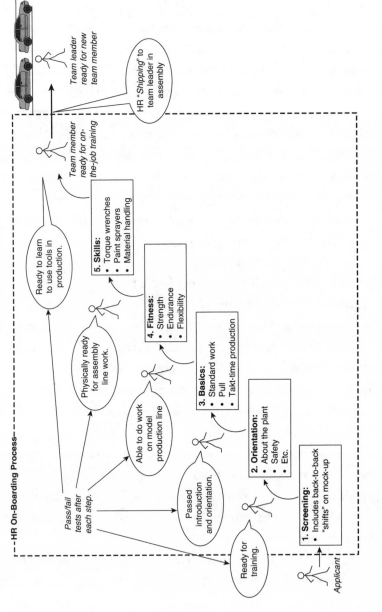

specified length of time for this training, but there was a specified outcome: New hires were to be trained until they could pass. No one was "socially promoted" and few washed out.

All this elaborate effort to determine what people needed to know to start their jobs successfully and to build a process that would ensure that they had those skills was not limited to shop-floor production work. For those joining the production engineering, equipment maintenance, and other technical departments, Toyota had contracted with a local college to develop training in electronics and other skilled trades. This was conducted along the same lines: Build knowledge in an incremental, layered fashion, rather than fully immersing someone in the real work environment all at once, and build tests into the training so that one stage is learned before the next is tackled.

I have described the training process in such detail because it is important to understand that high-velocity organizations do *everything* in this deliberate yet high-velocity way. Toyota makes cars, but it is as important that the training process be as rigorously defined by its output, pathways, handoffs, and work methods—with tests built in to tell when something wasn't succeeding—as it is that the auto-manufacturing process itself be rigorously specified with *jidoka* (self-regulation).

To illustrate the concept of designing systems of work with specificity and built-in tests, we started with relatively simple examples: the daily, repetitive work of an individual assembly worker and the on-the-job training he or she would receive. Then we looked at a more complex process involving more stages and more people—the preparation a new hire would receive as a prerequisite to being trained to do his or her work on the line. Now let's look at the same principles applied on a still larger scale.

Example: Managing High-Volume Mass-Customized Production

Aisin, a first-tier supplier of auto parts to Toyota, also has a consumer products division. In 1987, its Seiki factory, which manufactured mattresses, switched from mass production to mass *customized* production. Customers in furniture stores could test model beds and specify the size, cover fabric, lining material, quilting pattern, trim color, and firmness for a total of 850 alternatives and then have their customized mattress delivered in three days. This should have been a much harder operation to manage than simple mass production of fewer alternatives delivered with a longer delay, yet Aisin achieved remarkable increases in volume, variety, and productivity with simultaneous reductions in lead time and inventory, as shown in Table 6-3. What did Aisin do to achieve this enviable combination of variety, cost, and short lead time?

Like any product, mattresses are made in distinct steps (as shown in Figure 6-7), all of which are subject to fluctuations in demand, variations in process time, and other perturbations. In the framing stage, springs are coiled and joined into a frame. In quilting, liner layers are sewn to cover layers. In edging, the bolt of material for the circumference of a mattress is stitched. These three subassemblies are assembled into complete mattresses and then labeled, packaged, and shipped.

Table 6-3 Aisin Mattress Production: Variety, Volume, Inventory, and Productivity

	1986	1988	1992	1996	1997	Annualized Rate of Change
Styles	200	325	670	750	850	14%
Units per day	160	230	360	530	550	12%
Units per person	8	11	13	20	26	11%
Finished goods (days)	30	2.5	1.8	1.5	1.5	–24%
Productivity index	100	138	175	197	208	7%

Figure 6-7 Simplified material flow for mattress production

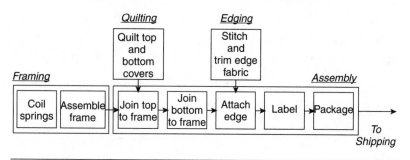

It sounds simple (and compared to jet-engine manufacturing, it is), but the simplicity of the material flows masks the difficulty of having information flow so that the various steps are integrated into a well-functioning process delivering the desired output. Who would think that information flow would matter that much in mattress production or that there even was much information to worry about? In fact, Aisin's success in converting its line from mass production to mass customization came as much from improvements and innovations in the information-processing side as in production methods.

For example, coiling, edging, and the other production centers originally received production schedules from a centralized production control center. Despite the effort that went into planning, these individual production schedules did not necessarily coordinate well. There was often a need for considerable inventory between successive production steps and between the plant and its customers. To solve that problem, Aisin adopted a just-in-time pull system, a method described earlier in this chapter. At Aisin, Taiichi Ohno's simple rule had multiple manifestations. Production schedules had been based on expected (rather than actual) demand. Now, customers would go into furniture stores and design their own mattresses. Those orders would be conveyed to Aisin, where daily production would be set. However, rather than broadcasting detailed production instructions to every work center, production control signaled the last step in the production line that another mattress had to be completed. As each mattress was completed and sent to shipping, the end station signaled the feeder stations (edging, quilting, and framing) to send the next piece forward. When those trigger signals arrived, each feeder station responded by sending one piece forward, now having room to work on the next, pulling on their own suppliers as they depleted material.

Figure 6-8 Connecting quilting, material ordering, and material supply

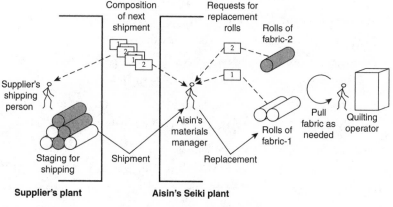

We see this simple exchange of trigger signals and material responses for the quilting feeder-line in Figure 6-8.

Why was it so important for Aisin to convert from a push system, in which production control sent detailed instructions to each locality, to a pull system, in which the people at each step set the pace of the steps on which they depended? This gets back to the basic problem of designing complex systems: It is impossible to design them perfectly. When Aisin depended on detailed production schedules, those schedules depended on inevitably flawed predictions of what customers would actually want and reflected flawed predictions of how a complex and therefore unpredictable operation would perform. Once the actual operation began to deviate from the schedule—which it almost always did—people would have to engage in workarounds or firefighting or heroics rather than previously tested best practices. In contrast, letting adjacent steps convey requests and responses directly to each other built self-regulation into the system—no more ad hoc regulation (firefighting) required.

But to be self-regulating, a system has to be both able to see problems and able to correct those problems as they occur. At Aisin this took many forms. For example, every two hours, production control re-established which customer orders were directed to each of the two assembly lines. With clarity of what was expected to be produced, where and by when, it was much easier to track whether the system was meeting those expectations. To highlight problems even further, display boards indicated whether the production lines were ahead of or behind their targets. When they fell behind the target pace, first- and second-level management were signaled to investigate why and to contain the problem.

Those were the diagnostics for the lines taken as a whole. Furthermore, each link between steps had a similar built-in self-diagnostic test. If the quilting subprocess fell out of sync with final assembly, it was obvious within a few minutes. One quilt too few or too many between one step and the other meant the two were no longer operating at the same pace; one had sped up or the other had slowed down. Without this homeostatic ability for self-diagnosis and self-correction, less effective approaches, such as maintaining extra inventory—which would have to be counted, recorded, tracked, and rotated—would have been needed to maintain a steady level of production.

To create this self-regulating, self-correcting capacity, Aisin had to make other design-related decisions. In order to have one process step pace the previous one, it was necessary to specify which people using which machines were supplying which other people. Thus, the flow of material along a predetermined pathway had to be specified; every person at every step had to know, for every handoff, who would supply him or her and whom he or she had to supply.

This is not an obvious approach for many organizations. For instance, at every step Aisin had more than one machine that could perform the same job: two devices to coil springs and build frames, five machines to prepare the top and bottom quilts, two lines on which the mattresses could be assembled. Since, for example, any of the quilting machines could do any of the quilting work, work flow could have been managed on a first-come, first-served basis the way bank customers get in one line and then go to whichever teller is free (see Figure 6-9). Instead, jobs flowed from one specified location to the next (see Figure 6-10) because Aisin did not want to forfeit the self-regulating (self-diagnostic and self-correcting) features of a work flow in which each step "pulled" what it needed from a specified previous step.

Recall that the basic problem in designing and operating a complex system is that no matter what effort has been put into

---

Figure 6-9 From any to any

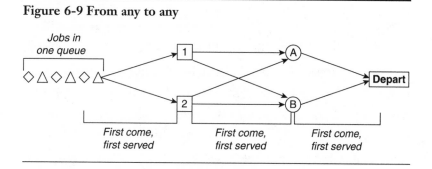

Figure 6-10 Prespecified flow

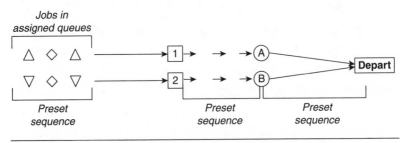

planning a design, there is still a lot that is not understood about how various elements interact with one another. Specifying the flow of material and information in advance, as shown in Figure 6-10, allows Aisin's designers and operators to be much clearer about their expectations: What steps do we believe are necessary for work to be accomplished? At each step, what are the speed and capabilities of the people using the equipment? At each step, what is the real work content of each job?

By making abundantly clear what is expected to occur, it is much easier to be surprised by the things that happen which have not been anticipated. Does that sound backwards? Shouldn't clarity make it harder to be surprised? The point here is that clear expectations don't, in themselves, make things go right. Clear expectations simply make it obvious when things do *not* go as expected. So it's easier to say, "Oh, that's not what I thought would happen. There is something about this process I don't understand and need to learn." This is exactly what Rickover was after when he insisted that Rockwell "know" how a meeting was going to turn out even before it started. It is the same discipline which Rockwell himself practiced when he insisted that before reactor shielding was tested, estimates be made of what every sensor on the surface would read.

Example: Consolidating Three Production Lines

We have now seen Toyota's *jidoka* approach applied very successfully to the hands-on work of a single individual, to the on-the-job training for a new hire, to the onboarding process for a group of new hires, and to an entire manufacturing operation. The usefulness of clarifying expectations in advance of action and building in tests to recognize when and where those expectations are proven wrong does not stop there. Here is an example of *jidoka* applied to the very opposite of repetitive work performed by an individual or small team; that is, to a complex one-time-only project carried out by a large and mixed group.

A Toyota supplier, facing reduced demand for certain parts, decided to consolidate three lines into one. The production-engineering staff generated a detailed 13-step plan for the consolidation process, indicating who would have to do what work, in what order, with what resources, and in how much time. Why bother with such a tightly choreographed routine for a task that would never have to be done again? Because the team responsible for the consolidation knew that, once the work began, they would start discovering all sorts of things they had not known and demands they had not anticipated. Even in the first step, they realized that certain work had to be performed that they had not thought of and that other work for which they had planned was not necessary. However, they did not content themselves with making do—doing the unexpected work, skipping the unneeded work, and carrying on with the original plan. Instead, every time their script proved to be flawed, they asked themselves what assumptions they had held that had led them to that choice. Typically, they realized that the same assumption was behind other steps in the plan, so they kept revising the later steps on the basis of discoveries made in earlier steps. One might think that specifying in advance what they thought would work and investigating every deviation from those expectations as they did their work would have made this one-off project take longer than necessary. In fact, it allowed the consolidation to be done more quickly, less expensively, and with better results than had been anticipated at first.

Example: New Model Launch

And this is not an isolated example. Paul Adler and his co-authors studied a series of new model introductions at Toyota's NUMMI joint venture with General Motors in California. Toyota was introducing a car to be produced both in the United States and in Japan. Although the car would be the same, much else was different. One plant had been designed by Toyota and operated by the company over many years; the other plant reflected its General Motors heritage in layout and equipment. The workforces had different mixes and degrees of skills and capabilities and the suppliers on which each plant depended were different as well. With so many differences, one approach would have been to let each plant develop its own launch plan. But that would eliminate the opportunity for one plant to learn from the experience of the other. Toyota decided to have the Japanese plant launch first. As that plant proceeded, it found that what it had anticipated was not always what happened, so it had to continually modify its script. Once that plant's launch was complete, it "loaned" its modified script to NUMMI. Not that the Japanese team felt its script had been modified to perfection, but it did reflect the best current understanding of how to introduce the product successfully. Before the NUMMI team even started its own launch, it modified the Japanese team's script based on what it knew of its own circumstances. Not that they cut out inappropriate segments and improvised to fill the gaps. They replaced those segments with their own tightly scripted segments. As the NUMMI launch proceeded, problems that occurred and were solved along the way prompted additional modifications that allowed for an even more successful launch the next time around.

Having looked closely at how work—from simple and repetitive to complex and infrequent—is designed and operated, we'll turn in Chapter 7 to how imperfect systems are continually improved, as are the people who improve them and as is the body of knowledge that will contribute to further improvement.

CHAPTER 7

CAPABILITY 2: PROBLEM SOLVING AND IMPROVEMENT

Chapter 6 conveyed my experience of working with experienced Toyota managers, realizing that their exceptional speed and facility in understanding, diagnosing, and designing systems depended on well-practiced, robust, reliable frameworks which they could apply broadly, rather than relying on a multitudinous library of best-practice analogies. In this chapter, we'll see a similar approach to problem solving and improvement—simple, robust frameworks which are used reliably by individuals and shared within groups that must solve problems collaboratively and cross-functionally. These frameworks both guide the direction of change—in the direction of an "ideal" system—and prescribe how change should be made—using the scientific method at high speed and low cost to solve problems while building ever deeper knowledge. Consequently, fixing something is both an end unto itself and also a means to two other ends—creating new knowledge which can be put to later, competitive use and developing greater problem-solving capacity in the people who are addressing the problem.

Let's take a closer look at what these frameworks are and how they are used to sustain a palpable sense of optimistic urgency. We'll visit several quality circles: groups of frontline operators whose responsibilities include not only doing their daily work but also improving their ability to do that work. One of the teams is at the Aisin plant that converted itself from a mass manufacturer characterized by delays and excessive inventory to a mass customizer that responds to customers' orders with exceptional rapidity (see Chapter 6). We'll also see how that plant's senior leaders practiced a similar discipline in problem solving and process improvement on a larger scale. We'll conclude by watching how Toyota leaders conveyed this discipline—work in such a way that you keep learning more about it and getting better at it—to the people for whom they were responsible. But first, let's get a preview of the discipline itself.

Problem-Solving Frameworks

Problem-Solving Goal: The "Ideal"

Once I realized that Toyota people discussed the design and operation of all processes in a patterned way (see Chapter 6), I also noticed a pattern in how they discussed improvement and innovation. For example, if I asked how a particular type of work was done, I got more than just an explanation of what was done. I also got an explanation of why it was done that way, according to the following pattern:

Ideally, here is what we are trying to accomplish at this step, *but the problem is* . . . (evidence of some particular difficulty: scrap, delays, strain, and so forth). We believe the problem is caused by (some particular factor or set of factors). Therefore, we are using this particular *countermeasure* to offset the causes that we have identified so we do not experience that problem again. As a result, we are able to do this work with fewer defects; quicker responses in reaction to customer need; smaller batches; less waste of time, effort, and material; and greater safety for those doing the work.

As I reflected on my repeated interactions with people at Toyota, who consistently answered using that same pattern, I began to recognize that this *ideal* was a "True North" beacon to which improvement efforts were oriented. This *ideal* implied that production and delivery should be:

- *Defect-free*—never compromising customer satisfaction.
- *On demand*—only in response to real need.
- *One piece at a time*—providing those who needed something exactly what they could put to use, not overburdening them with the obligation to hold things in anticipation of future need.
- *Immediate*—providing those who needed something what they needed without imposing any waiting time on them, but, if this was impossible, small batches of finished goods might be kept on hand to provide the illusion of immediacy.
- *Without waste*—never spending time, effort, creativity, and other efforts in ways that wouldn't be valued by someone else.

- *Safe*—so no one gets hurt physically or emotionally or is professionally threatened.
- *Secure*—so that things go only to those intended and not to others.

With this ideal as an absolute standard (akin to Alcoa's standard that the best production systems result in zero injuries), if a change advanced a situation along at least one of those dimensions, that was good. If it didn't, or if it caused a regression, that was not good.

Problem-Solving Discipline

As I reflected on this pattern of explaining how work was done, and as I was later exposed to the standard way of solving problems, I recognized another implication. It was insufficient to explain what was being done in terms of a gap with the ideal. It was also necessary to explain the rationale behind the approach—what had been addressed and discovered to reach the approach that was currently being used. Rationales took this form:

- *Background:* Why we were concerned about this situation.
- *Current condition:* How work was done and what problems (symptoms) were occurring.
- *Root-cause analysis (diagnosis):* What causes were discovered when the problems were investigated.
- *Countermeasure treatments:* How we attempted to offset the causes and eliminate the problems.
- *Target condition:* How work was expected to proceed with the countermeasures in place and the problems treated.

- *Actual outcome:* What was really achieved.
- *Gap analysis:* Why the reality differed from the expectation/prediction.

This thought process was often shown in a summary document, as in Table 7-1, that captured the entire discovery process.

Table 7-1 Problem-Solving Template

Background: Description of the process being improved and what motivated concern about it.

Current Condition	**Target Condition**
• Description/illustration of how work was being done.	• A prediction of how work would be done with the countermeasures in place.
• Description/illustration of problems that were being experienced.	• Description/quantification of expected effects of the countermeasures.
Root-Cause Analysis/Diagnosis	**Countermeasure Treatments**
• What factors were revealed by an investigation of the causes of problems.	• Changes in how work is done to offset the causal factors and prevent the problems from reoccurring.
Actual Outcomes	**Gap Analysis**
• Description of how the work system actually behaved. • Summary of how the work system actually performed.	• Investigation of the gap between what was predicted/expected and what was actually experienced.

Let's take a closer look at how this approach is learned and applied.

Example: Quality Circle at Taiheiyo

Taiheiyo is a first-tier supplier for Toyota's Tsutumi, Takaoka, Motomachi, and Tahara assembly plants. Its main processes are stamping, welding, and plating. A team member at Taiheiyo, Mr. Ohashi, explained to me a two-year problem-solving effort of which he was part. Not only did he and his colleagues create a better process, but they also built deeper knowledge about the process and built skills to improve other processes and solve other problems later on.

Ohashi was part of a quality circle that focused on improving the overall cleanliness and environmental quality of the welding department. Interestingly, as the effort was explained, it became clear that improving the process was not an end in itself. It was the means to another end: building the *kaizen* (improvement) skills of the operators. The particular problem that Ohashi's teams were addressing was the solid and gaseous pollutants created by CO_2 welding robots. Hot spatter from the welds increased the fire risk, crudded up the equipment with hard-to-clean residue, and created smoke so severe that operators had to wear uncomfortable masks.

Consider for a moment how such a problem might be addressed in other organizations. In some, workers might be expected to grin and bear it, wearing respirators, scrubbing the residue, and knowing that every day the job was going to be unpleasant, with lots of energy devoted to unproductive activities. In somewhat more enlightened organizations, responsibility for cleaning up the mess would be delegated to a team of experts. But because the number of experts is limited and the demands on their time are great, it might be a long wait before the welding problem was addressed—if ever. In the meantime, the unpleasant conditions would have to be tolerated. In the case of Taiheiyo, the idea was that if problem-solving capacity were developed throughout the organization, those affected by a problem could often solve it themselves—and immediately— relying on the experts only for problems of sufficient scale, scope, and complexity.

Mr. Ohashi was one of 10 who had dedicated time with their group leader to clean up the welding area. Though the group leader was more experienced and capable, his job was far more than being the project leader per se, divvying up work and assigning responsibility to this person or that for ideas he had generated and directing people to do what he thought was right. A fundamental element of his job was to be a Socratic teacher, asking them questions, pulling the team along by developing their abilities to think through situations, and teaching them how to resolve problems on their own by using the scientific method.

For example, he first led them in a series of exercises to figure out how to reduce the scattering of welding spatter. Even though he might have known better, the group leader let Ohashi's team try a domelike cover for the torch. It proved ineffective because the spatter accumulated inside the cover. An umbrellalike cover was tried next. It prevented the spatter from scattering above but increased the spatter to the sides. In a third attempt, the quality circle tried a bronze shutter that shielded the torch; this proved most effective in preventing spatter from accumulating on the welding arm.

But now they had another problem to solve: More spatter was accumulating on the base of the machine. Again, the group leader might have known which materials in which configurations would have made for easier or harder cleaning. However, the idea was not to impose his notions but to teach the quality-circle members to develop and test theirs. Their trials are summarized in Table 7-2. In conducting these experiments, the team concluded that the material had to withstand 1,000 degrees Celsius, that it had to have a heat capacity above 0.3 cal/°C, and that the material had to be formable.

Having dealt with spatter, and having practiced this knowledge-building approach to solving problems, the quality circle

Table 7-2 Taiheiyo Quality Circle Test Results: Base Covers

	Material	Melting Temperature, °C	Heat Capacity, cal/°C	Analysis	Conclusion
1	0.3-mm bronze plate	1,083	0.024	Made holes, spatter stuck	Rejected
2	1.3-mm bronze/zinc	1,083	0.102	Made holes	Rejected
3	3.0-mm tile	450	0.154	Dirty, rough, not formable	Rejected
4	1.2-mm stainless steel	1,450	0.103	Made holes, difficult to form	Rejected
5	1.8-mm aluminum	685	0.103	Dirty, made holes	Rejected
6	5.5-mm ceramic plate	400	0.102	Dirty, made holes, not formable	Rejected
7	4.0-mm bronze plate	1,083	0.320	Good	Accepted

developed alternatives for capturing the fumes generated by welding. Again, the group leader might have imposed his preconceived solution to the problem or the quality circle might have solicited solutions from other divisions or other plants. However, by doing that, they would have missed the point of solving problems for the sake of building problem-solving capacity rather than merely for the sake of making the problems go away. Instead, the team practiced the skills it had been developing in solving the spatter problem.

The team did trials for three types of intake mechanism and changed the shape and location of the vent cover to maximize the amount of fumes drawn in while minimizing the amount of spatter that dirtied it. But developing an effective ventilation system caused another problem: The vacuum used to draw in the fumes also drew in some of the spatter, risking damage to the vacuum fan and threatening to ignite a fire in the device. The team discovered that it had to develop a spatter filter in the ventilation mechanism. Here too they were given enough leeway to practice developing ideas and testing them experimentally rather than depending on established expertise for a turnkey solution.

The main issue was developing a filter that would stop the spatter without overly impeding the draw generated by the ventilating fan. The team began to test a variety of filtration materials (see Figure 7-1).

Drawing fumes through a container of pebbles proved ineffective because not enough air got through. Replacing the pebbles with golf balls was only partly successful. The golf balls accumulated residue and had to be replaced because they could not be cleaned. At ¥100 per ball, that was too costly. Metal ball bearings like Pachinko balls were too densely packed to be

Figure 7-1 Taiheiyo fume filter

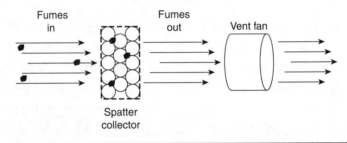

effective. However, glass marbles—like those used to seal certain soft-drink bottles—worked effectively. At ¥2 per ball—and the balls could be cleaned and reused—the price was right.

The team encountered other issues before arriving at its final design: how many layers of marbles to use—one, two, or three—and how to remove other contaminants from the fumes once the spatter was gone. In every case in which there was a question, the response was to generate an answer by conducting quick experiments, not by speculating. They finally arrived at a design that included a "marble-ator" to deal with the spatter and a static-electricity dust collector to get rid of the particulates. Again, speculating that they had "solved" the problem in its entirety ran against the grain of their approach, so they developed a simple test to prove the efficacy of their contraption. To test that the air coming out of the device was clean, they ran the exhaust tube into a fish tank, which, according to Mr. Ohashi and his assistant manager, Mr. Koiwa, was perfectly fine for the fish.

Taiheiyo's heavy investment in the problem-solving ability of its workers had multiple benefits. The problem-solving skills of the team were increased; the cost of equipment maintenance was reduced; the environmental quality, safety, and comfort of the work site were improved, earning the supplier an ecology award from the Ministry of Science and Technology; and the more technically skilled members of the maintenance-engineering department were unburdened of routine responsibilities and freed to address more challenging situations. Whereas the maintenance-engineering department had done 100 percent of the maintenance previously, the production workers were now able to do 80 percent of the routine maintenance themselves.

Example: Quality Circle at NHK Toyota

The improvement effort of Ohashi's quality circle at Taiheiyo had several characteristics:

- Process improvement was used as a mechanism to develop the abilities of line workers.
- Those affected by the problem were involved in solving the problem.
- Improvement activities were designed and performed scientifically, not arbitrarily, with structured tests of design alternatives.
- The improvement activity was guided by a capable teacher.

Here is an example from another Toyota supplier, NHK (Nippon Hatsujo Kabushiki Kaisha, or Japan Spring Corporation), which used the same approach to improve processes and to train workers to improve processes at the same time. We'll follow a quality circle working at a Toyota City plant, where they improved the quality of molded foam parts—the inside of armrests for the Crown, Celsior, and Lexus lines—and lowered the cost of producing them.

The quality circle had eight members, guided by a leader, Mr. Nagata, and a subleader, Mr. Mori. There were several specific problems. For example, the liner material they were using allowed the foam to bleed through the seams of the mold, resulting in time consuming, material-wasting trimming (both departures from the *ideal* of "immediate" and "without waste"). To resolve this issue, the quality circle didn't ping-pong, jumping to the conclusion that one or another alternative material would work. Rather, they set up a series of trials to see what material, at what thickness, would do the trick.

There was a related problem. The pin that ejected the parts from the mold had a tendency to weaken and tear the liner; this also affected quality and cost. As with the Taiheiyo quality circle, one approach might have been to delegate the problem to a technical expert or take a solution from some other armrest plant. Or they could have swapped one pin type out for another that they speculated would yield better results. However, even if this did improve the process, it would be by luck; it wouldn't develop the employees' problem-solving skills, and it wouldn't build deeper knowledge in pursuit of superlative cold-foam molding. With these multiple considerations in mind, Nagata and Mori led the team through a set of experiments, testing different combinations of pin shapes and material thicknesses to achieve the desired outcomes.

In one series, they ran 88 tests for different thicknesses of vinyl to find one that was both more durable and better at reducing leakage at the mold seams. In another series of experiments, the team adjusted the shape of the liner to achieve greater consistency. In a third set, they experimented with the number and location of ports in the mold to achieve a more even and consistent distribution of material. The experiments led to demonstrable cost and quality improvements. The defect rate was reduced by 89 percent and the number of parts that were too defective to use was reduced by two-thirds. The amount of material needed for each piece was reduced by 60 percent. And, of course, the team came to better understand its product, the material of which it was made, and the equipment used to make it.

We saw earlier that high-velocity organizations generate speed not only because they see and solve problems, but because the solutions quickly become incorporated into the *best known approach*—that is, the most up-to-date (and always improving) distillation of what the organization has learned *collectively* about how to do a particular piece of work with the best chance of success. This team followed the same pattern, concluding its improvement activities only after developing a set of standardized procedures so that the changes they had developed could be incorporated into the standardized work of the entire foam-molding department. Thus, they did not complete their work after discovering valuable changes; they completed it only after incorporating the changes into the regular work of the production setting.

Example: Quality Circle at Aisin

Chapter 6 included a description of the make-to-order system for manufacturing mattresses at Aisin. Over the course of several years, Aisin made enormous gains in productivity and product variety, with equally impressive reductions in inventory and lead time. Part of the improvement was rooted in switching from a functionally structured, push-based system to a process-oriented pull system. We'll see details of that system-level redesign below. However, Aisin's improvement could not be explained as a one-time change. The company's superlative levels of performance were rooted in a variety of improvement cycles, some carried out by senior managers when it came time to do large-scale reconfiguration, but many carried out more locally.

I had the privilege of interviewing members of Mr. Ito's quality circle at Aisin to learn about their experience of working in final assembly. According to Ito, there were compelling reasons to improve the line's capabilities. In 1993, the volume in the plant was growing, as was the number of workers. Each of the three production lines had the goal of reducing rejects to 250 in a six-month period (October 1993 through March 1994). Although Lines 2 and 3 met this target, with reject levels of 204 and 232, respectively, Line 1 had 258 rejects in the same period. For 1994, then, the goal was to reduce rejects on Line 1, increase productivity by reducing idle time, and "produce a workforce in which new techniques can be learned and applied." These objectives were quantified as follows: Reduce the number of defects from 258 for the six months ending in March 1994 to 170 for the six months ending in September (a 34 percent decrease) and 140 for the six months ending in March 1995 (for a total decrease of 55 percent). At the same time, the line was challenged to reduce the production time from 26.3 minutes per unit to 22.8 minutes in September (a 13 percent decrease) and 18.4 minutes in March 1995 (for a total reduction of 30 percent). Part of this improvement was to be accomplished by means of factory-level improvements, which we will explore in a bit, and part was to be accomplished by quality circles such as Ito's.

As these workers explained it, in the first phase of their employment, before joining the quality circle, they were responsible only for doing standardized work and calling for assistance when they were unable to do it. At first glance, this sounds like my experience at the Big Three plant, with the obvious exception that I hadn't even been armed with standardized work. When the quality circle was first formed, they were trained to distinguish between conditions that were and were not problematic, with the group leader challenging the team leader and team members to become more critical of the way in which their work was performed; this emphasis on seeing problems is a critical element of Capability 1, discussed in Chapter 6.

After spending a few months learning to do work according to a standard and to identify problems as they were experienced, the team was taught to suggest countermeasures to the problems they perceived. Having learned to identify problems and suggest responses, the team then learned ways to design, but not build, the countermeasures that had been suggested. The team members confessed that this became very frustrating. Why? At first, they had been "dumb and happy." Then they began to realize how much was going wrong. Now, they realized that there was a way to make things better, but they did not know how. Feeling constrained, they asked to learn skilled trades such as carpentry, electrical, plumbing, and automation so they would be able to fabricate countermeasures. Concurrently, other members of the team passed the qualifying test for assembly jobs that required higher technical skills. In other words, the team's capability increased in two dimensions. The sophistication of the production activities for which it could be responsible increased and, simultaneously, its ability to improve those activities increased.

Example: Comprehensive Process Redesign at Aisin

Mr. Ito's quality circle was a mechanism for increasing the ability of production workers to improve production activities while at the same time improving those activities. The progress it was making on skill development gave more senior people an opportunity to address more systemic issues such as line reconfiguration, rerouting of material and information flows, and modification of production equipment, knowing problems of smaller scope would be picked up and addressed by those, like Ito, who were confronting them daily.

I've paid three visits to Aisin over the years. On my first visit, the plant had three lines: small, medium, and large. On my second, it had consolidated the three lines to two, with each one capable of making any size mattress. As we'll see in this example, whether the changes at Aisin were large-scale or small-scale, conducted by experienced senior people or by less-experienced junior people, there was a disciplined problem-solving process.

Figures 7-2 through 7-4 are excerpts from process improvement summary documents prepared by Aisin managers to capture the logic of their discovery process. Several points come through:

- *Presentation of the information.* The summary is written as an experimental report, like the generic problem-solving template in Table 7-1. For example, the *before* condition lists five specific factors and the three negative consequences they cause. The *after* condition indicates the five specific changes and the effect each one had on performance.
- *Scale and scope of the problems being addressed.* The summary addresses the factors that only someone with boundary-spanning responsibility and authority is in a position to resolve, such as the layout of one process relative to another or the coordinating mechanisms between process steps.

Figure 7-2 shows the main sections of the improvement activity summary. The fact that the improvement activity is understood as an experiment can be seen in its use of several before-and-after contrasts:

- *System design*—before and after the improvement effort (sections 5 and 6)
- *System performance*—before and after the improvement effort (sections 4 and 7)
- *Gap identification*—predicted results compared to actual results (section 7)
- *Countermeasures*—changes in equipment, training, and methods (sections 5, 6, and 8)

Figure 7-3, focusing on section 5 of Aisin's problem-solving summary, shows the production system before it was changed. Several points are worth noting:

- The people who worked on the process improvement (group leaders, the assistant manager, and the Toyota Production

Figure 7-2 Aisin's summary of process-improvement effort

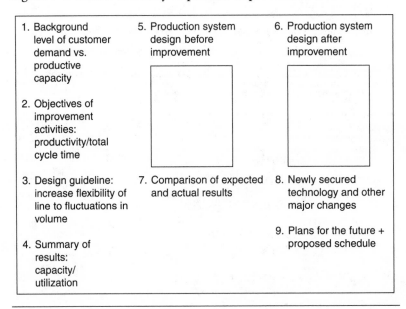

1. Background level of customer demand vs. productive capacity	5. Production system design before improvement	6. Production system design after improvement
2. Objectives of improvement activities: productivity/total cycle time		
3. Design guideline: increase flexibility of line to fluctuations in volume	7. Comparison of expected and actual results	8. Newly secured technology and other major changes
4. Summary of results: capacity/utilization		9. Plans for the future + proposed schedule

System promotion expert who, in his role as coach, was there to ensure that this system-level problem solving also developed leaderships capabilities) identified three symptoms that diminished performance: inability to respond to fluctuations in volume, volatility in cycle times, and inability to keep the production pace tuned to the rate of demand.

• Each symptom corresponds to some aspect of the ideal discussed in the start of this chapter. Inability to respond to fluctuations corresponds to inability to respond *on demand* and *immediately*. The lack of a pacing mechanism also compromised the system's ability to produce *on demand*. Volatility caused workers and machines to block and starve each other, a source of *waste*.

- For each symptom, the process redesigners identified at least one process feature as the root cause. For example, the diagram attributes the system's inflexibility to each line's size and specialization (a rise in the demand for small mattresses could not be absorbed by one of the other two lines). This diagram states the group's sense of cause and effect.
- Figure 7-3 shows where on the shop floor the root-cause feature is observable.

Figure 7-3 Section 5 of Aisin document (before-condition diagram)

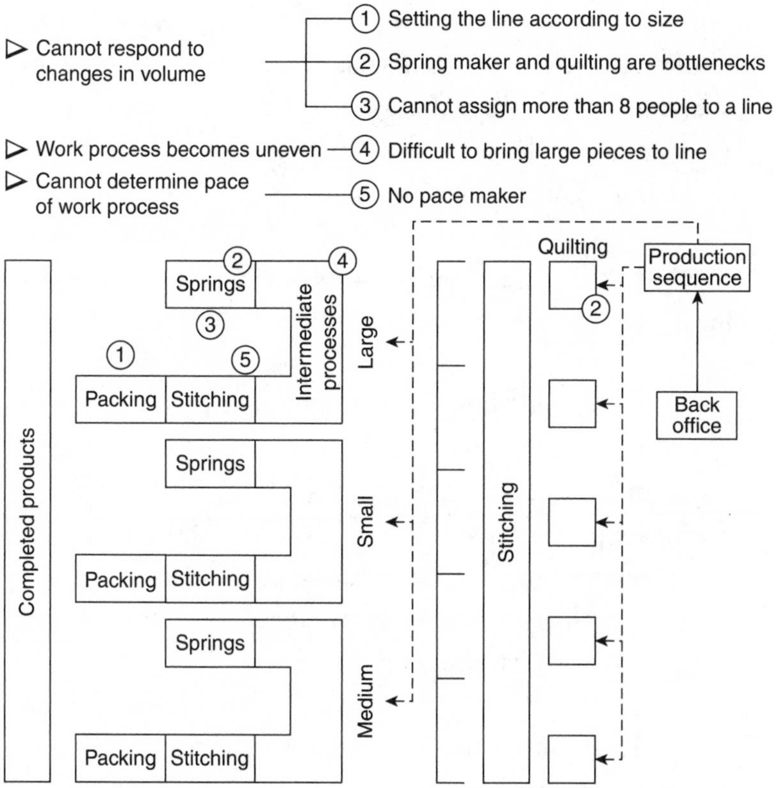

Figure 7-4 focuses on section 6 of Aisin's problem-solving summary. Again, several points are worth noting:

- For each root cause in the before-condition diagram, there is a particular change (countermeasure) in the design and operation of an activity (items 2, 3, and 4), connection (items 4 and 5), or pathway (items 1 and 2).
- Each of the countermeasures is credited with relieving a specific symptom that was identified in the before-condition diagram.
- The way each countermeasure was enacted is explained. Flexibility was achieved by altering the spring-forming process and separating spring-forming from assembly with a buffer, which prevented volatility in one activity from blocking or starving the other. Further flexibility was achieved by dividing work processes so that people could be added and subtracted easily.

In effect, this figure can be thought of in the following fashion:

> We redesigned the production system by conducting the following experiment. When we studied the system, we found three reasons to be disappointed with its performance. We traced these three disappointments to five root causes. Therefore, to improve the system's performance, we addressed each of these five root causes:
>
> - The countermeasure for cause 1 is redesigning spring-forming.

Figure 7-4 Section 6 of Aisin document (expected after-condition diagram)

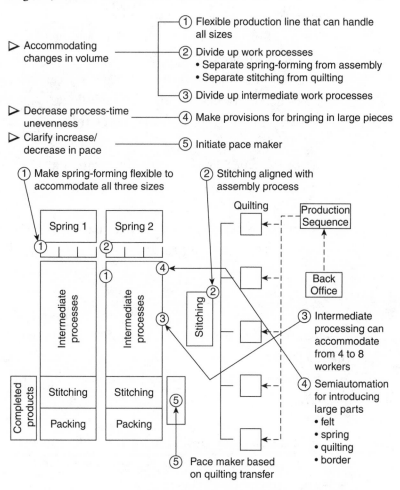

- The countermeasure for cause 2 is separating stitching from quilting and spring-forming from assembly by small buffers so that volatility from one does not block or starve the other.

- The countermeasure for cause 3 is redesigning work so that people can be added and
  subtracted more easily from the line.
- The countermeasure for cause 4 is adding
  some semiautomated equipment to make it
  easier for the operators to lift large, bulky
  pieces such as frames, quilting, and felt liners
  and carry them from line-side stores to the
  work site.
- The countermeasure for cause 5 is changing
  the information connection between assembly and quilting so that assembly (the downstream process) determines the pace of
  quilting (the upstream process).

The summary document captures the line redesign as an
experiment in which the "process scientists" quantified the
expected outcome (objective or goal) and compared it with the
actual change in performance.

Aisin's experience reveals several key points about improvement in general:

1. Building and exercising problem-solving skills is considered an important capability for everyone from top management to frontline workers.
2. Problem-solving skills are built by solving problems, so
   being responsible for doing work and being responsible
   for improving how the work is done are intertwined
   tightly. This is not scientific management in the Freder-

ick Winslow Taylor sense of having big dumb lugs doing the work prescribed for them by the brainiacs.

3. Problem solving is done in a disciplined fashion. Assumptions about cause and effect are made explicit and are stated clearly, then they are tested in a rigorous fashion so improvement efforts both make processes better and deepen process knowledge.

Several other points stand out, particularly in light of my third visit to Aisin two years later. Improvement and innovation never end, and they are always done in a disciplined fashion.

On a visit to Aisin subsequent to the one during which I learned about the consolidation of small, medium, and large lines into two "any-size" lines, I saw that both lines were still configured to handle any mattress in any order. Yet, they were no longer identical. At one step in the final assembly, one line completed the step manually while the other used a new piece of automated equipment. Why the difference? Why not both manual or both automated? The reason was that the new machinery had not been fully vetted. Therefore, rather than make the large investment (and gamble) of placing it on both lines, unproven, Aisin was trying it out on one. It was a deliberate attempt to try an idea in a less expensive and more reversible fashion.

A second image comes to mind from that visit. Consider two lines, each capable of making 100 units per day. On a particular day, there is demand for 180 units. How would you allocate demand across the two? You might argue for splitting it 90 and 90. You might also argue for assigning 100 units to one line to load it fully, with the remaining 80 assigned to the other line. Both would be reasonable approaches for most organizations, but not for the high-velocity rabbits that incessantly try to build useful knowledge that will make them even better performers. After all, at Aisin, they already knew how to handle 100 units a day on each line. What they weren't sure about was how to handle 110 or even 120 mattresses per day per line. But, if they were to increase their competitiveness, meeting the needs of more customers more quickly and more efficiently, they would have to. Therefore, on days when the lines were not fully loaded, they deliberately overloaded one, specifically trying to discover its failure modes. There might have been factors that didn't cause problems at a rate of 100 per day but did at a higher velocity. It was a stress test of the system, forcing it to reveal its vulnerabilities when the situation was not critical. The other line, running only 60 or 70 pieces, was there as a backup were the test to prove too stressful.

Example: Teaching Others to Generate Knowledge While Solving Problems

Let's take the perspective of a leader responsible for the development of others.

Hajime Ohba, general manager of the Toyota Supplier Support Center (TSSC), whom we met in Chapter 6, was visiting a factory in which one of TSSC's consultants was leading a training-and-improvement activity. The consultant was helping factory employees and their supervisor reduce the manufacturing lead time of a line and Ohba was there to evaluate the group's progress.

The group began its presentation by describing the steps by which the product was created. They went over a number of problems they had identified in changeover (the switch from making one part type to making another; for example, swapping out the die, scrap chutes, and metal coil on a stamping press) and explained the specific changes they had made in response to each problem. They concluded by saying, "When we started, the changeover required 15 minutes. We were hoping to reduce that by two-thirds—achieving a five-minute changeover—so we could reduce batch sizes by two-thirds. Because of the modifications we made, we achieved a changeover time of seven and a half minutes—a reduction of one-half."

Consider for a moment whether the team succeeded or failed. On the one hand, they had not achieved the goal of five minutes. On the other hand, they had cut the time in half, with all the attendant benefits of smaller batch sizes, less inventory, less cost and effort involved in material storage and tracking, and faster responsiveness to customer needs. That seems a victory.

For Ohba, it was true that they had succeeded, but not completely. Yes, they had made the changeover process much better than it had been. Their shortcoming was not that they had failed to reduce the changeover further. It was that they had failed to learn from not reducing it further. As Ohba pushed them with additional questions, increasing their understanding of the machinery and the work around it, the team realized where he saw a problem. They had not laid out clearly what they had assumed about the process—what could be changed and what was unchangeable. In other words, things could be changed, but by how much? In fact, the five-minute target was not a prediction based on a well-reasoned expectation; it was a goal based on desire. Thus, in falling short, they not only missed their target but missed the chance to push further to understand factors that they had assumed to be true but that their experience had proved to be false. The process had gotten better, but their understanding of it had not improved as much as it might have had they made clear their expectations at the start and the assumptions underpinning them, thereby having something tangible to investigate when those assumptions were proven false.

Example: Improving People While Improving Processes

In the next example, five small teams attempt to make improvements to a process. Four of the team leaders take the conventional approach: The point of process improvement is to improve the process. One team leader, the one with more experience in a high-velocity environment, takes a different approach: The point of process improvement is to improve the participants' process-improvement capabilities by coaching them as they try to improve the process.

MacDougal, Inc., employed 200 people and had annual sales of $20 million from remanufacturing damaged starter motors and alternators, which they acquired from auto repair shops. MacDougal would disassemble, clean, diagnose, repair, reassemble, package, and ship the items, which, in turn, would be sold by distributors or auto supply stores. Work was done on 10 lines, each of which was dedicated to a product family such as Chrysler alternators or Ford starter motors. Seasonal spikes in demand led to MacDougal having a broad, deep inventory. The fact that the inputs to this process were broken made the process hard to run. Reducing the burden of excess inventory while improving responsiveness to customer needs was the company's motivation for seeking Toyota's help. Toyota's motivation was that trying to improve such an unusual process would be a great learning experience.

This example is based on a three-day process-improvement exercise that included six people from the Toyota Supplier Support Center and ten from MacDougal. (TSSC supported Toyota Production System implementations at Toyota's North American suppliers and at other companies, such as MacDougal, which were not otherwise affiliated with Toyota.) Five teams of three were formed. Each had a Toyota leader and two MacDougal people as team members. The sixth Toyota person was the coordinator.

Each team was given the same initial assignment, to calculate cycle times for each of an assembly cell's 12 process steps. What was telling was the difference in approach and the difference in results among the teams. At one extreme, Team Leader 5, like three of the four other team leaders, adopted a divide-and-conquer strategy. These leaders assigned each team member to four of the 12 steps, took four for themselves, and set off to do the measurements. Team Leader 2 took a different approach. He kept his team intact and, starting at the last process step and working back, they calculated the cycle times together. While one might think Team 5's divide-and-conquer strategy would be the most productive, it was not. That team had calculated only three cycle times accurately (the ones studied by the team leader himself). In contrast, Team 2, though their approach was slower and more methodical, was 12 for 12 in getting accurate measurements.

This dichotomy in approaches continued over the course of the three-day exercise. When it came time to improve some of the process steps, Team Leader 5 divided responsibility among himself and his two team members. Team Leader 2 worked together with his team members. Team Leaders 1, 3, and 4 occasionally worked with their team members, but mostly held to an approach like that of Team 5. At the end of the exercise, when it came time to report out, the team leaders gave most or all of the presentation, except for Team Leader 2, who stood back, listened, and observed while his team members explained what they had done, why, and with what effect. Finally, during the wrap-up, when the MacDougal people were asked to comment on the experience, Team 5's two blurted out, "It was traumatic!" whereas Team 2's members gave the satisfied nod of someone who had just had a good experience. Again, the members of Teams 1, 3, and 4 were somewhere in between, expressing some hesitation and reservation in their posture and tone.

The obvious irony is that the four team leaders who tried to be efficient by dividing the task up among the team members achieved inferior results. In contrast, the team leader who actively coached his team got superior results. Why? For the teams that "efficiently" divided up the work, their team performance was, in effect, the average of their individual performances. Since the two MacDougal people were beginners and since they didn't get any better during the exercise, they brought the average down. The fifth team leader kept his team together almost all the time—seemingly an inefficient deployment of labor. But his approach was to increase the skill of the other two. In short order, he created a multiplier effect. The team's "average" kept going up as the two MacDougal people improved.

The difference in how the exercise was perceived and approached was even more pronounced when I asked the team leaders to reflect on what had happened and what would happen next. Four emphasized the process gains that had been made: smoothing of flows, reductions in cycle times, that sort of thing. For them, the natural next step would be to install permanently the modifications for which they had run trials. Again, this emphasized that they saw the purpose of the exercise as process improvement as an end unto itself. Team Leader 2 was different. Most important for him was the practice his team members had gotten in observing, analyzing, and piloting changes. For him, the next step would be to have them observe the efficacy of the changes under normal conditions rather than in this artificial setup; the measure of success would be whether they could apply their observation and problem-solving skills elsewhere. For him, the exercise was a means to an end, improve the process to improve the people, and, because you're never sure until you see, he couldn't be sure that what they had worked on was successful until he had watched it—and them—in normal conditions.

It was not lost on me that this team leader had the most extensive experience at Toyota, having been at some of its finest plants and having worked under the guidance of some of its most accomplished managers. His behavior reflected that of his mentors, who understood that, for an organization to be high-velocity, process improvement, however valuable, must also serve to improve the people carrying it out. If it does not, then the responsibility for seeing problems, solving problems, and generating useful knowledge that will reduce or prevent future problems will be in the hands of a select few, unused by most of the organization. The other team leaders hadn't had the same experience yet and their approach reflected a less complete understanding of what it meant to lead—not only to delegate and direct, but to coach and develop as well.

Looking Ahead to Capability 3

We started this book with the observation that a number of organizations get ahead and stay ahead of their competitors despite the difficulty of differentiating themselves or gaining a monopolistic advantage in their industries. For them, the way to stay ahead is not to find a better position and defend it, but to keep moving ahead with greater speed, agility, and endurance. We've just looked at how problem solving is conducted—in a disciplined fashion that solves the problems, builds deeper knowledge about the process, and increases the capabilities of those involved.

In Chapter 8, we'll look at another capability that leads to high velocity: the ability to take lessons discovered through local problem solving and make them useful throughout the organization, so that individuals learn not just for themselves but for their present and future colleagues. This turns out to be a decisive business asset.

CHAPTER 8

CAPABILITY 3:
KNOWLEDGE SHARING

Jared Diamond asks a provocative question in *Guns, Germs, and Steel*: "Why did Eurasians conquer, displace, or decimate Native Americans, Australians, and Africans, instead of the reverse?" The obvious answer is that the Eurasians had firearms, durable tools and weapons, and immunity to a host of terrible diseases. But this begs the question as to why. What led to those advantages? Positive outcomes depended on the ability of some peoples to compound knowledge more quickly and comprehensively than others. In Diamond's explanation, it was geography and, more to the point, the differential advantages that geography offered in accelerating a society's accumulated learning. Diamond's thesis is that travel across Europe and into Asia was conducted along an east-west axis in a narrow north-south band. As people moved, the climate was similar enough that what people knew about hunting, foraging, agriculture, housing, communication, and transportation in one place was useful in other places. Even if individual people didn't travel far, and most didn't, their knowledge gradually did, and it accumulated and compounded from the constant mixing and intermingling of one group's insights with those of others. Metal forging, animal husbandry, agriculture, and written language all benefited from a synergistic combination of ideas. It was not that individual Eurasians were brighter in terms of their capacity to retain existing information and invent new ideas. Rather, over the course of generations, Eurasian societies kept running into ideas that, when combined with what they already knew, were useful and allowed for the amalgamation of ever more complementary ideas that were of increasing value.

In contrast, the natural travel corridors in the Americas were north-south, not east-west. The geography of river flows and mountain ranges determined that situation. This had important implications for cumulative societal learning. Move too far north or south from home and you and your kin could not survive; your knowledge was not useful. The result: less migration, less intermingling, less mating of one idea with another. It was not that individual non-Eurasians were any less bright than anyone else, but the pool of novel ideas that their societies provided and from which individuals could draw was far smaller. Aspects of writing, metalwork, and animal domestication were found in particular places but did not come together synergistically. The lack of migration and travel kept those ideas in isolated ponds. Societal knowledge progressed, but not nearly at the same rate as it did in Eurasia.

What did this mean in practical terms? When the Spanish conquistador Pizarro faced off with the Incan king Atahualpa in Peru in 1532, one side was outnumbered by the other. It was not the Spaniards, even though they had only 168 "ragtag" soldiers "in unfamiliar terrain, ignorant of the local inhabitants, completely out of touch with the nearest Spaniards . . . and far beyond the reach of timely reinforcements." It was Atahualpa, even though he commanded an army estimated at 80,000.

How could this be? Behind every Spanish soldier stood the tens of thousands of Eurasians who collectively and cumulatively had devised the ocean-faring vessels and navigation systems that allowed the Spanish to land armed forces on foreign soil. Every soldier's head was covered with a steel-armored helmet, the result of the countless microinnovations that had occurred in metallurgy over many centuries; thus, an Incan club was not a terrible threat. In the Spaniard's hand was a sword, dagger, or lance that had a devastating combination of strength and flexibility so that it could cut but would not break. Incan fabric armor, useful in blunting blows from clubs, was easily slashed and pierced. The Spaniard might have been on horseback, thanks to centuries of domestication. The Incan had no beasts of burden and had neither the speed nor the endurance to outrun cavalry. The Spanish commanders did not have to improvise their tactics. They benefited from all the battle histories that were written, preserved, and studied in Spanish libraries, as writing, printing, and cataloging were collective achievements, not those of individuals. The Spaniards could improve and modify their tactics, but they did not have to start from scratch. With the cumulative expertise of all of Europe behind them, the Spanish routed the Incans without suffering a single fatality. Atahualpa was captured and held in exchange for an extraordinary ransom, which, even when it was paid, did not spare him from being killed by Pizarro.

Shared Knowledge: Fuel for High Velocity

What points can we take away from this? Success does not depend on a single event, just as catastrophe does not depend on a single failure. As we saw in Chapter 3, catastrophes can occur when enough small incidents come together in just the right way for the system to collapse or explode. A similar compounding dynamic leads to success as good outcomes build up over time. The leaders—the rabbit contestants—accumulate wins more quickly and with greater consistency and duration than the others. Speed and endurance tip the scales, and the winnings accrue to the group for which every step in the race increases the chance that the next step will be even faster and stronger. And this comes about when events don't transpire simply as successes and failures but transpire as successes or increases in the chance of success the next time. We saw this in detail with Alcoa and the nuclear navy in Chapters 4 and 5. One might think of a casino operating this way. For most players, a roll of the dice or a spin of the roulette wheel does nothing to change the odds on subsequent bets, and the odds are stacked in favor of the casino. For those who can count cards, however, what they learn playing one hand improves their odds on the next. By outlearning the field, they outplay the field.

Organizations, like the societies studied by Diamond, or like individual card counters, depend on their ability to accumulate useful knowledge more quickly than their competitors. The capacity to be faster and stronger in the design, operation, and improvement of complex systems depends on seeing where knowledge is needed (Capability 1), generating new knowledge (Capability 2), and sharing and intermingling that knowledge so that the expertise of the individual is a function of his or her experience combined with the experience of many others who have done related work. That is the essence of Capability 3, which we'll explore in this chapter.

We saw the consequences of not doing this in Chapter 3. In the case of Mrs. Grant, there had to have been repeated experiences showing that heparin and insulin were too easy to interchange. Yet that experience did not become cumulative knowledge embodied in changes to the packaging, labeling, or storage of those medications. In the case of the space shuttle, repeated experiences with foam failure and O-rings were not incorporated into NASA's procedures as cumulative insights into the system's vulnerability. Two crews were lost and billions of dollars were wasted recovering from accidents that should never have happened.

In contrast, Alcoa has compiled an enviable record of workplace safety in dangerous industrial settings. Why? Alcoa discovered that perfectly safe systems defy conceptual design but are very close to achievable through a dynamic discovery process in which (a) complex work is managed so that problems in design are revealed, (b) problems that are seen are solved so that new knowledge is built quickly, and (c) the new knowledge, although discovered locally, is shared throughout the organization. The same thing is true of the U.S. Navy's nuclear reactor program. The intense commitment to scripted procedures, incident reports about even seemingly minor departures from or failures of procedure, and the rapid update of procedures and of system designs more generally mean that a young crew and their officers setting out for their first cruise have over 5,700 reactor-years of experience underpinning their individual expertise.

Let's look in more depth at how knowledge is passed from those who have made a discovery to those who will benefit from it. We'll see a common theme: Just as discovering something for the first time is experiential—it involves solving a problem in context—so is teaching something. Those who do this well do not just broadcast solutions. They show the problem in context, find a solution, and indicate how the solution was discovered and why it will work. It is not just the outcome but also the discovery process that is demonstrated and shared, most often in an experiential fashion as well.

In this chapter, we'll see in more detail how a high-velocity organization—Toyota—multiplies localized learning into organization-wide knowledge. In the first example, we'll see how Toyota addresses a basic business problem that constrains business development—an inability to propagate know-how quickly enough in the production environment to sustain rapid growth. In the second example, we'll see how Toyota uses mechanisms for capturing and sharing knowledge to generate high velocity in new-product development. In the third, we'll look at a mechanism Toyota uses to foster collaborative learning in situations that are hard to define, codify, and explain for those who are not directly involved in them.

Case: Accelerating North America

Background: Global Localization

Success can present its own perils. That has been Toyota's experience as it tries to expand its business. Buoyed by outstanding sales in the late 1970s and early 1980s, it looked to the United States not just as an export market but also as a place to set up design and production facilities. As was explained to me by my colleagues at Toyota, relying solely on exports posed a financial risk, with the rewards of good planning and hard work compromised by uncontrollable fluctuations in exchange rates. There were also political factors. Too much success by Japanese firms had generated resentment in America's industrial heartland and retaliatory threats in Washington, D.C. There were commercial reasons as well. By being physically and culturally closer to the end customer, Toyota expected to be able to deliver products more in tune with the needs of local markets. Finally, there were practical reasons. Japan is a relatively small country; at some point Toyota would be bumping up against other companies in the quest to build new manufacturing facilities, hire new employees, and source from an expanding network of suppliers.

Global Localization First Steps: NUMMI

Expanding overseas presented a challenge, however. Toyota had been successful as an exporter of outstanding products because of the great management system it used domestically. Globally localizing production, as some within Toyota describe it, meant that the company would not be as dependent on exporting products, but it would have to learn to export the management system that made its products possible.

Toyota's first approach to this problem depended on simplifying the situation it faced. A manufacturer has to contend with many variables when starting a new facility: where to locate the plant, what to make, what production technology to use, whom to hire for direct labor, whom to entrust with management, from whom to source, and through whom to sell, among others. When Toyota created the NUMMI joint venture with General Motors in 1984, it kept many if not most of those variables constant, based on things it already knew. They used an existing GM plant and its equipment to avoid having to build a brand-new facility and the workforce largely was rehired from the GM labor pool, avoiding the need to bring novices on board. The plant's first Toyota product was the Corolla, which was already being manufactured in Japan and which already had a market presence in the United States. The one variable that would be different was using the Toyota Production System outside the comfortable, familiar confines of Toyota City.

In terms of how to address this challenge, Toyota could have flooded the plant's managerial ranks with experienced leaders from Japan, but that would not have been sustainable. The Japanese managers might want to relocate temporarily to the United States, but not permanently. If you have to make your leaders expatriates, that is not exactly global localization. It starts to have the look of colonization, and even if you're comfortable with a strategy of colonization, at some point you run out of administrators unless you can develop local ones.

What was the alternative? Toyota had to depend on Americans to manage other Americans, but for that to be effective, those Americans had to be trained. Consistent with the idea that training must be in context, coached, and learned by doing, Toyota arrived at a strategy. True, the site president would be a veteran Japanese Toyota employee. However, even for its first major manufacturing effort in North America,

Toyota hired managers from large American manufacturing concerns and established intensive mentoring relationships. But they wouldn't simply be dropped in to take charge. First, they would make similar products at NUMMI's sister factory in Japan, gaining hands-on experience with the way Corollas were built and the way that process was managed by Toyota in Japan. To use a sports metaphor, they would return to the United States not only having seen the plays, but also having run the plays over several weeks with the coaches and the first-string team.

Back on their home field, they would have continuous support. Toyota sent hundreds of coordinators from Japan to NUMMI to support the Americans. They shadowed and coached the Americans who had direct authority in the plant, coaxing them to look at this, try that, explain the reasoning behind something, and so forth. In Chapter 7, we saw this sort of behavior modeled by Mr. Ohba in pushing a team on the thinking underlying its process-improvement efforts. We saw a similar approach used by the experienced Toyota coach at MacDougal Automotive. He was the one who stepped back from improving production processes directly in order to use the process-improvement exercise to develop the team members for whom he was responsible. For Toyota more broadly, this intimate approach to coaching was how it developed hundreds of people at NUMMI. It was possible because there were enough coordinators to do it, from the most senior levels to the level of group leaders. This worked well initially.

The NUMMI start-up was a remarkable success. When the plant was run by General Motors, "sick-outs, slowdowns, and wildcat strikes frequently disrupted production, and daily absenteeism usually reached 20 percent. Alcohol and drugs were freely available on the premises." Furthermore, "in 1982, when GM closed the plant and laid off the workforce, more than 6,000 grievances remained backlogged in the system." How bad was it? "Frontline managers were known to carry weapons for personal protection."

However, in a seemingly overnight transformation, NUMMI scored remarkable successes. The MIT graduate student and researcher John Krafcik, who introduced the term *lean manufacturing* into the lexicon, documented the following comparisons: When NUMMI operated as a GM plant, its productivity and quality were as poor as those at GM's Framingham plant, the poster child for low-performing plants in *The Machine That Changed the World*. Under Toyota management, its scores outdistanced those of its GM sibling and approached those of Toyota's Takaoka plant (see Table 8-1).

It was not just the plant's speed off the starting line that was impressive. The plant has continued to perform well, earning awards from J.D. Power for initial quality and other accolades, as summarized in Tables 8-2 and 8-3.

When Toyota expanded its U.S. operations beyond NUMMI, it took a similar approach to product and process introduction, keeping a fair number of factors constant and experimenting with the smaller number that had been changed. For instance, when Toyota opened a new facility in Georgetown, Kentucky, it kept the novelty of the experience limited to a few variables again. It picked a well-designed, successful car already being made for the U.S. market in Japan— the Camry—and it had already created an approach for developing managers—the intensive boot camp in Japan fol-

Table 8-1 Productivity and Quality Comparisons among Four Automobile Plants

	Framingham 1986	GM Fremont 1978	NUMMI 1986	Takaoka 1986
Overall Productivity				
Hourly (hours/unit)	36.1	38.2	17.5	15.5
Salaried	4.6	4.9	3.3	2.5
Total	40.7	43.1	20.8	18.0
Corrected (Adjusted) Productivity				
Hourly	26.2	24.2	16.3	15.5
Salaried	4.6	4.9	3.3	2.5
Total	30.8	29.1	19.6	18.0
NUMMI's advantage	57.1%	48.5%		–8.2%
Quality Indicators				
GM audit	125–130	120–125	135–140	135–140
Owner survey	85–88	NA	91–94	92–94
Consumer Reports	2.1–3.0	2.6–3.0	3.6–3.8	3.8–4.0

Source: "Learning from NUMMI" by John F. Krafcik, unpublished International Motor Vehicle Program working paper (1986), cited in Charles O'Reilly, *New United Motor Manufacturing, Inc.*, Stanford Graduate School of Business Case Study HR-11, December 2, 1998.

Table 8-2 J.D. Power and Associates Initial-Quality Plant Awards

1994	*1995*	*1996*
North and South American Silver Medal	North and South American Bronze Medal	North and South American Bronze Medal
1999	*2000*	*2002*
North and South American Silver Medal	North and South American Silver Medal	North and South American Bronze Medal

Source: J.D. Power and Associates' press releases.

lowed by direct coaching that had been used for NUMMI. Now it could turn to new challenges, developing more local suppliers and developing workers less experienced in manufacturing than those who had joined NUMMI.

Packaging Toyota Know-How for Export

That approach ran into limits, however. Depending on coordinators to train people all the way down to the level of group leader limits the rate at which a business can progress; there are only so many coordinators and it takes time for a cadre of coordinators to be cycled from one plant to another. This can work if one new plant is opened every few years, but what if plants are opened on a compressed schedule or if several plants have to be opened simultaneously? Toyota needed an alternative to the coordinators.

And what if Toyota needed to introduce a product tailored to a local market, which was apparently one of the aims of the

Table 8-3 Awards for NUMMI's Corollas

1993:	J.D. Power and Associates' New Car Initial Quality Study: Among the Top 10 Models in Initial Quality
1998:	American Automobile Association: Top Car under $15,000
1999:	American Automobile Association: Top Car under $15,000
1999:	J.D. Power and Associates' Initial Quality Study: Best Compact Car in North America
1999:	R.L. Polk and Co.: Four-Door Compact Leader
1999:	*IntelliChoice Complete Car Cost Guide*: Best Overall Value in Compact Class
2000:	R.L. Polk and Co.: Four-Door Compact Leader
2000:	*Consumers Digest*'s "Best Buy"
2000:	J.D. Power and Associates' Initial Quality Study: Best Compact Car in North America
2001:	R.L. Polk and Co.: Four-Door Compact Leader
2001:	*Consumers Digest*'s "Best Buy"
2001:	J.D. Power and Associates' Initial Quality Study: Best Compact Car in North America
2002:	J.D. Power and Associates' Initial Quality Study: Best Compact Car in North and South America
2004:	J.D. Power and Associates' Initial Quality Study: Best Compact Car in North and South America
2006:	J.D. Power and Associates' Initial Quality Study: Best Compact Car in North and South America

Source: NUMMI Web site: http://www.nummi.com/awards.php.

global localization strategy? There would be no sister plant to turn to for support, equipment vetting, and standard work development.

Thus, success presented Toyota with a dilemma: If it could not export its management system more quickly than it had been doing, it might lose its hard-won reputation for quality, reliability, and affordability. But turning sales away for lack of reliable capacity wasn't acceptable either. It seemed that global localization of production could not be limited to cars, trucks, and minivans; it had to include local production of managerial talent.

The first step was to give production sites responsibility for developing their own talent internally. Chapter 6 discussed the approach taken at Toyota's Princeton, Indiana, truck plant to prepare new hires for assembly-line work. Although that was a step in the right direction, it ran the risk that every site would develop its own approach to skill development. If every site's approach were different, only one could be the absolute best, and perhaps none would be. There had to be a synergistic approach by which each site not only built its own expertise from its own experience but also made use of the cumulative experience of the whole company. In terms of Diamond's conclusion that the Incans lost to the Spanish because knowledge in the Americas was isolated in independent ponds, Toyota wanted to create the Eurasian dynamic in which all those ponds fed from and fed into the same ever-deepening pool.

Toyota's next steps in this regard began in 2003 with the creation of what is now called the Global Production Center (GPC), led by Yuichi Shibui, from the Tsutsumi plant, and staffed with trainers who each had 20 to 30 years of experience at Toyota manufacturing plants. The GPC trainers identified a set of critical production skills, including painting, welding, final assembly, tool and die maintenance, engine assembly, internal logistics, quality control, and equipment maintenance. Next, they identified group leaders known to be particularly knowledgeable about those skills. The group leaders went through the exercise of demonstrating their best practices, with GPC trainers repeatedly asking: What is the fundamental skill? What is the knack or key point? What method best demonstrates how to teach it?

Over many months, the GPC staff accumulated codified guidelines for fundamental skills. For example, with welding, they wanted to move beyond the touch, feel, and gut instinct of "master craftsmen" to identifying the three types of welding and, for each, the key process parameters such as weld-tip angle, height, speed, and torch intensity, and then quantifying what these needed to be to create successful welds.

Not only did the Global Production Center develop "recipes" for critical shop-floor production skills, they also observed the resident experts and interviewed them on how to train for those skills. For instance, one group leader had a series of repetitive exercises to teach bolt shooting. Another group leader had trainees fire bolts from different angles so they could link various postures and positions to outcomes. After gathering these multiple perspectives, the GPC team not only had recipes for production, but was ready to create standard work to teach those recipes. For instance, they developed standardized practice equipment for welding. For equipment maintenance, GPC developed a training tool kit so people could more easily learn predictive and preventive maintenance as well as temperature and vibration analysis. Of course, consistent with the emphasis we saw in Chapter 7 on Capability 2—problem solving—nothing was nailed down until it was tested. GPC conducted trials with team members from the plant in which it was housed. Then, they invited groups in from another plant to test the new production methods as well as methods and equipment for teaching those production methods. Then, more teams came from other Toyota plants to try the training methods at GPC before bringing them back to their own organizations. A timeline for GPC's activities is given in Table 8-4.

Table 8-4 Time Line of GPC Activities

Date	Event
May 2003	GPC started.
May 2003	First wave of group leaders to document best practice in a skill.
Late 2003	First version documented and defined.
2004	Documenting alternative approaches to skills started.
2004	Prototype of how to train completed.
2004	Skills-training prototype tested at Motomachi plant.
2004	Modification of skills-training equipment and approach.
2005	Release of new version of skills training.
2005	Deployment of new training technique to North American region followed by the European and Asia-Pacific regions.

Capturing knowledge so that it could be shared was hardly a trivial exercise. The GPC created 3,000 "visual manuals"—interactive Web-based demonstrations and explanations of critical skills. Each one took about 200 labor-hours to create, for a total of some 300 work-years. The content of the training was meant to be fairly comprehensive; that's why the visual manuals took so long and covered so many skills. That effort has to be placed in the context of the overall goal of halving the time required to develop thousands of employees.

GPC didn't stop at the practice and teaching of direct production tasks, such as welding and assembly performed by frontline operators. A critical role in the production environment is that of group leader, who is not only responsible for training people and developing their production skills, but who must also support problem identification and problem solving. Again, GPC tried to take the knowledge of Toyota's best and develop repeatable processes for managing the shop floor. For instance, they developed standard work for "abnormality management" (what to do when something goes wrong) and "change-point management" (how to prepare and train people for a change from one approach to another without the change being disruptive).

Exporting knowledge from GPC was not limited to Japan. After all, a big business-problem motivator for GPC was overseas business growth outstripping Toyota's ability to develop enough Toyota-style managers. Having honed and vetted its own approaches at Toyota plants in Japan, GPC invited representatives from Europe, Asia, and the Americas to Japan to learn the skills GPC had targeted, practice using the training techniques and equipment GPC had developed (see Figure 8-1), and

Figure 8-1 Knowledge-flow through the Global Production Center

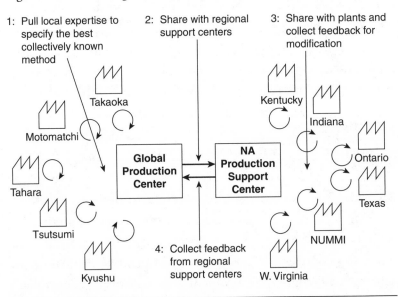

1: Pull local expertise to specify the best collectively known method

2: Share with regional support centers

3: Share with plants and collect feedback for modification

Takaoka

Motomatchi

Tahara

Tsutsumi

Kyushu

Global Production Center

NA Production Support Center

Kentucky

Indiana

Ontario

Texas

NUMMI

W. Virginia

4: Collect feedback from regional support centers

offer their own input. Here we see GPC engaged in a classic example of Capability 3. It had solved a problem and now it was sharing its newfound knowledge, doing so where the knowledge was discovered, and sharing the discovery process as well as the solution.

In February 2005, a team of managers and group leaders from Toyota's North American operations spent two weeks at GPC in Japan as a precursor to setting up a GPC-like organization to be called the North American Production Support Center (NAPSC) at Toyota Kentucky. This new group took the methods developed at GPC and tested them by training people and by training people to train other people at the Georgetown, Kentucky, site. Along the way, they made many modifications and tweaks, which would make the approaches more effective in the North American plants. Then, just as they had been invited to GPC to learn what GPC had discovered about training—where GPC had made its discoveries—NAPSC in turn invited colleagues from Toyota's plants in Indiana, West Virginia, Ontario, and elsewhere to Kentucky, as a precursor to creating their own training centers. Before moving on, let's look at some examples of GPC's handiwork.

Example: Final-Assembly Skills

GPC training was designed to allow learning incrementally, iteratively, and with hands-on learning by doing. In the case of final assembly, training started with fundamental skills such as how to grab a bolt and how to use a torque wrench. Those elements were combined into work elements such as shooting a bolt into a vertical plate, at an angle, into an enclosed space, and the like (see Figure 8-2).

The training explained not only what to do but why. I remember standing in front of the practice stand for shooting a bolt and being told how and why to cradle bolts in my left hand—palm up as I moved the bolts up to my fingertips, not down, so if I lost my grip, the bolt would fall back into my hand and not to the floor or onto the car. I was also instructed

Figure 8-2 Example of setup for best-skills training: Assembly

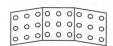

Shoot bolts
into a panel

Shoot bolts
at angles

Shoot
Interior bolts

to hold my wrist in a neutral position to avoid undue strain. This was a prelude to practicing those fundamental skills and isolated work elements on a moving assembly line. In a sense, first the fingers and hands were trained individually, then the hands together and in concert with the arms, and finally the arms in harmony with the torso and legs.

Example: Welding

At another station, a group leader with 20 years of experience at Toyota explained the training that had been developed for welding. GPC had identified eight fundamental skills that had to be mastered for resistance, arc, and acetylene braze welding, including items such as setting parts, establishing data points, and taking measurements. Just as training for work on a moving assembly line is progressive, incremental, and hands-on, so is training for welding, starting with the basics (CO_2 welding, equipment, and safety), moving on to simulated training and practice, and concluding with practical welding. Table 8-5 shows the steps in welding training.

Example: Group-Leader Training

As mentioned previously, training was not limited to physical work, but was also developed to teach how to be a competent shop-floor manager at the group-leader level. Caren Caton, an assistant general manager at NAPSC, explained that group leaders were pretty good at watching team members and team leaders for departures from standard work, but they were not as good at seeing how the standard itself might be flawed. By

---

Table 8-5 Steps in NAPSC Welding Training

Phase I: Basics of CO_2 Welding and Safety

1. Purpose
2. Training plan
3. CO_2 welding
4. Equipment
5. Injury prevention
6. Safety

Phase II: Simulated Training and Practice

7. Basic training with dummy

Phase III: Practical Welding Training

8. Initial inspection
9. Training in welding sequence

Built-in Test

10. Overall evaluation

---

training group leaders to be both more critical and more supportive, NAPSC began to see group leaders become refreshed in their role of solving problems. If you define a problem only in terms of whether you have adhered to the standard, you set a low bar for a pass, but if you define a problem by the much more rigorous criteria of whether the work is being done without delay, without waste, and without strain of any kind, you set a much higher bar and create more reason to try to improve on what you are doing.

Progress to Date

Reflecting on the progress of the North American Production Support Center, Latondra Newton, the general manager at NAPSC, stated:

> Toyota needed to create a way to help people best understand the intent of the Toyota Way and accelerate their development over what mentoring alone could achieve. We've certainly learned a lot from the know-how captured at GPC [in Japan], but we've been responsible for adding to that as well. The key is to build on the principles we learned from them and apply the same way of thinking to what's unique in our region.
>
> Sometimes we had to modify some of the techniques they developed to account for local conditions. In paint, for instance, they had people spraying parts closer to the ground by doing deep knee bends. That's fine in Japan, where people tend to squat from an early age, but our folks needed a different approach. We had to account for some other ergonomic issues.
>
> But we also had to invent some things. For instance, we do aluminum wheel casting here, and they don't, so we had to develop our own approaches to training and training the trainers.

Case: High-Velocity Product Design

In the late 1980s, researchers at the MIT International Motor Vehicle Program and elsewhere identified the first "Toyota paradox." Although Toyota plants were doing work similar to that of their competitors, they seemed to be generating twice the output in half the space with half the people and inventory and in half the time. Some years later, researchers at the University of Michigan identified a second Toyota paradox. The Michigan team found that Toyota was designing customer-pleasing products and bringing them to market with greater ease of manufacturability in less elapsed time and with fewer engineering hours—without adhering to some of the best practices others had been trying to adopt. When we look closely at the Toyota paradox research, we once more find that Toyota's excellence comes, in part, from organizing its efforts in order to (a) create knowledge by solving particular problems and (b) make that new knowledge part of the company's collective expertise.

As for the nature of this second paradox, the Michigan team compared Toyota's approach and performance with that of Chrysler's successful LH program. (LH referred to an underbody and chassis that would be common to a series of midsize and large automobiles, including the Chrysler Concorde, New Yorker, and LHS; the Dodge Intrepid; and the Eagle Vision.) According to MIT graduate student and researcher Gregory Scott, the LH was the first new platform for Chrysler since the K-car in 1980 and was the "first major fruit" of a new approach to new-product development. The attributes of this approach included "multidisciplinary platform teams, a strong commitment to simultaneous or concurrent engineering of distinctive vehicle designs, greatly increased manufacturing and supplier involvement, and the introduction of the Chrysler Technology Center as a centralized facility for the company's technical activities." This approach was aimed at allowing more design discretion at lower levels of the organization while ensuring successful integration of the entire project. "[I]mprovements in communication, teamwork, and ownership among all new-product development] personnel" were expected to reduce development costs, cycle time, and time to market while increasing product quality. "[T]he firm appears to have taken strong steps away from a pure functional organization by investing substantial responsibility in the hands of relatively heavyweight project managers and project organizations. These managers, in turn, have increased the amount and breadth of team-based decision-making to achieve substantially higher levels of design consensus, synchroneity, and coordination." In short, LH was Chrysler's best shot at doing the "right thing" in product design by using techniques championed by a number of researchers, such as teams that were (a) co-located for brisk, frequent collaboration, (b) cross-functional to bring multiple perspectives to bear on problems, (c) with heavyweight project managers to assure alignment of objectives across disciplines. Despite this, Toyota well outperformed Chrysler, with substantial differences in quality, cost, and time (see Table 8-6).

It was not just that Toyota was better at doing what Chrysler was doing. Toyota seemed to violate best practices. Toyota had a far "lighter-weight" approach to project management, with experts largely answerable to their functions and with chief engineers exerting persuasive, coordinative, and integrative but not coercive influence on the flow of work. Toyota also seemed to delay decisions more, allowing uncertainty about critical design parameters to persist, and it toler-

---

Table 8-6 Process Superiority: Product Design

Quality of design	In 1993 and 1994, 6 of the top 10 cars of the J.D. Powers' initial quality survey were Toyotas.
Elapsed time	Toyota required 27 months from concept approval to full-scale production, nearly one-third less than the 37 months required in Chrysler's LH program.
Cost	Toyota used 500 people per program, in contrast to 750 used by Chrysler in the LH program.
Cost	Toyota consumed 50% fewer person-years per program than Chrysler did in the LH program.

---

ated a far greater number of expensive, time-consuming prototypes. Toyota even started designing and building stamping dies before the final design was specified.

It seemed crazy, but those differences, summarized in Table 8-7, were part of a knowledge-building, knowledge-sharing approach that allowed Toyota to rapidly generate and accumulate knowledge—useful for creating competitive advantage about how individual components should be designed and especially about how the component pieces would come together harmoniously in a well-integrated system.

Knowledge Generation: Organized for Discovery

Let's look first at some of the knowledge-generating techniques and then at how the new knowledge was captured and shared. The Michigan research team discovered that Toyota's approach reflects the reality that early in the design process, the "right answer" cannot be known. Instead, it must be discovered

Table 8-7 Comparing Toyota and Chrysler

	Concurrent Engineering at Chrysler	Toyota's approach
Program management	Heavyweight	Lightweight
Assignments	Designers assigned to a particular model or platform	Designers managed functionally, being assigned to vehicle programs as needed, working on the program full-time only during peak periods, then moving on to other programs and answering to different chief engineers
Interactions	Multifunctional, co-located design teams	Teams neither co-located nor dedicated
	Highly structured design processes	"Unstructured" design processes
	Intense communication among team members	Intense communication among fewer members of design team and supplier base
Prototypes	Three one-fifth-scale clay models	Five to 25 one-fifth-scale clay models
	One full-size clay model	Two full-size clay models
Design commitments	Early freezing of hard specifications by the design team	Late freezing of hard specifications
	Point-by-point iterative search for solutions	Convergence on the final solution from a gradually narrowing set of solutions (including part specifications and price)

250

through repeated trials. Exactly what customers want must be discovered, along with ways to embody what they want in components and subsystems, build those components and subsystems, and join them together. Therefore, rather than specifying a single solution early on, Toyota's chief engineer was specifying a broad range of product solutions within which engineers could explore. Engineers responsible for systems, such as the power train or the styling, were breaking down their responsibility into smaller bites, giving junior engineers broad ranges in which to explore solutions. The examples of this approach are many: suppliers presenting many alternative subsystem designs, stamping-die designers beginning to develop tooling before final "hard points" were specified, and sets of parts being produced and tested, with the easier-to-modify dies being adapted to match the harder-to-modify dies. The idea was that by starting with many potential solutions, the group was more likely to converge on the correct solution that was superior and feasible for all parties involved (see Figure 8-3).

Figure 8-3 Set-based design: Convergence on mutually feasible solutions

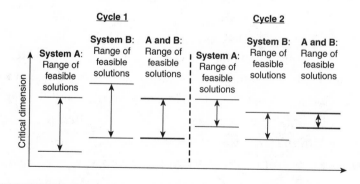

There were other examples. The Michigan authors reported that Toyota had two full-size clay models when the design was handed from the stylists to the manufacturing people, whereas Chrysler and others had a single full-size clay model. In effect, the Toyota approach acknowledged that the stylists can accept a final product that is within a range of physical dimensions and manufacturing can produce a physical product within another range of dimensions. The key is to allow the stylists and the manufacturing engineers to explore the feasible space that is common to both functional specialties before committing to a single final design. Other examples of experimenting as much as possible, to learn as much as possible before committing to one design, included:

- The large number of one-fifth-scale and full-scale clay prototypes
- The large number of prototypes developed by partners and mature suppliers
- Continued refinements of intermediate and final clay models until 27 months before production (versus 37 for Chrysler's LH)

In contrast to these approaches at Toyota, the Michigan researchers found that the Chrysler designers were quicker to settle on critical design parameters without going through the trial-and-error experience, the experimentation, and the rapid cycles of conceptualization and validation/refutation—as if they could *think* their way to the right answer rather than *discover* it. That assumption was wrong, of course. Chrysler engineers made early commitments in pursuit of speed, discovered they had made the wrong commitments, and quickly jumped to new commitments, only to find that these were wrong too. Toyota engineers on the other hand allowed themselves to smoothly converge on solutions that were agreeable across disciplines. They hadn't really delayed making decisions and commitments; they had given themselves a window to learn as much as possible about a number of different options.

Knowledge Capture: Codifying Discoveries

The commitment to discovery partly explains why Toyota chose to delay decisions while conducting repeated trials and experiments. What remains unexplained is how Toyota managed to enjoy the advantages of a lighter-weight management approach to product design. Rather than having co-located, dedicated cross-functional teams, Toyota kept its functional specialists fully loaded and practicing their specialties by moving people into projects when their skills were needed and moving them out when they were not. Yet, Toyota seemed to avoid the disadvantages of this approach, such as lack of coordination and risks of local optimization.

The key to Toyota's project management approach was that experiments and prototypes were never for the sake of the current project alone. Toyota had a fastidious discipline of capturing the results of each experimental cycle in a variety of lessons-learned books. When a designer in one area started to work, he or she could draw on deep wells of knowledge about what sets of solutions had worked or failed in the past and why. Thus, a stylist did not necessarily need a manufacturing expert in the room while developing the contours of a fender or a roofline. The lessons-learned book told the stylist which curvature radii could be manufactured and which could not. Stay within those boundaries and all is fine. If those boundaries appear too constraining, then it's time for collaborative problem solving. But cross-functional collaboration is done on a case-by-case basis to solve new problems, not all the time just in case two people have to resolve a problem, the solution for which has been lost. The "second paradox" researchers explained:

> Lessons-learned books describe the current company capability, including feasibility ranges. For example, a Toyota die designer showed us a lessons-learned book for a fender design. The book, ten to twelve pages long, contained approximately sixty to seventy different ranges of specifications that would ensure the fender design's manufacturability (e.g., intervals of acceptable curvature radii for angles). Developed during the past fifteen years, these books of every body part give a very detailed definition of what can be done from each functional area's viewpoint.

The Michigan authors went on to emphasize that the knowledge in the lessons-learned books is not static:

> Each deviation from the lessons-learned books is noted on an audit sheet, the primary communication between affected groups. These sheets give the nature of the problem, a countermeasure suggested to alleviate the problem, the suggesting department,

and a sign-off for the affected functional areas. Often the suggestions resolve the problem to all parties' satisfaction. However, if they are unable to find a common ground, a functional group (say, die design) may develop a new technology or process advance to make the design feasible, and then revise the lessons-learned book.

Case: *Jishuken* Activities

The examples discussed so far have a common characteristic: Someone has experience that leads to expertise. That expertise is converted from tacit knowledge to explicit codified knowledge, which can become someone else's expertise through practice. But this is not the only way in which Toyota transfers wisdom. Another approach is called *jishuken* (pronounced "jee-shoe-ken"). The literal translation of *jishuken* is "self-study." We'll see why that term is a surprisingly accurate description of a process that places so much emphasis on collaborative problem solving. The object of *jishuken* is to move knowledge from those who have it to others who can put it to good use. However, *jishuken* is not a broadcast mechanism. It is a way of sharing knowledge through collaborative problem solving for situations in which problems are messier and the knowledge needed to solve them is not transportable enough to be written in a lessons-learned book or practiced in a training center.

The basic setup of a *jishuken* is something like this: People from different sites are teamed with each other. Periodically, they converge on one location to tackle a particularly vexing

Figure 8-4 *Jishuken* **organization**

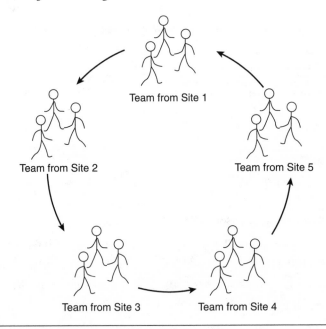

Team from Site 1

Team from Site 2

Team from Site 5

Team from Site 3

Team from Site 4

problem, progressively making their way to all the sites, as in Figure 8-4.

I'm sure you have encountered many forms of shop-floor problem solving and collaborative improvement that have a variety of names, such *kaizen* blitzes and rapid work-cycle improvements. What is the difference between these and *jishuken*? The key differences involve the means and ends of the activity.

Kaizen blitzes often take this form: A group is gathered to focus intently on a process with problems, whether the process contributes directly to production and delivery or to a supporting function such as administration, customer service, or payroll and accounting. The blitz lasts a few days, the objective is process improvement, and the means are the concentrated use of people from outside the process to advise those normally inside the process. The blitz team will gather information through document reviews, interviews, and personal recollections and will act on that information with varying degrees of process redesign. Their legacy will be a new aspect or a new approach: new layouts of equipment, new means of conveying material and information, a more organized workspace, or standardized work. They may also leave behind a to-do list of changes to be made down the road; these are carried out with varying degrees of fidelity. What *kaizen* blitzes typically do not leave behind is greater capability to design, operate, and improve processes on the part of the people who work with the target process every day.

On a research trip to Japan, I visited several Toyota suppliers. For them, *jishuken* was something quite different. It took place on several levels. There were teams consisting of people from different parts of the same plant. Those teams rotated among several plants in the same company, and the company had a team of people who partnered with teams from other participating companies and rotated among them. One *jishuken*, for instance, included companies that specialized in electronics, forging, stamping, and machinery construction. Someone from Toyota facilitated and coordinated the *jishuken* process, dealing with scheduling, site selection, and protection of proprietary information. Aside from those administrative functions, Toyota might spend months supporting a supplier, pushing it to do its "homework"—improving its process-improvement capabilities.

What does it mean to be part of a *jishuken* process? Put yourself in the position of the plant manager at a manufacturer that specializes in injection molding. The key processes in your plant are molding, assembly, material handling, production engineering, and shipping. As a plant manager, you would support the group leaders and department heads from these areas as they work together on particular process problems such as reducing setup times in molding, reducing cycle times in assembly, or improving the quality and timeliness of equipment maintenance. When group leaders from one department visited another, they would apply the expertise that they have developed solving their own problems to the resolution of another group's most challenging problems.

It is a bit different for the group leaders and department heads who are acting as hosts. The *jishuken* team is focusing on a problem on which the host has already spent considerable time and effort improving. They are not there to focus on problems that the host could have solved independently. Therefore, the hosts begin by demonstrating how the process currently works, what problems it experiences, and the root causes for those problems that have already been discovered. Then, the host details the countermeasures that have already been tried and the results of those tests.

Only with that background will the guests start taking a close look at the process, bringing their expertise and understanding to bear. However, it is not just the production work they are observing and critiquing; it is also the host's problem-solving process itself. After all, if the hosts have a problem persistent enough to merit *jishuken*, it is because they have applied their own problem solving without achieving a resolution.

The host's problem-solving process is problematic. So the guests will try to find out where it can be improved. What was not looked at? What was not tried? What was not examined? What was not considered? For this approach to work, the hosts have to be ready to show their best game, their highest level of preparation, and then have the guests pull at the threads that remain loose.

Of course, if you are a plant manager, you are not off the hook. Not only will you have supported internal *jishuken* conducted by group leaders and department heads, you will have had to be involved enough to represent your own plant at a companywide *jishuken* with other plant managers. If you are a guest, you need to have made enough improvements with your people and on your own that you can coax even greater accomplishment from people who have reached the limit of their capabilities. To be a host, you need to have done enough homework to have pushed yourself and your team to their maximum.

That is why the translation "self-study" is an appropriate description of this highly collaborative enterprise. Its success rests on your willingness, energy, and drive to do your own homework so that you are pushed to the edge of your abilities and are therefore receptive and positioned to benefit from feedback, critique, and coaching (see Figure 8-5).

One supplier told me about having to do 10 to 20 "home-works," during which his team achieved a 30 percent reduction in machine cycle time—and that was before any formal *jishuken* even took place. Another supplier was working on a single machining process; the machine was too dirty from coolant oil that was spraying because the line pressure was too

Figure 8-5 *Jishuken* **dynamic**

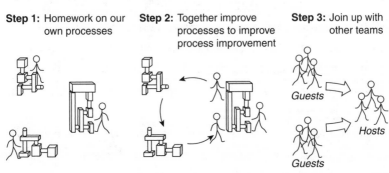

Step 1: Homework on our own processes

Step 2: Together improve processes to improve process improvement

Step 3: Join up with other teams

high. That affected part quality, safety (slipperiness), and process control (you couldn't see through the window on the machine). That supplier had the objective of achieving 50 modifications on a process but had achieved only 36 because the goals for improvement were so ambitious. Another supplier had accomplished a reduction in die changeovers from 13 minutes to 3 minutes as a result of internal *jishuken*, and that was just the precursor homework for company-level and corporate-level *jishuken*.

Then there was the supplier who was thrilled to be part of a cross-company *jishuken* after years of internal and company-wide improvement efforts. I remember him gushing with enthusiasm about how exciting it was to work so hard in so many different venues and describing the different situations in which he and his colleagues had participated.

"When did you host a *jishuken*, and what was the theme for you?" I asked.

He grinned and nodded his head knowingly. "Oh," he replied, "we haven't hosted a *jishuken* yet."

"Why not?"

"We haven't done enough homework. We still have to learn before we can host."

CHAPTER 9

CAPABILITY 4: DEVELOPING HIGH-VELOCITY SKILLS IN OTHERS

It is an understandable view that leaders are responsible for setting objectives, allocating resources for the pursuit of those objectives, and establishing an emotional tone for the organizations they lead, including establishing the right combination of incentives to achieve the objectives. Leaders in high-velocity organizations do all those things; their combination of perspective and authority makes them the only ones who can. However, it is what they do in addition that sets them apart from their non-rabbit counterparts. One difference, of course, is that they must be system-oriented—responsible for the design and operation of processes at levels of aggregation for which others have insufficient perspective and authority. We saw that kind of boundary-spanning responsibility exercised by the senior leadership at the Aisin plant described in Chapter 7. Quality circles and other mechanisms could have been used to make the component modules of the process self-correcting and self-improving, but only those who were more senior were in a position to make the major line reconfigurations that were described in that chapter. We'll see another example of a leader owning some aspect of a system's design, operation, and improvement in this chapter when we describe Gary Convis's experience leading Toyota's facility in Georgetown, Kentucky.

Leaders in high-velocity organizations must play yet another role: They must develop those for whom they are responsible so that the organizational capacity to be self-correcting, self-improving, and self-innovating is distributed and practiced widely and consistently. We have already seen some examples: middle and higher-level managers who were responsible for developing quality circle members at Aisin, NHK, and Taiheiyo, the standout team leader at MacDougal.

In this chapter we'll see how high-velocity rabbits consider leaders to be both mentors (or developers) and process managers. Let's look over the shoulder of Bob Dallis as he learns to lead at Toyota.

Learning to Lead at Toyota

Bob Dallis was an accomplished auto-manufacturing manager who made a huge career shift. He spent several years at a Detroit Big Three company, where he led the turnaround of an 1,800-employee assembly plant and ran a new-engine design program as well as leading an engine plant through its design, ramp-up, and first years of operation. His accomplishments before age 40, interlaced with engineering and business degrees and honors from great universities, would be noteworthy for most people in their fifties and sixties. But in the face of down-sizing and offshoring—and always dreaming of helping reinvigorate American manufacturing—Dallis left for Toyota, the automaker that was most aggressive about increasing design and production in North America. Their shared objective was that, after a period of initiation, he would become a senior leader, probably at Toyota's flagship plant in Georgetown, Kentucky.

One might have expected a quick transition for someone with Dallis's credentials—perhaps a round of cursory walkthroughs and introductions. Given Toyota's emphasis on shop-floor operations, perhaps he would also do some hands-on line work and visit dealerships for direct customer contact, but soon he would have substantial managerial responsibility. However, that was not the case. Learning to lead at Toyota was a months-long effort managed by a more experienced Toyota veteran, Mike Takahashi. And although we will be following Bob Dallis, in some ways this is also Mike Takahashi's story. Bob learned a lot from Mike, and so can we.

Learning to See and Solve Problems

Takahashi first assigned Dallis to Toyota's West Virginia engine plant, not to Kentucky, to improve the work of a 19-member group on three dimensions: ergonomic safety, efficiency, and operational availability. For six weeks Takahashi emphasized observation, seeing the reality of the "current condition"—how work was actually performed and what problems actually affected it. Then he emphasized making changes so that maximum insight would be generated about the complex system of work. This was not a matter of making arbitrary modifications but of predicting clearly what was expected to occur before those alterations were made. With cause and effect articulated—out in the open—if a modification did work, Dallis would truly understand why. If it did not work, he would at least have some idea of where he had gone wrong, having put his reasoning "on the table" from the start.

For six weeks, Dallis focused on the work of the individual operators. He implemented some changes that seemed laughably minor in comparison to his past and future responsibilities: reconfiguring line-side parts racks so that material was more accessible, repositioning the handle on a machine to reduce ergonomic strain, and so forth. Others were more substantial and required shifting work among the workstations. That meant coordinating with material handling about part delivery and with maintenance to relocate light curtains, so those changes were completed over a weekend, when the plant was shut. With those changes, Takahashi reinforced the importance of tracking actual results against predicted ones, watching with Dallis to see what the real effect would be in comparison to what Dallis had predicted. Productivity and ergonomics had gotten better, but operational availability—the proportion of the time that a machine ran without delay—declined (see Table 9-1). Of course, the employees had not sabotaged the equipment. Instead, with the group working more fluidly and productively, problems with the machines which hadn't previously seemed significant now seemed like real impediments.

So Takahashi redirected Dallis's assignment for the next six weeks. Rather than focusing on people, he was to focus on the machines, looking for ways to improve their reliability and availability. Takahashi insisted that Dallis not speculate but

Table 9-1 Before-and-After Comparison of Assembly Line's Performance

	Before	After
Productivity		
Number of operators	19	15
Cycle time	34 seconds	33 seconds
Total work time/engine	661 seconds	495 seconds
Ergonomics*		
Red process steps	7	1
Yellow process steps	2	2
Green process steps	10	12
Operational availability	≈ 90%	≈ 80%

*The difference in the total number of processes in the two ergonomic columns reflects the reduction from 19 to 15 in the number of process steps. Process ergonomics were rated from worst (red) to best (green) on the basis of a formula that considered the weight lifted, the difficulty of reaching, the need for twisting, and other risk factors.

wait to see real-time failures so that he could investigate problems when and where they had occurred. This seemed awfully inefficient because machine failures did not occur frequently and machines could not participate in analysis and correction the way people could, but over time, the power of this approach became more evident. In one case, a switch was in a position where workers could brush it accidentally, activating the machine before a jig was loaded. After investigating several faults in another machine, Dallis discovered that the shape of an interior bumper allowed pallets to ride up and get out of line. Direct observation of the machines, root-cause analysis and recreation of each failure, and immediate recon-figuration to remove suspected causes raised operational availability to 90 percent, but this was still below the 95 percent target Takahashi had set.

Dallis spent 12 weeks learning about the importance of observation as the basis for improvement and of using the scientific method of being clear about expectations before making changes and following up to observe the results of those changes. Having learned these skills, while significantly improving the process on which he had been working, wasn't it time for him to begin his "real" work at Toyota? Or would he first have to practice the same skills on a larger scale, given the responsibilities for which he was being prepared? Neither. Instead, Takahashi and Dallis flew to Toyota's Kamigo engine plant in Japan. Takahashi had worked there, but more significantly, it was the storied plant where Taichi Ohno had first scoped out the basic elements of the Toyota Production System and just-in-time manufacturing. For engine and manufacturing people, Kamigo is not just a destination but a pilgrimage, like visiting Kitty Hawk or the Wright Brothers' lab in Dayton, Ohio.

On arriving, Dallis learned his assignment: For three days, he would work with one operator in one machining cell. In three shifts, they had to put in place (not just plan) 50 changes to reduce the "overburden" on the employee—anything that was taking more effort than was really needed. The cell would be "on-line" with daily production demands. The Kamigo team member spoke no English, and Dallis spoke no Japanese. Dallis applied the lessons he had learned in West Virginia about using direct observation to see a process's failures and

⌘

rapid experimentation to arrive at better approaches, but with far greater acuity and speed than he had done before. Despite the imposed pace, Takahashi insisted that Dallis not speculate but always ground alterations in observed data and always test against well-articulated expectations.

Dallis came to see subtleties he had not appreciated before. For example, relocating a jig was not a matter of making a single change. Whether it was to the worker's left or right, how far away it was, and the angle at which the elbow and wrist had to be bent to grasp it all mattered. He also learned that the demand for speed and the insistence on discipline were not irreconcilable if he could construct high-speed, low-cost prototypes to test an idea. As he explained to me, "If I had an idea to relocate something, Takahashi would challenge me." If something required welding, was it possible to bolt it in place to test the idea? If it could be bolted, could time be saved with temporary taping? Instead of taping, could it be held in place to see the flaws in the idea with extreme speed? "Mike," said Dallis, "was trying to get me to go quicker, quicker, quicker, making as little investment as possible in an idea so I could try it and discover its strengths and shortcomings first, before making more of a commitment. It was all about learning at maximum speed." Dallis was learning how to minimize the trade-off between speed of testing and discipline of learning.

After three days, Dallis had identified 50 problems with the cell's quality checks, tool changes, and other work. To deal with those problems, he had made 35 changes, with 15 suggestions still to be implemented (see Table 9-2).

With the shop-floor changes done, Takahashi had Dallis present his work to the plant manager and the machine shop's

Table 9-2 Summary of 50 Changes Made by Dallis in the Machining Cell

	Quality Checks*			Tool Changes*			
	Walking	Reaching	Other	Walking	Reaching	Other	Other Work
Number of changes	8	8	13	7	4	5	5
Effect of changes	20-meter reduction (50%) per check	2-meter reduction	Remove trip risk; organize tools to reduce confusion, risks, etc.	50-meter reduction per tool change	180-cm reduction in reaching	Improved ergonomics; organization to reduce confusion and risk, etc.	Remove trip risk; simplify oil change

*Quality checks were performed two to three times an hour and tools were changed hourly. Together, Dallis's changes cut approximately half a mile of walking per shift while also reducing ergonomic and safety hazards.

manager and group leaders. Two things struck Dallis. The first was the discipline with which he had to prepare and present the report. Dallis and the two team leaders who had been going through a similar experience in adjacent cells had to explain the changes they had made in context; the presentations took place on the shop floor alongside the work cells in question. They had to explain what they had observed of the process, the problems they had found, the causes they could assign to those problems, the changes they had made to remove the problems, what they had expected the results of the changes to be, and the outcome they had achieved. They could not simply report changes or results; they had to make very clear the entire thought process underlying their actions. This emphasized the importance of using the scientific method to (a) solve problems, (b) build deeper process knowledge, and (c) spread what was learned by showing the discovery process, not just the solution. Dallis was also struck by the detailed questions he was asked. "The plant's general manager, the machine shop's manager, and its group leaders were engaged in what the 'lowly' team leaders said. They busily took notes during the presentations, asking pointed questions, constantly challenging our thinking."

With the work at Kamigo behind them, Dallis and Takahashi visited several other plants to learn how group leaders managed a variety of improvement projects. One project involved reducing changeover times and establishing a more even production pace for an injection-molding process, another focused on reducing downtime in a machining operation, and a third sought to improve productivity and quality in final assembly. Another project focused on proactive maintenance, finding ways for operators to distinguish "normal" from "abnormal" in a machine so that maintenance would be able to solve real problems, not just take preventive actions whether they were needed or not. In all those projects, the group leaders followed the same disciplined approach of explaining the entire discovery process, both to provide instruction and to invite critiques.

Bob Dallis's takeaways from his first several months at Toyota included:

- The importance of direct observation so that problems are seen in the idiosyncratic context of person, product, process, place, and time in which they occur and are investigated while they are still hot. This is the way to improve complex systems of work while creating deep knowledge about how those complex systems actually work.
- The importance of structuring all improvement efforts so that assumptions embedded in the work and in the changes could be tested.
- The lesson "to bolt rather than weld, to tape rather than bolt, and to hold rather than tape," so there need be no trade-off between speed and problem-solving discipline.
- The importance of reporting not only your actions and their results but also the reasoning that led you to take those actions and to expect certain results (which may or may not have been what actually happened).

Add it up and we see that Dallis was being introduced to the first three of our four capabilities—process design and operation, problem solving that is also knowledge building, and knowledge sharing. In fact, as we will see, he was also being introduced to Capability 4, learning to lead others through his relationship with Takahashi.

The "Process" of Leadership

Dallis found that these practices of observation, experimentation, and speed were ubiquitous in Toyota, used not only for manufacturing but also for intangible processes such as training. In preparing Dallis to be a Toyota manager, Mike Takahashi was applying the very process he was trying to instill in Dallis. For example, before Takahashi ever met Dallis, he had plenty of data—résumés, references, and anecdotes—concerning Dallis's career and accomplishments. But he had never *seen* Dallis in action. Just as he didn't want Dallis to speculate about what to do on a manufacturing process before seeing it in action, he was not prepared to "develop" Dallis until he had seen him in action. Therefore, following his own formula, he first observed Dallis at work in a fairly controlled situation (in West Virginia). It was a familiar technical setting (an engine plant), but on the simpler side of things (assembly, not machining). There were only 19 in Dallis's group and the experience itself was professionally safe. Dallis could make mistakes, be corrected, and be directed, but not in front of people he might later be leading in Georgetown, Kentucky.

Takahashi had reduced the complexity of the situation so he could focus on how Dallis solved problems and how he involved the people with whom he was working. Because he was seeing Dallas in action frequently, he was able to adjust his coaching appropriately by seeing problems with the training process and quickly trying changes rather than trying to think his way through a whole high-level training program in advance; in other words, there was the familiar emphasis on rapid discovery rather than planned design. It was the equivalent in Takahashi's own work of holding rather than taping rather than bolting rather than welding.

In short, to enhance Dallis's ability to learn about processes and his own ability to learn about Dallis, Takahashi took an incremental but intensive, immersive, high-speed approach to Dallis's development, much as he had had Dallis break down shop-floor processes into their microelements. He might have thrown Dallis into an unfamiliar environment—paint rather than power train—or started in Japan with its attendant language and cultural differences, but that would have introduced too much novelty. If Dallis struggled, what would it indicate? With so many factors in play, drawing conclusions about what caused the trouble would be terribly difficult. Table 9-3 shows the process of introducing novelty in small increments.

Although Dallis took away many important lessons about problem solving and knowledge sharing, the lessons he learned about leadership were the most compelling. Each level of the management hierarchy was part of a cascade that developed the problem-solving process-improvement skills of the people for whom it was responsible. Consider the colleagues he met at Kamigo. First there was the team member with whom he worked for three days. Dallis discovered that this frontline operator was not only capable of doing work in what must have been an already finely tuned, slack-free environment—after all, this was Ohno's old stamping grounds—but was also able to be an active participant in making improvements to such a well-tuned system. Then there were

Table 9-3 Introducing Novelty in Small Increments*

	Last Employer	*West Virginia*		*Kamigo*	
Product	Engine	Engine		Engine	
Management system	Old employer's	**Toyota's**		Toyota's	
Processes	**Assembly** and machining	Assembly		**Machining**	
		First: Work methods	**Second: Machine problems**	First: Improve work-space and methods	**Second: Learn about machine improvements**
Plant workforce's experience and process knowledge	Less than 10 years	Less than 10 years		More than 30 years	
Problem-solving support from skilled trades	1-week lead time for changes	Changes tested within a day's time		**Several changes tested every hour**	
Familiarity of plant	Dallis's work site	Known by Takahashi		Takahashi's former work site	

*Items in **boldface** refer to something novel.

the team leaders who were having a similar training experience in cells near Dallis. To get to that position, they would already have to be capable of supporting team members (frontline workers) in doing their daily work. However, they were also exceptional problem-solvers in their own right. On the first day, Dallis was delighted to demonstrate seven changes that he had put in place, only to learn that one team leader had nearly 30 to explain, while the other had more than 30.

Then there were the group leaders at Kamigo who participated in the wrap-up. They displayed detailed process knowledge and knew how to help Dallis and the team leaders learn even more from their experiences by asking them challenging Socratic questions: How did you observe? What did you see? Why did you do this? Why did you try that? What did you expect? What did you get? What was the gap? What do you think might have been its cause? What might have you done differently? The constant challenges that these group leaders and the production and

---

Figure 9-1 Managerial cascade of training and assistance and the supporting infrastructure

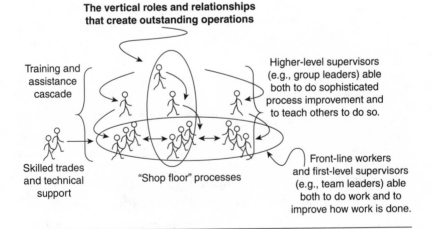

plant managers were able to provide and that Takahashi provided ceaselessly were part of the development program.

We can draw the following conclusions, summarized in Figure 9-1:

- Frontline workers, like the one with whom Dallis worked for three days in the Kamigo plant, were so accustomed to change that production could continue even when a non-Japanese speaker was making changes in how work gets done several times an hour.
- First-level supervisors (the team leaders who were receiving the same training as Dallis) were capable problem solvers in their own right, able to conceive and execute many changes in rapid succession.
- Second-level supervisors (the group leaders who explained their discoveries) were capable of facilitating larger-scale process innovations that were at the very least akin in scale, scope, and impact to what Dallis—an exceptionally accomplished manager—had done during the first 12 weeks of training.
- Senior management within Toyota was building the process-innovation capabilities of those less senior, much as Takahashi had been doing for Dallis.

Dallis now saw important contrasts. So many people had characterized Toyota by emphasizing a handful of shop-floor tools for managing the flow and transformation of materials—value-stream maps, pull systems, standardized work, production cells, and "5S" workplace orderliness. These are aspects of managing the horizontal flows of material from receiving through shipping. However, Dallis came to appreciate how sharply this contrasted with the top-down cascade of training and support, the daily development of people's skills in designing, operating, and improving systems, as shown in Figure 9-1. This is how Toyota created operating velocity and improvement-and-innovation velocity. If one contrast was between Toyota's practice of developing people and its imitators' inordinate emphasis on product and process, there was also a contrast between how many companies thought about responsibility and how it was carried ou at Toyota. Dating back to Frederick Winslow Taylor and before, there is the view that management is responsible for designing systems, solving problems, and ensuring "compliance" with procedure, leaving it to subordinates to work around problems until something goes so badly that management can't ignore it any longer. That wasn't the way at Toyota.

HOW I LEARNED
TO LEARN

My own experience during the six months that I worked at Toyota was that my managers led me by directing me to situations in which I could learn, just as Takahashi did for Dallis. For instance, in my first days at Toyota, I was assigned to a team responsible for developing a first-tier supplier of stamped parts. I asked my boss, Mr. Ohba, what I was supposed to do. He said, "Go find out what they make." (It was not until later that I realized I was learning to observe a system at the four levels—output, pathways, connections, and activities—and according to the two criteria—specified in design and operated with built-in tests—that we encountered in Chapter 6).

I came back later that day with a list. "How did you get the information?" he wanted to know. I explained that I had interviewed managers, including the plant manager and the sales manager. "You don't really know," he said before turning to other matters. I came back the next day with a different list. "How do you know this is what they make?" he asked again. I explained that I had gone to the supplier's accounting department to see what had been invoiced as shipped. I had figured that those guys would not invent phantom shipments. "You still don't know," he told me. I went back to the plant the same day and returned some hours later with a third list. "How do you know this is what they make?" he asked yet again. This time I had not counted on invoices; I had asked accounting to let me see what Toyota had actually paid for. I did not think they would pay for materials they had not received. I should not have been surprised when he said, "You still don't know."

The next day I came back once again. It had taken longer than the previous tries, but the list was quite different. Ohba asked, "How do you know this is what they make?" I was ready this time. "Well, here's what I did," I said, thinking to myself, "I'm on to your tricks and games."

I explained that I had stood at shipping and, as each box was about to be loaded onto the truck for delivery, I had written down the part number. Not the number on the kanban card (the shipping label), mind you; I had checked the part number stamped into the metal. I had done that for both shipments. I had also confirmed that for each part there was a stamping die in the plant that could make it. Not that I had ever suspected that the supplier was reselling parts made by someone else, but now I *knew*. I told Ohba, "I know there are still some holes; there may be ones I didn't see yet, but these are what they make, I'm pretty sure."

Ohba nodded his head for a moment and looked at my list again. The he looked at me and said, "Well, that's probably not wrong. But I have another question: How are these parts made?"

A Toyota Leader in Action

Some years ago I had a chance to shadow Norm Bufano, a senior manager at Toyota's assembly plant in Indiana. That plant does an exceptional job of manufacturing top-rated products; it has proved itself capable of rapid expansion in production capacity, flexibility in terms of the product types it can make, and quick assumption of responsibility for testing new manufacturing equipment and developing new manufacturing techniques in preparation for the launch of a new model.

Bufano, like the others there, had specified his work: what he was going to do, when, with whom, where, and with what expected outcome. If something ran early or late, an explanation was called for: What had unexpectedly happened along the way? Typically, his morning began with meetings on safety, production, and similar issues. Then he would visit one of the several improvement projects being undertaken in his plant or at nearby suppliers. The basic format of each visit was the same: Those involved in the project explained how the process they were trying to fix had worked at the time of the senior manager's last visit, the problems that had been experienced then, the root-cause analysis that had been conducted, the countermeasures that had been tested, the target condition that had been predicted, and the actual results that had been achieved. The presentation always made explicit the experimental design of the improvement efforts.

Here are my reflections on watching this leader in action:

- Visiting these projects was part of Bufano's daily work. He visited each project every two weeks or so, not quarterly or for annual reviews.
- The review occurred where the problem was being solved, not in a conference room, office, or off-site location.
- The entire hierarchical chain that linked Bufano to the group leaders who headed the improvement effort came to the review.
- Everyone in attendance took notes and asked questions about the problem, the attempted solutions, and the results.
- Toward the end, Bufano would always say, "Thanks for the [technical] explanation you've just given, and congratulations on the results you've achieved. But let me ask you, aside from what you accomplished [with the process], what did you learn?"

This is the quintessential Toyota leader question. It comes from the most senior level and cascades down to the front line. It is asked regularly and is based on a manager's direct experience with the person doing and improving the work. It emphasizes the importance of continually building knowledge and expertise.

Leader as Capability Developer

I've been fortunate that so many people have been willing to share their experiences with me over the years. What is striking about Toyota is that when I ask people to describe a seminal experience with a leader, almost all the stories revolve around the leader doing something that helped develop the storyteller. The story is almost never about the tough call or the brilliant move the leader made; I didn't encounter the common view of managers as decision makers who tell others what needs to be done. When Toyota people tell these stories, it is not a dispassionate, academic recollection. Inevitably, at some point midway through the telling, they have to stop and collect themselves because the experience still has deep emotional resonance even though it happened even decades before. Here are some examples.

Ken Kreafle was with the Georgetown plant from its earliest days. He shared his story with me:

> I remember when I was running a paint shop for the first time. We were told a senior manager from Toyota City was going to visit. We spent a day

searching for the finest example we could find of a painted vehicle. We pulled it off the line, set it up in an undisturbed part of the facility, lit it with bright lights, and roped it off so no one would touch or otherwise mark or mar it. The only thing that made it different from a Hollywood big shot on Oscar night is that we didn't actually have a velvet rope or a red carpet, but not for lack of trying.

The Japanese manager who was my "coordinator," mentor, guide, and coach asked me what we were doing. I explained that we wanted to show off the best example of our work. We had a lot to be proud of. It was the early years of the plant, we were Toyota's first greenfield site in the United States, and we had worked very hard to get the plant up and running with what had started as an inexperienced workforce.

He said, "That is not the one he wants to see." We didn't understand. "What does he want to see?" we asked. He said, "I'll show you." He closed his eyes, turned on his heels, and pointed. When he opened his eyes, he said, "That one!"

"That one?" we asked. He had taken a body at random.

"That's not all," he continued. "He'll want to see what you found wrong with the car."

We did not get the point at first, but over the next several hours we were scouring that car for every slight imperfection, scratch, dust spot, and blemish. Not just on the visible areas like the hood, trunk, and fenders. We were crawling under and in the car, places you would only see if the car were on a lift or disassembled (or not yet assembled, like this one was). By the time we were done, marking each flaw with a Post-it, the car looked like an especially large piñata.

"Now," our coach added, "you're *almost* ready. When he gets here, he'll not only want to see what you found, but also what you think caused those defects and what you think you can do to prevent them from happening again." The next day, when he showed up, I couldn't believe it. I had worked for one of the Big Three. When an executive came, it was all about showing him the good news, and the questions were all about the numbers. Did we meet our targets? What was our scrap, our overtime? It was all stuff that got measured right on the bottom line but that we couldn't touch directly. Not this guy. He wanted to know all about the process and more, all about what we knew about the process, the stuff that eventually reached the bottom line but the stuff that we *could* touch directly. When we got to a bump or a mark that we couldn't explain, we didn't leave it there. We walked back and forth between the car we had examined and the line, trying to find the link. I'll never forget it.

Kreafle recounted a story with another leader:

Then there was my first annual review with Mr. Cho, now Toyota's chairman but then the president of Toyota Kentucky. When we started the year, he asked me to lay out the agenda for our department. I did, but he kicked it right back to me, asking, "Where is the business case for these changes? Even if we hit these goals, are they enough to succeed?" We spent the next hour working our way backward: what the market demanded of us to be a top competitor and how that translated to quality, productivity, lead time, and all the measures relevant in my department. Then we set some marks for where we had to be to be top in our class. It seemed impossible, but every day we went at it, trying to hit those measures.

At the end of the year, it came time for my annual review. At Toyota, reports are pretty simple: For almost every measure it is red, yellow, or green. As I started going down the sheet, I started looking at all the red, the preponderance of yellow, and a paltry amount of green. I had known all along where we were, but this was the first time I had confronted the reality of how far we were from the objectives we had set many months before. Right before my meeting, I stopped for a minute and called my wife. "I'm going for my review right now," I explained. "I may be out of a job this afternoon." With that, I walked into his office.

I started by apologizing. He listened for a while and asked why I was being so contrite. What had I done wrong? I started to show him my summary sheet, all the red and yellow and the marked lack of green. The year was pretty much a failure as far as I could tell.

"No, the year was a success."

"Excuse me?"

"You made a lot of progress—"

"But," I interrupted, "the goals we set when we started. . . ."

"Those were what we had to achieve to absolutely delight the market. Those are real targets. We set those so we wouldn't fool ourselves into thinking we are better than we actually are. We weren't good enough then, and we still aren't good enough. But we are much better. And I know what is going on in paint. We are going to be even better yet. Don't worry. The year was a success. We're just not done."

Process-Excellence Boot Camp

In any sophisticated organization, one would expect to find experts in particular technical specialties. At an auto company, for instance, there would be experts in styling, design, power trains, and so forth. Within the manufacturing portion, there would be experts in stamping, forging, molding, welding, paint, assembly, and so on. At Pratt & Whitney there are experts on various parts of a jet engine—compressor, combustion, and turbine blades—and the various disciplines required to make those elements work—materials, aerodynamics, controls, and the like. High-velocity organizations that outpace, outrace, and outdistance the competition have all these same experts—and something more. They have people whose specialty is the art, science, and discipline of processes: the harmonious integration of specialties and functional pieces into coherent wholes.

We've already visited Aisin several times in this book. Aisin has an organization called the Operations Management Consulting Division (OMCD). Think of it as the home of the Toyota Production System experts of the organization, a place where people have a chance to step outside their normal line responsibilities and have a deep, intense boot-camp experience in designing, improving, and innovating processes and—equally important—teaching others to do the same thing.

At the time I was studying Aisin's OMCD, it had three general managers, three assistant managers, and 88 other members. Some of them were technical experts who were past 55 years old and permanently assigned to OMCD. Some were at OMCD for a two- to three-year stay, during which they deepened their TPS knowledge before returning to their home plants. The rest of the 88 had graduated from Aisin College, a developmental program for those hired into Aisin with no advanced education. OMCD members participated in improvement activities that lasted from one to three months. Upon completion of their tenure there, the temporary members were reassigned to Aisin plants as TPS promotion experts, a resource something like Alcoa's environmental, health, and safety experts whom we met in Chapter 4, available to advise and assist at every level and scale of aggregation—plant, location, business unit, and corporate.

According to Aisin's OMCD head, Mr. Torii, the three-year curriculum had a logical progression. In the first year, students focused on process improvements, smaller-scale work like that done by Bob Dallis in West Virginia and Kamigo. In the second year, they advanced to system-level projects, progressing from component work methods to problems of connections and pathways, the interfaces and architecture of work systems. For instance, they might have participated in the line redesign at the Aisin plant, which I described in Chapter 7. In the third year, the students would oversee improvement activities, both to solidify their own knowledge and to practice transferring similar skills to others, much as Mike Takahashi had done with Bob Dallis and as Dallis was learning to do with others.

As a training ground for process experts and a supplier of process expertise, Aisin's OMCD played several critical roles. It evaluated the effectiveness of each production line, established performance-improvement goals, and supported improvement efforts by identifying opportunities for fruitful change. Each of those activities was a venue in which people could hone their problem-solving skills while removed from their positions of operational responsibility.

Toyota, of course, has its own Operations Management Consulting Division. Toyota's OMCD supports plant-improvement activities and provides a venue in which people can become more expert through frequent problem solving. For example, during one of my research trips, one of my hosts was Mr. Numa, who had worked for Toyota for 16 years, much of it in the quality-control division, and was in his first year at OMCD. He had projects at three sites where he developed his own problem-solving skills and practiced developing those skills in others.

Leader as Process Owner

Gary Convis is someone with a unique perspective on Toyota. He worked at Big Three firms for nearly two decades before coming to NUMMI. There, he worked with and was responsible for people who, like him, had seen what it was like to work in a low-velocity environment like the one I described in Chapter 3 and who now knew what it is like to work in a high-velocity organization. Convis helped launch Toyota's Georgetown, Kentucky, plant and became the first non-Japanese president of a Toyota manufacturing site.

Convis described to me an occasion on which he had had to take charge of a process change, not because others were unwilling or incompetent, but because of the number of boundary-spanning issues involved. As with many of Toyota's problems, this one resulted from its success. The Georgetown plant had to increase its productive capacity because of increasing demand. What is the solution for such a problem? In part, you continue to make progress on the way people work with machines, seeing if more speed can be squeezed out. However, there may be limits with existing equipment, or the speed of improvement may not match the speed needed for growth. Georgetown had reached the point where it needed more equipment, but where to put it? Expanding the plant was neither a low-cost nor a quick solution. That pointed to the next question: Where was space used unproductively? The answer: in parts storage.

This might seem surprising in light of Toyota's reputation for small inventories that turn over very quickly, but there is still line-side storage of the minimum number of parts needed to tide production over while material is replenished. In certain areas, those parts are big and even minimal storage requires a big footprint. Consider body weld. If a station needs one or two beams per cycle and each beam is 2 to 3 feet long by a few inches wide, that requires a few square feet of floor space. Keep enough on hand for even a small portion of an hour's worth of work before material handling returns with a refill, and the footprint is several feet by several feet. Multiply that by the many workstations in the shop and you have consumed a lot of space for storage. Factor in that the parts come in sets of 5 or 10 at a time and that each set has a carrier and the work area gets even more congested.

Probing questions were asked: Why do you need carriers for several parts? Can't parts be conveyed in lots of one? Why must the parts be carried and stored horizontally, consuming even more space? (These parts could not be stacked, so the more there were on a conveyer, the wider that conveyer had to be.) That inquiry helped establish a goal of transporting one piece at a time; even when several traveled together, each would have its own small conveyor. Added to that was the objective of moving and storing them vertically, not laid flat.

These objectives were not as easy to reach as they sound. Working from the point of customer contact—the line-side location where the parts were used—it meant reconfiguring workstations to accept material presented in a different fashion (the domain of production engineering) and reconfiguring the way in which the pieces were accessed and handled by operators (the realm of the production supervisors and managers). When material handling moved long beams upright, they had a tendency to wobble. Could they be transported vertically without danger of being damaged? Transport would have to be altered, as would the way in which parts were loaded at the suppliers and unloaded at Toyota. There were a lot of organizational boundaries over which collaboration and coordination of effort and innovation would have to be managed. This made it Convis's job.

What makes the situation so different from what might take place in other organizations is that Convis himself felt that this was his job. He never saw it as something "below his level," nor would he have concluded that if moving parts vertically instead of horizontally was going to be this much trouble, then it just wasn't worth it. This points out another critical difference between the manager in a high-velocity organization and his or her counterparts elsewhere. If a problem makes it way up to his or her level, the high-level manager has to be part of its resolution. Either the problem spans boundaries over which no one else has authority and responsibility, or it doesn't, but it is challenging enough that it could not be resolved at lower levels. Either way, the senior leader has to be a process improver, which depends on seeing problems when and where they occur.

Who Is in Charge of Whom?

If the goal is to design work to see problems and then solve them where they are seen, a leader must be in a position to see problems as they arise. The higher the level of authority, the harder it can be to do this because much of the work itself is less tangible. "Normal" may be harder to define, which makes departures from normal harder to see. Convis reflected that one of the most difficult conceptual challenges is finding abnormality in things that one cannot see. They may be intangible, they may just be far away. Nevertheless, if they go wrong and the problem is not detected, they cause trouble. If they are seen as they start to go wrong, their effects may be mitigated quickly and the organization may learn from their occurrence.

In most organizations, the more senior person tells a less senior person what to do and the less senior person confirms that what has been mandated has been completed. This system is inverted when the objective is to ensure that problems are seen and solved where they occur by and with the people affected by the problem. If those less senior people cannot solve the problem, they have the right and the responsibility to pull on someone more senior for help and he or she is obliged to provide that help. Put bluntly, the most senior manager is the most subordinate person. Everything is done in support of shipping product to customers. Problems pull support from successively higher levels; in effect, the senior person's pace of work is determined in large part by the needs of people many years and many ranks his or her junior. The same thing is true in a design or service situation. There is much that the senior leader must do in terms of directing, expanding, and contracting people's behavioral latitude: We're working on this, not that; you're needed here, not there. However, in an organization managed to see and solve problems, it is the occurrence of problems and, more to the point, the occurrence of problems that cannot be reconciled that determines where a manager's efforts are directed. And that's just what we saw earlier in this chapter in the attitude of the visiting senior manager who didn't want to see the perfectly painted car. He wanted to know where the struggle points were so he could do his job—helping those below him improve their own work. Convis has addressed this point:

> I remember when Mr. Higashi became the second president at NUMMI, following T. Toyoda, I was promoted to VP of manufacturing. Mr. Higashi had exactly the same philosophy I had heard from Mr. Ikebuchi and T. Toyoda. He said this to me during one of my earliest meetings with him:
>
> "Everyone knows you're the boss. But I want you to manage as if you had no power over your subordinates." He explained that I couldn't just mandate things. He wanted me to go out on the shop floor and sell my ideas. To do that, I had to get out of the office and down on the production line. That's the only way to understand the issues.

In Chapters 6 through 9, we've looked in detail at Toyota in order to see examples of the four capabilities that characterize high-velocity organizations. Those organizations are quick to meet customers' needs; they reach that speed with an intense commitment to specifying how work is expected to proceed to ensure that the best known approach is used. However, they couple that commitment to specificity with building tests into the work (Sakiichi Toyoda's *jidoka* principle) to ensure that problems are seen when and where they occur. When problems are seen, they are swarmed, investigated, and solved—not just to make them go away, but to replace the process and/or system ignorance that allowed them to occur with useful knowledge about how to operate better. That knowledge is not kept locally. It is shared so that individuals' experiences contribute to the expertise of their colleagues as well. Finally, leaders of high-velocity organizations play roles not often seen in those organizations stuck in the pack, racing for second or third place. These high-velocity leaders manage processes, designing and improving at the level at which no one else has the necessary perspective, responsibility, or authority. Most importantly, they are personally responsible for establishing the cascade of capability development throughout the organization that makes the organization a rabbit.

Before we leave Toyota, we'll look in Chapter 10 at what it means for an organization to use these capabilities not only for routine situations but also for crises. In the examples that follow, Toyota was hit by seismic disruptions, yet recovered quickly through the agility of its responses. We'll come to see that when you are seeing and solving problems every day all day, there are no crises per se; there are just some problems that are bigger and more demanding than others.

CHAPTER 10

HIGH-VELOCITY CRISIS RECOVERY

The Crisis That Wasn't

On Tuesday, February 4, 1997, *The Wall Street Journal* reported the following:

> TOKYO—Production at Toyota Motor Corp.'s plants in Japan, which build 16,200 vehicles a day, has virtually ground to a halt and could be suspended for up to a week or more after a fire at a brake maker's plant cut off the supply of three brake and clutch parts.

The crisis was huge. The incinerated factory, which belonged to the Toyota supplier Aisin Seiki, made P-valves, which control fluid flow and pressure in hydraulic brake lines, as well as clutch parts for manual transmissions. Although only a $5 to $10 part, the P-valve was critical to safety, its design was patented, it required precise machining, the hundreds of specialized machines devoted to its production were destroyed in the fire, and there was no backup—Aisin had nearly a 99 percent share for this item.

The *Journal* estimated that a shutdown could cost Toyota $40 million a day in lost profits, a particularly galling blow because Toyota had ramped up to accommodate a peak in demand. Toyota offered a reasonably optimistic prediction of recovery, but others were not so sure. An expert quoted by the *Financial Times* predicted the following:

> If Toyota resumes 15 percent of its production within the week, and raises this to 60 percent next week, the cost of lost production would be ¥162 billion in sales and ¥33.1 billion in operating profits.

For victims of Japan's manufacturing triumph over the previous decade and a half, the *Wall Street Journal* article added what must have been a sweet consolation:

> Toyota's trouble also shows the continued vulnerability of Japan's industrial titans to their heralded "just-in-time" inventory systems, even two years after the Kobe earthquake stopped production of key parts and reminded them of flaws in the system. Under just-in-time manufacturing, suppliers deliver parts as often as hourly so the manufacturer does not have to keep expensive inventories. That makes for tiny reserves.

One can imagine more than a little delight around some breakfast tables and over some coffeepots in Detroit and elsewhere that morning, but one hopes they did not start opening the champagne that night. By the next day, the *Journal* ran a story that was headlined "Toyota Sees Output Recovery by Friday, but Many Parts Suppliers Are Hurting":

> TOKYO—Toyota Motor Corp. expects to resume "near normal" production by Friday at 20 Japanese assembly plants idled after a fire destroyed a supplier's factory last weekend. . . .

How could Toyota rebound so quickly? The experts in the previous article had been predicting 15 percent by the end of the week. The *Journal* reported:

> Toyota, Japan's largest manufacturer, said several parts makers have stepped in to make three critical brake and clutch parts that Toyota previously procured solely from Aisin Seiki Co., a supplier that lost a key plant to a fire Saturday.

But what about the unique, specialized, patented precision equipment that had been destroyed? As perplexing as this might have been, at least there seemed to be some doubts about the scope and quality of Toyota's surprisingly swift recovery:

> Mr. [Tatsuo] Ushijima [a senior associate at Mitsubishi Research Institute, a Tokyo think tank] questioned whether the quality of the alternative parts would equal those produced by Aisin Seiki, which

manufactured exclusively for Toyota. "I don't think the recovery will be as smooth as Toyota has announced," he said.

Observers eager to read accounts of profuse corporate apologies and resignations over the disaster, and more predictions of dire circumstances, found nothing in Thursday's or Friday's *Journal*. It was not until the following Monday that the story was picked up again. Buried in news summaries, between paragraphs about telecommunications in Japan and the Russians selling from commodity reserves to close budget gaps and others blurbs about a French defense contractor's plan to offload shares in a bank, an appreciation of Polish privatization vouchers, and fraud in Albanian financial markets, was the following brief item:

Toyota Resumes Most Production

Toyota Motor Corp. of Japan said it resumed 90 percent of its normal output Friday, almost a week after a Feb. 1 fire at an affiliated parts producer hobbled the auto maker's domestic production of 14,000 vehicles a day. The blaze at Aisin Seiki Co., which supplies most of the brakes and clutches for Toyota cars, forced the auto giant to halt production for two days, set up temporary parts-making lines and seek parts from other companies.

How could the company have rebounded so quickly? A few months later, a hint appeared in the *Journal:*

By the following Thursday, the 36 suppliers, aided by more than 150 other subcontractors, had nearly 50 separate lines producing small batches of the brake valve.

Through that collective effort, supplies resumed and production gradually restarted:

> Trucks bearing the first 1,000 usable P-valves rolled in late Wednesday. On Thursday, 3,000 more arrived, and on Friday, 5,000. Slowly, Toyota's assembly lines started up again.

With P-valves available, Toyota began reopening plants as early as Thursday, and by the following Monday all Toyota plants were back to normal production even though Aisin was able to provide less than 10 percent of the valves, not reaching 60 percent of the supply until more than a month after the disaster.

If you haven't started *Chasing the Rabbit* with Chapter 10, you probably have a few more hints as to how Toyota pulled this off. But before we delve into it, ask yourself how likely it is that your organization could add a new product to its existing line by the end of the day tomorrow. Could a commercial airline launch a new route in a day? Could a hospital add a new service overnight? If you cannot do that now, what would you have to change to be able to do it someday?

For some clues to answering that question, let's entertain alternative explanations for what happened within the Toyota network. One possibility is that either Toyota or Aisin assumed a micromanaging command-and-control posture, telling some 200 other companies exactly what to do in order to produce P-valves exactly as Aisin had done. This explanation may seem plausible, but it doesn't really hold up. The first problem is the basic impossibility of such micromanagement in such a short time. In addition, as accounts of the recovery emerged, they did not accord with such an explanation. According to the *Journal*, "The secret lay in Toyota's close-knit family of parts suppliers. In the corporate equivalent of an Amish barn-raising, suppliers and local companies rushed to the rescue." In an in-depth case study published a year after the fire, Toshihiro Nishiguchi and Alexandre Beaudet found that recovery from the fire was achieved through an "immediate and largely self-organized effort" with companies that "generally [had] no previous experience with P-valves." (Nishiguchi and Beaudet estimated the number of participants at over 200, with 70 directly responsible for production.) Significantly, and contrary to the alternative posited above, that was done with "very little direct control from Toyota."

These accounts suggest another possible explanation: the extraordinary element of trust built into the Toyota supplier network, derived from years of close cooperation. One supplier was quoted as saying: "Toyota's quick recovery is attributable to the power of the group, which handled it without thinking about money or business contracts." Nishiguchi and Beaudet agreed that the recovery had been accomplished without "haggling over issues of technical proprietary rights or financial compensation." Certainly, that loyalty was repaid, for when the dust had settled, Toyota gave its suppliers a bonus amounting to 1 percent of their sales to Toyota from January to March, a total estimated at $100 million.

Trust and rewards to the loyal may explain the effort, but they cannot explain the outcome. Toyota could have turned to many individuals and organizations during the crisis and not gotten the same response. If micromanagement by Toyota or Aisin is not a feasible explanation and trust is not a sufficient explanation, how else can we explain how thousands of people from several hundred organizations could create a new production and logistics system in a matter of days? The key lies in the concept of being self-organized. So let's look more closely at what "self-organization" implies before we turn back to the fire recovery story.

Self-Organization: Complex Results from Simple Rules

In a variety of domains, designers are increasingly aware that the size, scope, and complexity of the systems on which they work make it increasingly difficult to plan systems that are reliable and robust, able to do what they are supposed to do, able to survive their own flaws, and able to adapt to changing circumstances.

Software designers, whose systems have to be dynamic and responsive, have been struck by systems in nature that seem self-organizing and self-regulating without any command and control or centralized decision making. With this apparent paradox in mind—coordination in the absence of a coordinator—computer-graphics expert Craig Reynolds set out to create a program that imitated bird flocking. He didn't program each "bird" with complex flight patterns, the command-and-control approach, akin to the frame by frame drawing that old-school animators must have done. Managing the detailed trajectories for each individual bird, once a number of them began flocking together, would have been overwhelming. Instead, Reynolds programmed three simple rules into each bird: Avoid obstacles (including other birds), fly in the same direction most of the other birds are going, and try to stay in the middle of the pack. Those simple rules worked well and scaled reliably. They were the backbone for the computer-generated animation of bats swarming in a *Batman* movie and the stampede in *The Lion King*.

Although the swarming of bats in the Bat Cave is nothing like the swarming of problems at a Toyota plant, the underlying principle that complex successful behavior can arise from a few simple rules is the same. Throughout this book, we keep coming back to the four capabilities that helped Alcoa and the U.S. nuclear navy stay accident-free, that helped Toyota get ahead of overwhelming competitors, and that helped Avenue A and Pratt & Whitney turn tangled or plodding internal processes into lean, mean, profit-generating operations. Here are the four capabilities expressed as rules:

1. *Design:* Specify work systems in terms of what output is being pursued, who will perform what steps in what sequence along a pathway to generate that outcome, how exchanges of materials and information (including the informational triggers to start work) will be made across the connections between steps, and what methods will be used at each step. Design systems with tests built in to immediately identify any gaps between what was predicted and what happens.

2. *Improve:* Swarm problems the moment they are seen so that they can be contained, investigated, and resolved

quickly. Involve those affected by the problem in resolving it, using the discipline of the scientific method to ensure that solving problems also builds additional useful knowledge on ways to increase the chance for success in the future.

3. *Share knowledge:* Share throughout the organization whatever is learned locally. Share the discovery process as well as the particular solution, so new insights can be put to wider use and have broader benefits.

4. *Develop problem-solving capabilities:* Develop these core capabilities in those for whom you are responsible as a leader.

If we look closely at the Aisin fire recovery, we'll see that the self-organizing effort succeeded because these four straightforward capability rules were followed with great discipline even before the fire was brought under control.

First, of course, was the recognition that there was a problem that had to be addressed. Within an hour of the fire starting, before it was under control, Aisin had created a "war room" stocked with several hundred cell phones, an additional 230 land lines, and sleeping bags to accommodate a round-the-clock operation. (By 8 a.m. that morning, Toyota was racing 400 of its own engineers to Aisin.) Immediately, Aisin began establishing new processes with which to supply its customers. This task was divided into four subprocesses: setting up alternative production sites, establishing logistics networks to handle material flow to and from those sites, working with customers (Toyota was the plant's largest but not its only major automotive customer), and working with unions and neighbors, among others.

Aisin and its customers started inventorying the types of P-valves for which production capacity had to be reestablished; there were over 100. This inventory was itself no trivial task, as Aisin's part-numbering system did not match Toyota's. Aisin and its customers determined the priority with which supplies had to be provided. If a customer used P-valves on more than one car model, it had to determine which model had higher priority.

In other words, the first task was to specify what output had to be achieved by the system overall—how many of which parts to which customers by when? All other decisions would support that one. Objectives could now be set for the firms that had offered to help. Aisin began faxing drawings of particular parts by early Sunday morning, within a day of the fire. This delegation of responsibility continued through the network. For example, the Toyota supplier Somic Ishikawa Inc. was farming out its own production to its suppliers to free capacity for the assignment it accepted from Aisin. Taiho took a mixed approach, offloading some of its normal work and some of its P-valve work to 11 of its suppliers. Kayaba, another supplier, parceled out responsibility to three of its suppliers on the basis of equipment availability and appropriateness (the largest had approximately 100 employees and the smallest only 6), helping them ramp up but doing no P-valve production in its own plant. Toyota itself took some responsibility for P-valve production, creating "temporary production sites" in a department normally responsible for experimental processes and equipment maintenance.

Regardless of where production responsibility landed, each of the autonomous elements within the self-organizing network followed the same rule: Given the abilities and constraints of the available people and equipment, establish production flows that generate defect-free P-valves. From site to site, the steps would differ, but the output would be reliably the same. Whereas Aisin had depended on automated high-speed transfer lines dedicated to P-valve production, Denso had to reconfigure its machining centers for P-valve production. Brother had not made auto parts before the Aisin fire; it had to "cobble together a P-valve production line by adapting computerized milling equipment that usually makes sewing machine and typewriter parts."

We've seen that high-velocity organizations are set apart by their capabilities to design systems, improve systems, and share what one has learned so that each person or organization can perform as if in possession of everyone else's experience. If there was ever a time when this capability for sharing was needed, it was in the first few hours after the fire. Outside of Aisin, the cumulative experience of P-valve production was nearly zero. However, since Aisin had not made those parts in machining centers as the substitutes were doing, it was not the best source of advice. Aisin therefore organized problem-solving sessions in which one plant could transfer what it had learned to others. Denso not only shared the insights it had gained by solving bottlenecks, but "also modified Aisin's design drawings and process instructions to make them more appropriate for machining centers." Although the speed and urgency were unusual, the basic approach of collaborative problem solving, cross-site learning, and leveraging local learning into system-wide gains was very familiar.

For decades, Toyota and its suppliers have honed their skills in designing exceptionally reliable processes, improving them quickly, and, as they make improvements, sharing what they have discovered along the way. Remember that Capability 4 is the development, by a leader at any level, of just these skills in the people for whom that leader is responsible. So when Toyota affiliates were faced with the challenge of reconstructing—or constructing for the first time—production lines to make a vital precision part, it was not an abrupt departure from what they normally did. Command-and-control micromanagement was not necessary because employees at all levels had been trained every working day to be quick problem solvers. What might have been crippling for some organizations was, for Toyota and its suppliers, a challenge of the sort they already knew they could handle.

I interviewed a member of the Aisin fire recovery effort. He explained that the hours were long and the pressure was high, but what was most noticeable was that, despite all this, people seemed to be having fun. They had practiced their skills at discovering great systems at exceptional speed and this was a chance to test themselves, like a sports team playing for the championship.

Now we'll look at a few more examples of high-speed crisis recovery to show the variety of situations to which this sort of agility can be applied and to emphasize the point that the capabilities needed for "normal" high-velocity management—creating and delivering an organization's products and processes—are the same as those needed to handle larger disruptions. In fact, we'll see that the difference between "normal" operations and "crisis" response is not a distinction in type, only in scale and scope.

Before we do that, let's consider a contrast between Toyota and one of its direct competitors on something much simpler, the day-to-day work of digesting small, local shop-floor process improvements and the steady redistribution of work to keep the line in balance. When we consider how different the attitude toward such a challenge is at the two companies, we'll be better able to appreciate the idea of crisis recovery as normal work.

On my first visit to Toyota, a group of us toured an assembly plant and were learning from those responsible for logistics how they managed the inbound and internal flows of parts and materials. To put some perspective on this, the plant used a vast number of parts on a just-in-time basis; some suppliers were delivering up to eight times per day. So tight was this operation that they were currently dealing with the "problem" of some suppliers' trucks arriving a minute or more *early*, causing congestion and delay in the unloading area. Their goal was to have trucks arrive within 30 seconds of the target time so as to avoid creating bottlenecks.

Despite how tightly wound this system was, we were told that there were daily reassignments of "line-side stores," the points in assembly where parts were distributed, because of the need to rebalance and shift work. These reassignments, normal for this plant, happened up to sixty times per day. The consequence was not only that some workers had to pick up the tasks previously assigned to others, but that parts and materials had to flow without delay or interruption to their new locations.

When one member of our group, a senior manufacturing manager at a Toyota competitor, heard this, he couldn't believe it until he saw documentation indicating what had been moved where over several days. Then, he explained his disbelief. Had one of his plants tried something similar, even with the cushion of inventory it normally held, the plant would be paralyzed for hours.

With that contrast in mind, let's look at the types of disruptions a high-velocity organization can handle on a regular basis.

Crisis Recovery as Regular Work

It might seem that events like the Aisin fire are rare, but a complex system, particularly one as sprawling as Toyota's, is constantly buffeted by disruptions and disturbances. The question is how to handle them. If the organization's activities are sufficiently limited, it might rely on redundancy—backup equipment, spare capacity, and extra suppliers. But that type of safety can exact a competitive price: the cost of extra resources, the space they take up, the inventorying and maintenance they require. There can also be an impact on quality. To the extent that redundancy protects an organization from problems, it also protects the organization from opportunities to solve those problems and from all the practice, learning, and improvement that come from that.

If system stability is to be maintained without compromising cost, quality, and product variety, it cannot be because the system has been dumbed down in its simplicity and bulked up in its redundancy. It must be because the system is good at seeing and solving problems, not only on a small scale, like a high-functioning immune system, but also on a larger scale, able to repair itself even when seriously wounded. For such an organization, responding to crises is not idiosyncratic work. It is something that is done all the time. It is this responsiveness that is their source of reliability.

Let's look at some other examples of dealing with abnormal situations in a normal way.

Example: Port Lockout

After the Aisin fire, the loss of a single supplier had to be countered by a self-organizing network. If that seemed challenging, what if the entire supplier network went off the grid? That is exactly the situation that confronted Toyota when 29 ports on America's West Coast were shut down from September 29 to October 8, 2002, due to labor-management conflict. Diverting ships to Canada would not necessarily do the trick because Canadian longshoremen were affiliated with and sympathetic to the American longshoremen. Mexico also had limitations: Once the ships were there, the infrastructure of roads and railways was insufficient. Even diverting to East Coast and Gulf ports would be problematic: Some of the cargo ships were too big to pass through the Panama Canal.

Let's look at how Toyota self-organized to solve this problem.

The strike was not entirely a surprise. But the truth is that the union and management had been negotiating and most people thought the two sides would stop playing chicken soon enough to avoid a collision. That was not to be, however, and now Toyota's ability to produce and deliver vehicles was going to be impaired.

A decade earlier, when more Toyota cars were imported from Japan fully completed, the problem might have been less severe. North American dealers would have had some leeway, thanks to the inventory on their lots. But in 2002, Toyota was manufacturing nearly 1 million autos per year in North America. A disruption in shipments from Japan would affect North American body shops, engine production, and final assembly as well as many suppliers that used foreign-sourced materials.

There was little time to act. Toyota had already been increasing the frequency and decreasing the lot size of shipments between its suppliers and itself within North America. It had been pushing the same effort with supplies coming from Japan. True, there had to be some accommodation to the scale economies of packing things in containers and the vagaries of ocean travel times, but many of those issues had been addressed by bundling small batches of different types of parts on shipments. So there was little inventory for certain items. If supply networks could not be reestablished quickly, plants might have to shut down. With so many companies dependent on the West Coast ports, there was going to be a mad dash to lock up alternative routes. Toyota was looking at a winner-take-all contest.

The shutdown came on Sunday. Within hours, experts in supplier relations, production planning, control, and logistics on both sides of the Pacific were assembled into a working team.

The first priority was building a "bridge" from Japan to the United States to replace the stranded fleet. Without a means of moving material, all else was moot. Space was lined up on cargo-carrying 747s (ultimately, more than 100 flights were used, nine or ten per day). That was to be the pipeline. Meanwhile, other groups were establishing what had to flow through that pipeline by calculating what materials were expected at what plants by when (establishing the target "output" for this temporary shipping system). One team was tallying what was onboard ships waiting to dock along the West Coast. This was critical information. First, it gave them a measure of the volume and weight of what had to be transported. Second, they could start setting production priorities for supplier plants in Japan. Materials manufactured but not yet loaded could be diverted, but materials already at sea had to be replaced.

Still more needed to be done. Not enough 747s were available on short notice to move all the supplies that were needed to keep Toyota's plants running. A massive Antonov transport plane, so big that it had its own internal block and tackle to move shipping containers, was available but was not cleared to land in the United States. Separate routing had to be created to transport cargo from its landing field in Canada. One ship operator stranded off the West Coast got fed up and dumped 200 cargo containers in a port in southern Mexico. That was both a hassle and an opportunity. The situation necessitated creating an unloading-and-transport mechanism, not only to accommodate the infrastructure in an out-of-the-way place, but also to move the material through the Mexico–United States border crossing without undue delay or cost. But at least those parts were now part of the lifeline if they could be delivered quickly enough.

Toyota's Glenn Uminger, who was in the thick of this crisis, explained to me how this was handled in a plug-and-play fashion:

The person that we sent there had a proven history. He was from the Georgetown [Kentucky] plant and he was a guy who can just get things done. He can make decisions on his own. Send him into this hole—into the unknown.

He had had experience with U.S. ports, so he could handle the technical difficulties of getting the ships unloaded, and the inventory accounted for, tracked, loaded onto trucks, and sent on its way. That was "normal" process to him. But then we had to insert another step into the flow—clearing customs—so we had to plug in the other piece, having a group of customs experts support him on how to file the right paperwork to transit the border. These people didn't typically work together, but with a common approach to jump-starting a process and solving a problem, they meshed perfectly. We never missed production except for a few of the trucks in Indiana, where it didn't make economic sense to airlift heavy engines and transmissions.

Uminger reflected on managing abnormality as a normal occupation:

It is never routine, but it is repeatable. We follow the same formula.

[In the moment,] you are looking to people because they have faced things and are prepared for this right now, so the leaders are very important. They are the ones with the experience, so we try to team up people who have been through some small problems over the years at different levels, for instance, very experienced people plus experienced people on their staff plus less-experienced people to give them experience who can learn how to manage the situation and run with it.

He then discussed the alternative of running operations with more slack:

We get this [criticism] all the time. The whole discussion of how just-in-time doesn't work. People comment, "This is stupid. Why not just carry inventory?" From our perspective, it's better to have a tightly linked supply chain and manage disruption when it occurs rather than carry fat all year round. If you do that, you lose your ability to see problems and solve problems. Instead, we practice on real problems all the time, so when a big problem hits, it's just a matter of degree.

Example: Finding a New Permanent Supplier

While a port's closure is a dramatic example, complex systems are constantly dealing with crises as events occur, conditions shift, and plans go awry. Being able to respond in a dynamic fashion is what converts crises into an exercise in building and ramping up new systems in a methodical fashion (albeit at great speed) rather than a potential derailing of the enterprise. Here is another example.

313

Kirk Manley, a manager in Toyota's Production Control Division who specializes in project planning management, is another of those Toyota people whose normal work is dealing with abnormal situations. One arose when a supplier to three of Toyota's North American factories requested that it be freed of its obligations. It fell to Manley to manage the transfer of production from that supplier to an alternative, all the while ensuring that there would be no interruption in supply to the customer plants. Time and execution were critical. With the supplier eager to end its obligation but with little inventory in the system, any glitch could be serious.

Manley was in no position to solve the problem on his own, and even the permanent staff with which he worked was too small and lacked the particular skills to make this bad situation good. So Manley had to build a virtual organization to handle the challenge.

He started by outlining the large objectives he had to meet and the key process steps that had to occur. First, someone had to identify alternative suppliers that had both the technical skills and the physical capacity to pick up responsibility for new production in midmodel, well after they had made the budgeting decisions and space, equipment, and labor allocations to support their current commitments. Second, a gap analysis had to be done: What were potential new suppliers capable of doing and what resources would have to be transferred from the existing supplier? There was also the technical challenge of dismantling, transferring, and reinstalling specialized production equipment. Then there were logistics considerations: Raw materials would have to be diverted from their current paths to new destinations and finished product originating from these new production facilities would have to get to Toyota's plants.

Within weeks, the new suppliers were ready to go. Not only had the crisis-management team generated a design, it had also done a number of validation tests—its version of the hold, not tape, not bolt, not weld approach Bob Dallis had practiced. Mock-ups had been created at the new production sites to ensure that ergonomics, material transport, plumbing, wiring, lighting, and other factors could be fine-tuned before the equipment arrived. Representatives from the new plants had worked on the equipment at the current supplier's plant before that equipment was disconnected, establishing standard work processes for both production and preventive maintenance, with people from production engineering learning from the experiences of their counterparts at the current supplier and reviewing that supplier's maintenance logs. When it was their turn to solve problems, they would not be starting from scratch but would benefit from the experience with the equipment that had already accumulated.

With a plan in place and its key elements tested, the current supplier ramped up production, building a buffer inventory that could be stored at the new facility to cover the transition. Moving that inventory to the new site also provided a chance to debug material handling, shipping, and other logistics problems before responsibility switched from one site to the next.

With everything in place, the production at the original site was stopped and the choreography of who was to do what commenced. Of course, things happened that had not been anticipated, but those problems were swarmed and solved with equal acumen. For the plants dependent on these suppliers, the transition appeared to be completely seamless. Not because the system was simple enough to rearrange easily. Nor because the system was complex but had wisely built up enough protective layers of redundancy. Rather, the system was well-practiced and well-honed at being self-correcting and self-improving and at treating *anything* that happened as an opportunity for additional self-correction and self-improvement.

Example: Finding a Temporary Supplier

Kirk Manley's colleague, Matt Buckenmeyer, has led similar efforts, dealing with abnormal out-of-control situations in a normal, in-control way. For example, a supplier of wheel rims suffered a fire; it had sufficient capacity to restore production, but it would take several days before the fire-damaged equipment was repaired. In the meantime, five of seven machining lines were unusable. A few days might not seem like a lot, but it is when the system has been chiseled lean.

Wheel rims might seem like a relatively simple part of an automobile, but in fact they are the product of sophisticated forging, machining, and powder-coating processes. What's more, because customers get to personalize their rides, rims and wheels have to be matched to particular vehicles. Because they are big, bulky, and expensive, they cannot be stored in anticipation of demand. With one supplier down even temporarily, it was not sufficient merely to have other suppliers lined up to pick up the slack. To maintain sequence and timing, logistics had to be ramped up so that the suppliers could produce and deliver exactly what was needed when it was needed, loaded and presented in just the right sequence.

This takes us back to the concept of self-organizing systems and how Toyota's high-velocity way of doing things allows it to benefit so much from self-organizing systems when something goes wrong.

Outside the Toyota system, it might be common for each pair of supplier plants and customer plants to have its own approaches to placing orders and responding to them. Some customer plants might broadcast a production schedule days or weeks in advance, others have electronic ordering systems; some might convey orders to headquarters, others to individual supplier plants, and still others to specific lines, bypassing any centralized system. Imagine trying to solve a supply problem by unplugging one supplier and temporarily plugging in the next. It would take a huge effort just to establish how orders would be sent and received. It would be like getting PC peripherals to work with Macs and vice versa, but much worse.

That's not how it is within a Toyota supplier network. In accordance with the "rule" of specifying connections, or hand-offs, Toyota and its suppliers develop "interfaces"—standardized ways in which orders are exchanged. When a plant needs something, it must ask for it directly from the designated supplier for that item and the designated supplier will deliver only when asked. It is Ohno's rule from his Kamigo engine plant days applied over great distances. But if one supplier cannot do the job, the plant can easily ask another without having to learn a whole new ordering procedure. The forms of the requests and responses have already been agreed on; all that has to be worked out is how much of what is being requested by when. It's like living in a world in which every computer peripheral connects effortlessly through USB ports, but much better.

For another automaker, the loss of a wheel-rim supplier for a few days could have been an enormous hassle, if not a crisis. Alternative suppliers would have to be found and, in each case, the complex mechanics of getting the right rims delivered to the right places at the right times would have to be mastered— all that trouble for just a few days until the old supplier came back on line. For Toyota, it was as easy to order rims from one supplier as from another; capacity might be a problem, but logistics would not be.

Example: Crisis as Improvement Opportunity

You might think the Buckenmeyer family pet was a Dalmatian, the way Matt kept having to respond to fires, both figuratively and literally. An oil-pan supplier had been building up an inventory buffer to create a bit of breathing room. Planned installation of new equipment and modification of existing equipment would require some downtime, as would the investigation of some process issues, such as excessive scrap. In January 2007, the supplier had a fire. Thanks to the buffer inventory, oil-pan deliveries were not interrupted, and the supplier was up and running within two days. But now, rebuilding the buffer meant delaying the expansion, modification, and improvement efforts.

For Toyota, the immediate problem was coordinating accurate deliveries out of the buffer inventory, while the longer-term problem was that this supplier was less agile than needed. To deal with the immediate problem, Toyota's purchasing department, responsible for relationships with suppliers, managed coordination with the engine plants that depended on the part to ensure that there were no stockouts while the plant got back on line.

At the same time, Matt Buckenmeyer was sent in to deal with the longer-term situation. The production problem had been precipitated by the fire, the recovery from which had wiped out the supplier's backup inventory. Without that buffer, the supplier faced a dilemma. It couldn't afford to put off the equipment upgrades and modifications long enough to rebuild a large enough buffer to carry it through. But if it did shut down for upgrades without having built up a buffer, it wouldn't be able to make delivery of parts. Neither option was acceptable. But for Toyota, and for Buckenmeyer, the real question was: Why couldn't this supplier manage upgrades and the like without building up an inventory and shutting down? Why couldn't it do normal production and normal improvements simultaneously? What was so fragile about the system that both couldn't happen at the same time?

With some investigation, Buckenmeyer and his team realized the sources of vulnerability. Although the supplier was linked to its Toyota customers with a just-in-time pull system and therefore had a clear view of its immediate production demands, it did not have an equally simple, reliable system for coordinating its internal flows of material and information. Within the plant, it wasn't absolutely clear what had to be made because external customer demand wasn't reliably setting the pace of final production, in turn setting the pace of upstream processes. So one reason the supplier felt it necessary to build a store of finished goods before the equipment upgrade was that it was never entirely sure that it had made what it needed to make. (As we saw in Chapter 6, this was the very predicament that motivated Taiichi Ohno to develop a just-in-time pull system. We also saw how such a system helped Aisin Seiki be far more responsive to its customers, making custom mattresses in response to actual orders and shipping them right off to customers rather than making them in response to anticipated orders and piling them up in a stockroom.)

Not only hadn't the supplier developed the capability to follow the rules for designing a system, but there was also a second problem. Because the supplier was unable to track what was needed and what was available with ease and accuracy, it was difficult to detect abnormal situations. This compounded the need for extra inventory "just in case" a problem came to light—a problem that might have existed for a while before being discovered.

The solution to both problems, of course, was to help the supplier's management develop their capabilities to design and operate reliable systems and to solve problems as they occurred, so the production system would be more reliable, more agile, and less vulnerable.

Crisis? What Crisis?

Many people think of work as having a demarcation between the normal demands, in which people stick to a groove, and the crisis situations, in which the rules have to be thrown out the window to make do. Let's consider an alternative view. Not that there are two categories of work—regular and crisis—but that there are two categories of organizations—those for which everything feels like a crisis and those for which everything feels regular.

In some organizations, the processes are so poorly designed that, even on a routine day, they regularly generate problems. Because the problems are so hard to see (the processes not having been designed to make problems visible), they can be exceptionally disruptive by the time they are recognized as problems. Even then, they are not contained and resolved effectively; they are bandaged and worked around and are sure to pop up again. Lessons learned by one person are rarely of use to someone else. The result is constant firefighting just to get the job done each day.

Then there are the organizations with well-honed, broadly shared routines for accomplishing work, improving work, and continually learning how to accomplish and improve even more. Processes are detailed in a methodical fashion while they are being designed; when they are in operation, there is constant attention to perturbations. When perturbations are experienced, they are swarmed and investigated; problems are resolved through high-speed, low-cost cycles of discovery. When discoveries are made, there is an organization-wide protocol for sharing them. Every situation requires people to design and operate, improve, share knowledge, and develop these skills in others; the only difference between glitches and crises is one of scale and immediacy, not approach. That is the situation Toyota tries to create for itself and for its suppliers. That is the situation its competitors have been unable to create, much to their detriment.

Now, let's look at some health care organizations that have tried to do the same for themselves as well.

CHAPTER 11

CREATING HIGH-VELOCITY
HEALTH-CARE ORGANIZATIONS

Chapter 3 related the sobering story of Mrs. Grant, the woman who was recovering from successful surgery but who was killed when a nurse inadvertently injected her with several doses of insulin rather than the anticoagulant he had intended to administer. This chapter looks more closely at the complex systems of work used to deliver care to people, showing how organizations that once were stuck in the pack—working too hard and delivering too little—achieved high velocity. In doing that, they not only improved the care provided to their patients and bettered the lot of those who provided that care, they also set an example of how other great organizations—health-care and otherwise—can catch up and win the race.

The American Health-Care System
Is Too Dangerous

The American health-care system is at once exhilarating and exasperating. Because it is staffed by exceptional people who have chosen careers in which they provide care, comfort, and cure to others, who are well educated, well trained, and have the best science and technology at their disposal, one's expectations should be optimistic. But the reality is far from what one would expect. Access to care is often hard to secure; when it is obtained, it can be prohibitively expensive; and even if it can be afforded, there is a good chance that something will go wrong. The Institute of Medicine released a study indicating that up to 98,000 of the 33 million people hospitalized each year die as a result of the mismanagement of care, with an equal number succumbing to infections acquired while being treated. An estimated five to ten times as many are injured through mismanaged care. These figures do not extend beyond acute care, nor do they include the waste of time, money, and other resources. The total damage is surely astronomical. It is also demonstrably avoidable. This chapter will show how.

In Chapter 2, we looked at an example of how the increased sophistication of medical science and the consequent complexity of medical treatments require ever more sophisticated approaches to management. In Chapter 3, with the story of Mrs. Grant, we saw how, even in the controlled setting of a hospital, the management of care can break down catastrophically. Then there is the world outside the walls of a hospital, which is where most of the care for chronic conditions such as asthma, diabetes, heart disease, hypertension, and depression takes place. In those situations, it is even harder to pull the pieces of expertise together into effective holistic systems.

In 2007, I was part of a panel discussion, sponsored by the MacArthur Foundation, on the poor system management endemic to health care. As an opening question, we were asked what our biggest fear was—the situation that would keep us awake at night with worry. For me, as the father of three small children, it was the prospect of taking one of our kids to an emergency room. This fear had both conceptual and practical origins. I was remembering back some years to a presentation at Harvard Medical School by Dr. Lucien Leape, a pioneer in the patient-safety and quality-of-care movement. On a blackboard, he listed a variety of activities according to the risk of getting hurt or killed. On one end were very safe undertakings such as flying on a commercial airliner and going for a walk. Bike riding was a bit more dangerous. Moving toward the other end, there were parachuting and hang-gliding. At the far end of his list was "base jumping," which includes parachuting off buildings, bridges, and the sides of mountains. With only a few seconds of drop time, no time for a backup parachute to open, and a real chance of slamming into the building or mountain from which you jumped, the odds of injury and fatality are enormous, far greater than with regular parachuting. The odds, it turns out, are about equal to the odds of getting hurt or killed in a hospital, and while most of us wouldn't think of base jumping—or of strapping a family member into a parachute and throwing him or her off the roof for sport—we will all encounter a hospital at some point.

Imagine, then, a great hospital, 20 stories high, staffed with dedicated and expert doctors and nurses and equipped with all the best technology. If you get in, your prognosis is fantastic. But you can't just walk in the front door and get care. No, first you have to climb to the roof and parachute down to the entrance. If you survive that, your first-rate medical care can begin. It's outrageous, but that's what most American health care is like today.

Dr. Leape's statistics became quite real to me several years ago when our son, Jesse, was two months old. He had a lung infection of some kind and his breathing was so labored that my wife, Miriam, took him to the emergency room of a major teaching hospital. No end of interns, residents, and nurses filtered in and out of the exam room, some from the emergency department, some from pediatrics, and some from internal medicine. Each one questioned and prodded, but what each one learned or was thinking didn't seem to be shared and amalgamated with what everyone else was thinking. Sure, they were recording information in the chart, but the chart wasn't going to do the interpretation or explanation. Shift change was even worse. The basic lack of structure and discipline in the handoff meant that a new group of people were all starting from scratch. If that wasn't bad enough, no one could find the test kit to determine which one of two illnesses our son might have, so they managed his symptoms, but without actually starting a treatment. It all ended well enough, but years later, when the panel moderator asked me to name my health-care nightmare, I didn't have to think twice.

Another participant in the meeting—a nurse—had had a different but equally illuminating and disturbing experience. She had gone to visit her aging parents and decided to check on the care they were getting. Several days later, having talked to her parents' primary-care physician, cardiologist, pulmonologist, diabetologist, and other specialists, she had found only one person in the entire health-care system who had anything approaching a holistic view of her parents' conditions and treatments. That was their local pharmacist.

The American Health-Care System Can Do Better

I know we can do much, much better because it has already been done. A number of health-care organizations have gone out of their way to learn from high-velocity organizations, though not by trying to make medical work—which has to be adapted to individual patients—rigid and repetitive. Instead, they have been learning how to replace their old approach to managing with a more sophisticated approach to designing and operating complex processes, improving them when their flaws are found, and modifying the systems as appropriate when circumstances change. I trust this all sounds pretty familiar by now—and pretty encouraging. Here are some examples:

- Ascension Health is the largest Catholic health-care system in the United States. In 2002, Ascension articulated a Call to Action for health care that works, is safe, and leaves no one behind. The objective was to have fewer patients die in their hospitals from preventable causes such as pressure ulcers (bedsores), falls, surgical errors, birth trauma, hospital-acquired (nosocomial) infections, and medication errors. After six years of effort, Ascension estimated that 2,000 lives a year were being saved. Pressure-ulcer rates are 93 percent lower at Ascension facilities than the national average, patient falls are 86 percent lower, and birth-injury rates are nearly three-quarters lower.

- Virginia Mason Medical Center (VMMC), which is discussed in more detail below, has targeted a range of issues. By teaching migraine patients how to avoid pain in the first place and how to manage it when it first starts up, VMMC has cut emergency-room visits for migraines by half and reduced the use of expensive diagnostic tests. Efforts to speed up patient flow through the gastroenterology department have saved VMMC from having to expand the facility and buy new equipment, yet it has been able to keep up with an increasing number of patients. This is a perfect example of "doing more with less"— one of the hallmarks of high-velocity organizations.

- The Mayo Clinic has reported a reduction of more than half in medical injuries at its hospitals.

- Hospitals that have participated in the Institute for Healthcare Improvement's 100,000 Lives Campaign to prevent avoidable deaths and its more recent 5 Million Lives Campaign to prevent avoidable injury have recorded excellent gains in patient safety by reducing surgical-site infections, medication errors, surgical complications, and bedsores. An estimate at 18 months into the program was that more than 120,000 deaths had been avoided.

- Hospitals in the Pittsburgh Regional Healthcare Initiative reduced the rate of central-line infections (those caused by catheters snaked into patients' veins) by 68 percent overall, with some hospitals reducing it by 90 percent and more.

- The pathology department at the University of Pittsburgh Medical Center cut the error rate in a screening test for cervical cancer by half.

- Endoscopes—tubes inserted into the body to take images or biopsy samples—are easily damaged, not only during use but even more so while being cleaned and maintained. A New York hospital reduced the number of endoscope repairs from three a day to three a week. At $5,000 per repair, this has led to an annual savings of $3 million. Beyond that, it means greater availability because fewer endoscopes are being fixed at any given moment. Furthermore, less effort is needed to keep track of backup endoscopes, since fewer are needed in the system.

All this shows what can be done. If we extrapolate these results, we find that a hospital visit does not have to be as dangerous as parachuting off a cliff, crippling both physically and financially to the individual and the larger society.

Case: Improving Primary Care

Boston's Massachusetts General Hospital (MGH) has been building its capability for process excellence in primary care. For example, the adult-medicine practice at its Revere Health Center was able to increase the productivity of its flu shot clinic 500 percent in three two-hour sessions. They did this by following the approach of the world's best organizations. Before they began their work, they "scripted" as well as they could the way they thought check-in, inoculation, documentation, and checkout should proceed. They did this for two reasons. First, they wanted to be sure that they started with their best collective understanding of what would work and what would not. Second, by defining what was normal ahead of time, the staff would find it easier to detect abnormal situations while doing their work. Was this out of the ordinary? Not for the Revere team. Having devoted their professional training and practice to understanding what is normal for complex biological systems (people) so that they could detect abnormalities (symptoms of illness) easily, they found that the same discipline applied to the complex system in which they were embedded—the daily work processes on which they depended to provide care to people.

By specifying ahead of time what they were going to do, seeing problems as they emerged, and treating them in real time, the practice generated terrific results. Whereas in most years the practice was challenged by fitting its flu-shot clinic into an already full schedule, this time lengthy waits for patients were virtually eliminated. The work was easier for the staff. Efficiency, as measured in terms of flu shots per clinical staff hour, increased fivefold, as shown in Table 11-1.

Table 11-1 Flu-shot clinic improvement

| | MGH Revere Flu-Shot Clinic | | |
	Session 1	*Session 2*	*Session 3*
Hours per session	2	2	2
Flu shots administered per session	43	71	151
Clinical support staff FTEs involved	3.5	2.5	2.5
Flu shots administered per hour of staff time	6.1	14.2	30.2

The basic principle was that when a problem was identified, the staff did not "make do," work around the problem, or cope to get by. Having practiced the skills of process design and operation improvement on other "routine" work, they were in good shape to do the same thing at an accelerated pace (just as we saw with Toyota's crisis recovery in Chapter 10). When something went wrong during the clinic, they had a momentary huddle and a rapid redesign of a piece of the process, then continued almost without hesitation with a new specification in place. Changes were from stem to stern, affecting the work methods of individual people, the handoffs between one step and another, and the sequencing of work. For instance, check-in for the clinic collided with check-in for regular appointments; lines formed while nurses waited. A modification was put in place. Flu-shot patients were steered directly to the inoculation area; they filled out a simple paper "encounter form," and the front-desk secretaries entered the information into the computer during slow times and at the end of the day.

Another slowdown involved asking about allergies. Revere's patients speak English, Spanish, Arabic, Khmer, and Portuguese, with a smattering of French and Russian. Trying to get verbal confirmation on allergies created a huge bottleneck. Quickly, the nurses polled the center's interpreters and generated simple "point to" signs in each language. Another problem solved and then another one seen. Normally, patients coming for an examination or consultation went into an examination room and had a chance to hang up their coats and prepare for the examination or treatment. The flu clinic was not in a typical exam room, and patients were not there as long as they would be for a regular exam. More time was spent fumbling with personal items and trying to find somewhere to place them than giving the shot. Another quick modification was made to the work area so that patients could disencumber themselves, get the shot, and be on their way quickly. In three shifts, totaling six hours, the staff made more than 20 process changes (approximately three times per hour) that allowed a fivefold increase in productivity.

As staff members were celebrating its success, they began speculating about the next year's clinic. They realized that the biggest bottleneck was patients trying to park in the health center's small lot. "How about a drive-through shot clinic?" someone suggested, not entirely facetiously. "We could have the patients queue around the block, where they could pick up the encounter form on a clipboard. At the right time, signs would advise them to take off their coats and turn up the heat in the car. As they got closer, another sign would tell them to roll down the window, and at the last minute they could stick their arms out."

Revere's efforts were not limited to the flu inoculations; these were part of a common approach to getting better across the board. In such a multilingual setting, having interpreters in the right place, at the right time, speaking the right language to support clinicians was essential for quality of care and efficient patient flow. Rejecting the alternatives of "we need more people," "we have to try harder," or "we just have to accept the disconnects," staff worked with the secretaries who scheduled appointments to better level the demand for language services, streamlined flows, better-partitioned time and responsibility for "on-line" work (real-time interpretation) and "off-line" work (follow-up on correspondence, lab results, and phone calls) more effectively, and built a better signaling system to call for language assistance. They discovered and showed that there was no problem of unavailable interpreters. There were myriad problems that made it too hard for interpreters to be available and too easy for them not to be.

The unit's medical director commented:

> We became used to inefficiency to such a degree that we actually accepted it as the norm. It is only when these inefficiencies are removed that we realize just how great a burden they've been. The changes we have made are often subtle, but the cumulative impact of all these little changes has significantly improved efficiency and quality of life within the practice.

At MGH's Back Bay primary-care practice, the clinical staff members took Mrs. Grant's experience to heart and committed themselves to a simple doctrine: no ambiguity in work design and no workarounds of problems when they are seen. The staff members started by shadowing one another, with the practice manager shadowing the medical director and a licensed nurse practitioner tailing a medical assistant (MA). The shadows took minute-by-minute notes about what factors caused a disruption in the flow of work. In four hours, they together found nearly 300 instances in which the doctor and the MA had to work around a problem. Armed with those insights, they made it a weekly ritual to peel items off the list. The results included halving the distance the medical assistant had to walk each day, increasing the time per visit that the physician was in the exam room with patients, and decreasing the number of interruptions.

They then applied the same approach to patient scheduling. Rather than contend with the fact that some patients were allotted too little time and others too much, doctors started tracking how much time was actually needed and what patient characteristics drove that need. Then, secretaries, doctors, and nurses developed an interview script for front-desk employees so that they could better determine the amount of time a patient needed for his or her next appointment. Rather than a one-size-fits-all standard appointment length in which too little time was allocated, forcing the doctor to run late or the patient to leave prematurely, they gave themselves the flexibility to match the time provided with the time needed.

The successes at Back Bay and Revere are significant examples because primary care is a critical link (but often the missing link) in the American health-care system. Good primary preventive care keeps people well so that they do not need other forms of care. For those with illnesses that cannot be cured and have to be managed, such as asthma or diabetes, good chronic care can greatly improve the quality of a patient's life while avoiding expensive and often ineffective acute (hospital) care. In reality, our health-care system often undermines primary care and is therefore hard on patients and providers alike. Patients have trouble gaining access to practices in many areas, and primary-care doctors work long hours for far less pay than specialists such as dermatologists and plastic surgeons. Part of the cost of poor-quality health care is the toll that working in broken systems takes on doctors, nurses, pharmacists, technicians, aides, administrators, and others. Like the Big Three autoworkers I described in Chapter 3, these health-care workers have to go to work every day knowing that to do what they aspire to do, they will be firefighting, working around problems, and depending on their own and their colleagues' beyond-the-call-of-duty efforts just to keep frustrating situations from becoming tragic ones. And they still know that no amount of heroism will ever be enough.

All the success stories described above turned on an organization's decision to (1) switch from managing functions in isolation to managing the provision of care as a coherent, integrated start-to-finish process and (2) switch from making do when problems are discovered to designing work so problems are immediately visible, swarming those problems when they occur, and involving those who are affected by a problem in solving them and improving their own work processes. Let's watch this approach in action in the realm of acute care.

Case: Putting an End to Hospital-Acquired Infections

The medical staff at Allegheny General Hospital (AGH) focused on the problem of bloodstream infections related to central lines, which are catheters snaked into a vein in order to deliver medication very quickly into the bloodstream. These infections add $3,700 to $29,000 to the cost of care for patients who become ill. Much worse, they kill 14,000 to 28,000 patients a year in the United States. Allegheny General's chief of medicine, Rick Shannon, and his colleagues wondered whether a systems approach similar to that of companies such as Alcoa and Toyota would allow AGH to eliminate central-line infections entirely.

Allegheny General started by reviewing the medical records of every patient who had passed through its intensive-care and cardiac critical-care units in fiscal year 2003. They wanted to determine which factors had caused individual central-line infections and use those discoveries as the basis for process improvement.

Their effort had two surprising results. First, the medical records said little about what caused infections. Although the records documented the treatments that had been ordered and those that had been carried out, they did not capture the subtleties that cause infection, such as inadequate hand hygiene, a catheter accidentally draped across a ventilator tube, or shared equipment that has not been properly sanitized. The second surprise was that AGH's rate of central-line infections was far higher and the consequences for patients far worse than they had realized. AGH had been recording infections related to subclavian placements—catheters snaked past the collarbone and the sternum—but had not been tracking the more infection-prone femoral placements—catheters snaked through the groin. They also had not counted AGH patients who had been readmitted to other institutions for treatment of central-line-related infections. AGH's infection rate was double what had been assumed. More significant were the human costs: Among the 1,753 patients admitted to AGH's intensive care units in 2003, 37 patients had been infected, of whom 19 died.

Realizing the limited utility of retrospective reviews of aggregated data, AGH created a central-line team with the mission of observing every central-line placement and every incident of line maintenance to see the microbreaks in routine that might lead to an infection. They found that doctors, nurses, the materials distribution staff, and others were working hard, but in isolation from one another. Each work "element" was not well-integrated into the system, leading to problem after problem. There were problems rooted in ambiguous assignment of responsibility (pathway problems, as discussed in Chapter 6), unreliable handoffs and exchanges of information (connection problems), and individual work methods that were not dependable. The one point on which all could agree was the desired output of the process for placing and maintaining lines: No one should be harmed.

In terms of the system breakdowns, the team observed a resident who was on call in the intensive-care unit (ICU) placing a femoral line in a patient, a particularly surprising move given all the attention that had been given to the risk and cost of infections. True, it is easier to insert a central line on the inside of the thigh—a femoral line—than near the collarbone—a subclavian line. There is less twisting and turning required. But in the long run, a femoral line is much more dangerous because the inner thigh is a much "dirtier" part of the body than the neck; there are many microbes in that area that are happy to take advantage of a puncture in the skin and invade the body.

This is basic information that any medical resident knows. Why, then, had this resident placed a femoral line rather than a subclavian line? Certainly, he was neither lazy nor stupid. Rather, he was forced into a dilemma. Those responsible for creating training rotations, and those responsible for scheduling residents within a rotation, had done so without taking into account the specific needs in that particular unit. They had done their work, but without a clear understanding of how it fit into the system as a whole. He hadn't had specific training in how to place central lines. He did his best under the circumstances, using the femoral placement because he did not feel confident doing a more difficult subclavian one.

However, the problem went beyond that. If the femoral line had subsequently been replaced with a subclavian line, there would at least have been less time for microbes to take advantage of it. But that was unlikely to happen; there was no one specifically designated to move lines from high-risk to low-risk locations. The more experienced specialists in intensive-care medicine were the obvious choice, but there were poor mechanisms for the night shift to indicate to the day shift that a line should be replaced. In other words, the connection—the handoff of responsibility (in the form of information about high-risk lines) from one shift to the next—was underdesigned.

Idiosyncratic and plentiful as those problems were, once they were seen, they could be solved. AGH developed training for all residents rotating through the ICU and adjusted its schedules to make sure every shift had someone capable of placing subclavian catheters. While those responses were being developed, every day shift had a person responsible for replacing femoral lines with subclavian lines (the specialists mentioned above) and the team worked out a set of simple signals to indicate when such work had to be done.

Once a central line is put in, it needs to be maintained. The line itself needs to be checked for kinks, the puncture needs to be checked for infection, and so on. And here, too, the team observed breakdowns as nurses tried to do their work but couldn't find bandages, gloves, gowns, or hand sanitizer where and when they needed them. Rather than continue the traditional nursing practices of hunting and hoarding or "being careful" (for example, changing a bandage while standing on tiptoe as far from the patient as possible because you can't find the gown you should be wearing when you work close to a patient), the team worked to integrate nursing and materials distribution into a reliable system to help determine what items were needed in what quantity, in what form, and at what location by whom and when, to ensure that catheter-wound sites could be cleaned and rebandaged without running the risk of infection.

No one ever found a silver-bullet solution to the problem of infections. Rather, the line team and the ICU staff made dozens of changes in the way they did their work and the results of their 90-day effort were spectacular. In 2004, the number of patients and the severity of their conditions increased at Allegheny General, but the number of infected patients dropped from 37 to 6 and the number of deaths plummeted from 19 to 1. The record of success continued through 2005 and 2006 (see Table 11-2).

Case: Stress-Testing and Improving Medication Administration

In the previous example, problems occurred often enough that it was possible to see them just by watching the system in action. The University of Pittsburgh Medical Center (UPMC) South Side hospital took this approach a step further by creating a high-speed mock-up of their own pharmacy in order to see problems that would be much harder to spot in

Table 11-2 Eliminating Central-Line Infections at Allegheny General Hospital

	FY 03	FY 04 Year 1	FY 05 Year 2	FY 06 Year 3 (10 months)
Intensive-care-unit admissions	1,753	1,798	1,829	1,832
Central lines employed	1,110	1,321	1,487	1,898
Line days	4,687	5,052	6,705	7,716
Infections	49	6	11	3
Patients infected	37	6	11	3
Rates (infections/ 1,000 line days)	10.5	1.2	1.6	0.39
Deaths	19 (51%)	1 (16%)	2 (18%)	0 (0%)

real time. South Side had decided to deal with the persistent problem of missing meds: the disruption caused by nurses going to the place where medications were stored in the nursing unit, only to discover that what was needed was not there. The subsequent waste of time and emotional energy to restore the system by chasing down a pharmacist to chase down the pill was extraordinary. I remember watching one nurse finding that a med was out of place. She called the pharmacist who was to have dispensed the medication, but that person was not in the room. Another pharmacist did his best to track down the order, but to no avail. After an hour of churning, the original pharmacist returned to the department. In fact, the medication was not missing; it was stocked out and on order from the distributor. Obviously, there were several problems here. The first, of course, was the problem of stockouts and the second was the difficulty of making visible the fact that the medication, though late, was on the way. Even in the absence of the drug, that information would have saved hours of wasted nursing and pharmacy time.

Fatigued and frustrated by situations of that type occurring too often, the staff members challenged themselves with the following question: Why isn't medication administration *ideal?* That is, why can't the pharmacy deliver one order at a time when it is requested and when it is needed, without defects or delays?

They had some insight into the problem. Medication administration was done in batches. Physicians made their rounds early in the day, with occasional follow-ups if patients' conditions changed. Medication orders would be collected and delivered periodically to the pharmacy and entered by the pharmacists, who would look for potential problems with dosages, interactions, and allergies. Orders would accumulate until the afternoon. The next day the pharmacy staff would begin filling the orders, assembling the proper mix and volume for each patient. This was done by the afternoon, at which point a "delivery tech" would run things to their point of use in the hospital. There was a separate "first orders" process for getting at least one dose to a patient after an order was written, but that did not account for the bulk of the deliveries and, anyway, it was in effect a redundant workaround solution to the problem that the main process was too balky to be relied on for speed. Because so much time passed before medications were delivered, there were double workarounds: getting additional meds to fill the gap between when the first order drop-off was made and when the regular deliveries occurred and returning medications to the pharmacy because patients' conditions had changed in the meantime.

To get to the root of the problem, the staff set up a prototype process. They took a real pharmacist, a real pharmacy tech, and real orders—although from the previous day—and tried to fill those orders one at a time (one every three minutes, as it worked out), delivering them to a cardboard box rather than to the unit. With everything in place, they started the test, stopping every time the pharmacy team could not maintain the pace and investigating why they could not. There were printer jams, stockouts, excessive walking distances, and so forth. Within a few hours, they discovered dozens of factors that made keeping up impossible. Some were easy fixes, such as storing drugs in accordance with how frequently they were used rather than alphabetically. Others were more difficult, such as changing the time that deliveries were made to nursing units so as not to interfere with meals and patient hygiene. Together, these changes had a large cumulative effect.

Delivering one order at a time ultimately was not feasible because the doctors did their rounds within a narrow period in the morning and the evening—before or after their scheduled surgery and clinical hours—and some units were quite far from the pharmacy. Still, there were remarkable gains. Before, a whole day's worth of orders would not be delivered until the next day. Now, every order was being delivered no more than two hours after it was placed. The rate of missing meds fell 88 percent, search time went down 60 percent, stockouts were cut by 85 percent, and the need to dispose of intravenous medications that had been mixed but not used was reduced significantly.

Case: Stopping the Presurgical Madness

It used to be that on a typical day, 40 patients or more came to the West Penn Allegheny Hospital ambulatory surgery unit. The staff made heroic efforts to have the patients ready to go whenever the surgical team was ready to take them. The patients, on the other hand, spent hours waiting for their surgery, wearing their embarrassing hospital gowns. But after some months of high-velocity effort, the situation there was entirely different, as can be seen in Table 11-3.

The difference between the before and after conditions was due to Gloria, the nurse in charge of presurgical nursing. Having heard fellow Pittsburgh resident and Alcoa CEO Paul O'Neill's admonition that the way to get close to zero injuries at Alcoa was to see problems, solve problems, and share what was learned, Gloria had an epiphany: "I always thought I was a problem solver," she confessed. "But then I realized I had been 'solving' the same problem every day for 20 years." She decided that enough was enough. She declared to her staff that, starting the following Monday, she would not help them work around problems as in the past. Instead, she wanted them to call her immediately when they experienced a problem so that she could help swarm it and solve it and it would not recur, needing to be solved again every day for another 20 years. There was an important qualification. She understood that, at

Table 11-3 Presurgical Nursing at West Penn Allegheny

Metric	Before	After
Time between signing in and starting registration	Up to 2 hours	0
Time patients spent registering	12 minutes to 1 hour	3 minutes
Time spent assembling patients' charts	9 hours each day	2.25 hours
Number of charts with unstamped pages	35	Less than 1
Nurses' time wasted as a result each day	70 minutes	Negligible
Number of gowned patients waiting on chairs in hallway	4 to 7 at any given time	0
Time spent waiting in gowns in public	25 minutes on average	0
Number of patients whose lab results are incomplete	7 out of 42	0
Availability of supplies	Some unavailable; others overstocked but past expiration	What is needed is available when, where, to whom, and in the quantity required
Number of unnecessary blood-bank reports issued	10 to 11 per day	0

Toyota, a fundamental part of the work of team leaders and group leaders is problem solving and process improvement. Yet she knew that she could not make an abrupt change, flipping

180 degrees from working around problems to solving them. Even half a day would be too much. After some reflection, she decided to start with a 15-minute period in the afternoon (2:00 to 2:15), after most of the surgeries had begun.

At 2:00 p.m. on Monday, Gloria stopped her usual frantic fire-fighting, stationed herself in the center of the unit, and waited. That Monday was like any other Monday, with the normal need to chase down lab results and supplies, yet no one reported a problem. On Tuesday, Gloria reexplained the concept, but again there were no problems reported. On Wednesday, a nurse came running to Gloria with a problem. Eager to rush to it while it was still hot, Gloria was disappointed, though not terribly surprised, to find that the problem already had been worked around.

It was not until the next Monday that someone brought a live problem to her. In taking a patient's history, a nurse had found that the chart was missing forms and had other defects. Immediately, Gloria huddled with the secretary who built the charts every day to help establish what it meant for a chart to be defect-free and investigate what it was about the job that made creating a defect-free chart so difficult. Needless to say, they did not resolve that on Monday, and even Tuesday's and Wednesday's 15 minutes were not sufficient. However, by pounding away at the problem day after day, they developed myriad countermeasures: how to organize the workstation, how to access documents, how to create consent forms, from where to gather patient information and previous lab results. Chart building went from taking nine hours a day to taking two, and nurses no longer needed to fix broken charts on the fly. More to the point, they had freed so much time that it was like having an extra secretary in the unit and a lot of additional nursing time. Now Gloria was free 30 minutes a day to see a problem and solve a problem rather than helping with workarounds. Registration popped up as the next problem to solve and when the dust had settled, the unit ended up with the equivalent of yet one more secretary. Within a few months, a unit that had been hard on patients and staff alike was functioning like a well-tuned machine. The key was taking that first step of breaking the workaround habit—even if only for 15 minutes a day, during a slow time—solving problems, stabilizing and improving the process, and gaining bundles of time for nursing the patients rather than nursing a broken process.

Case: Total Dedication to High-Velocity Health Care

There are many health care providers testing the waters, experimenting with managing the complex processes needed to deliver care in the same fashion as the world's greatest organizations. A few have taken the plunge. One is Seattle's Virginia Mason Medical Center (VMMC), a 300-bed teaching hospital that employs 5,400 people, has 400 doctors, admits 16,000 patients a year, and has more than 1 million outpatient visits. Struggling with problems of staff retention, quality, safety, and cost, VMMC's leadership got interested in the Toyota Production System in 2001 when they started learning about the great results local businesses were getting by upgrading the way they managed their complex work systems.

VMMC dipped its toes in the water with a few pilot projects. Then, in 2002, the hospital's chairman and president, along with its senior administrative and medical leadership, made a two-week visit to Japan. They visited factories, worked on the line briefly, and participated in an improvement project at a Toyota affiliate. They were blown away by the discipline with which work was done and the flexibility and agility with which it was improved and adapted with fluid grace. Upon their return, VMMC's leadership made a commitment to provide the same high-quality work environment to their staff and the same quality of service to their patients that they had experienced in Japan. They also made a commitment to retain all employees; they didn't want people to conclude that finding ways to accomplish more work with less effort would be rewarded with a layoff.

VMMC began training *everyone* on the staff, from frontline workers to the most senior executives and even members of the hospital's board. Then it tackled head-on the coupled problems we saw in the Mrs. Grant tragedy: operating complex processes as if managing the functional pieces were sufficient and tolerating (even encouraging) workarounds when the system was crying out about the flaws in its design. To complement the deep clinical expertise in its various departments, Virginia Mason created a "*kaizen* promotion office" as a place to develop expertise in process management; in other words, it had its medical professionals develop their expertise within functional specialties (the vertical perspective to which we referred in earlier chapters) while home-growing expertise in the horizontal perspective of crafting high-performing boundary-spanning care-delivery processes.

These process experts have led hundreds of rapid-improvement projects, attending to sick processes with the urgency that traditionally was reserved for attending to sick people. To ensure that care-related problems did not remain unaddressed, VMMC instituted its Patient Safety Alert System. When an employee notices that a process has an urgent condition—a failure or aberration that might lead to patient harm—that employee has the right *and the responsibility* to report the problem on a 24/7 hotline, invoking a drop-and-run commitment from the department chief and vice president to swarm the situation, stop the process if necessary, and ensure that the situation does not deteriorate further or recur. (In other words, just what happens when a patient has an urgent condition and a doctor or nurse calls a code.) To fulfill its commitment to managing work so that problems are seen when and where they occur, the senior leadership does safety walkarounds, seeing for themselves how processes really operate rather than how they are supposed to operate and creating more opportunities for staff to report the difficulties, impediments, obstacles, and inconveniences that compromise their best efforts to provide perfect care. Virginia Mason has enjoyed the financial benefits of greater efficiency—such as eliminating budgeted construction projects, as mentioned above—and its patients have had better clinical experiences, as with migraine management and a host of other conditions.

Process Management as a Problem of Medical Education

I have already offered several examples of how the frameworks presented in *Chasing the Rabbit* apply to much more than the manufacturing operations from which it originated. We saw in

Chapter 5 that they can be used to understand, diagnose, and improve a product-development process (Pratt & Whitney) and a service process (Avenue A), not to mention the nonprofit and very dangerous work of the navy nuclear propulsion. We saw in Chapter 6 how well the framework for process design can be applied to workplace training. We have been seeing in this chapter how it applies to another very complex service process—health care. Now I would like to show how useful it is for understanding a process about as far from manufacturing as you can get—medical education.

Remember my friend Mark Schmidhofer, mentioned in Chapter 3, whose long medical training did not address the management responsibilities thrust upon him as a specialist in a hospital? Not only does an American medical education fail to include training in managing processes, one could argue that it is not even managed as a process itself. Yet it certainly is a process—a sequence of steps intended to produce certain results. As a process it has been criticized for its cost, its length, and the mismatch between what medical students are taught and what new doctors need to know. My colleagues Elizabeth Armstrong of Harvard Medical School and Marie Mackey, at the time a researcher at Harvard Business School, and I decided to examine the medical educational process with the same framework/discipline I have been describing throughout this book, starting with Mr. Ohba's questions: What results or outputs is the system meant to achieve? Who is responsible for performing what sequence of steps to achieve those objectives? How are handoffs managed across the connections that link individual steps? What methods are used within a step to achieve success? We also asked: For every level of specification, are there built-in tests to indicate when the system or process is failing?

We discovered that medical education is underdesigned in comparison with the system design and operation criteria of Toyota and other high-velocity organizations. In other words, the preparation for doctoring is not even as well-thought-out to achieve its ostensible aims as the training for an assembly-line worker at a Toyota plant (described in Chapter 6). Of course, a medical student is intensely trained. The question we were left with was whether the training was as effective as possible, done with the least waste and the least risk to patients and students. Let's take a look.

When we surveyed medical-education reform proposals, we found that they focused on expanding the curriculum with courses such as medical ethics (adding steps to the pathway) or changing the teaching approach from lecturing to case studies (a change in the method within a process or pathway step). And despite concerns about cost and duration, some reformers think a medical education should last even longer. For Armstrong, Mackey, and me, such proposals set off warning bells. This is a classic trade-off that assumes that we are getting as much yield as possible from the current investment and therefore have to give up something good (time and money) for another good (quality of educational experience). It is just the sort of thinking—in order to have perfect safety, we'll have to take a hit in productivity—that Alcoa soundly rejected. Our examinations of exceptionally high-performing organizations would lead us to wonder: What's to stop us from getting more for less? Why can't a medical education be shorter, cheaper, *and* better?

To answer that question, Armstrong, Mackey, and I looked at the first four years of medical education, leading up to the M.D. degree, and wrote a paper about a representative student, "Emily Wilson." What we see from her experience is that she—along with her peers and instructors—is subject to a system in which individual educational experiences are not managed as pieces of an interdependent system, leaving those responsible for the pieces (teachers and students alike) to cobble together coherent approaches in an ad hoc and very suboptimal fashion. This process seemed less analogous to the training at Toyota, Indiana, than to the process chaos Avenue A experienced in its early days.

Like other students during her first and second years at medical school, Emily Wilson took basic science courses such as anatomy, physiology, biochemistry, epidemiology, microbiology, pathology, and genetics—and also received some teaching about the doctor-patient relationship—as preparation for her clinical training. Her third and fourth years were quite different. Training was done in teaching hospitals, where students were to leave behind the conceptual frame of the classroom and instead learn by seeing the practical reality of patient care. In her third year, Wilson had clerkships in internal medicine, obstetrics, pediatrics, psychiatry, and surgery, delaying family medicine until her fourth year. In contrast, the sequence for one of her classmates was psychiatry and family medicine followed by surgery, pediatrics, and obstetrics, with internal medicine at the end. A third had a completely different sequence. The fact that the clerkships were at several different hospitals added variation, as did the fact that, regardless of the rotation, Wilson was never teamed with fellow students with whom she had trained previously. Much of the training depended on a downward flow of direction and critique—students reporting to residents, residents reporting to attending physicians—but there was little continuity. Students' rotations were not synched with those of the residents or those of the attending physicians, so the students frequently changed instructors in midstream.

Thus, as Wilson cycled through the system, the people responsible for her training and evaluation came and went, not only between rotations but during them. The fourth year repeated this pattern, only more so. For their fourth year, medical students plan clinical rotations on the basis of the specialty they want to pursue and the experiences, grades, and evaluations they will need in order to be accepted by a desirable residency program. It was hard to have confidence in the process. For instance, in an anesthesiology rotation, Wilson had to shadow a different physician each day (there were 45 in the department, plus 24 residents). In a lecture-based radiology clerkship, there were different lecturers each session and attendance was never taken, let alone practice provided.

Emily Wilson's experience (and therefore the experience of her instructors) was echoed in the stories of 10 other current and former students from seven medical schools whom we interviewed. Interviewing medical educators revealed similar patterns and themes. When we shared Wilson's case with 68 participants in a program for medical educators at Harvard Medical School—participants who came from 31 institutions and 16 of whom came from outside North America—64 of the 68 agreed that Wilson's experience could have been that of one of their own students.

When we reviewed Wilson's case, we could not help noticing the role that chance played in what she learned, how well she learned it, and how she was evaluated. Because clerkships in the third year were assigned on the basis of room in a department, without regard to sequence, there were 720 different ways to complete the six requirements. In a class of 150, it was unlikely that any two students would encounter the same material in the same sequence. The fact that clerkships were at different hospitals, with residents and attending physicians changing according to their own schedules, increased the randomness of the process. The unsynchronized staffing schedule meant that responsibility for training within a rotation was somewhat arbitrary as well.

As tough as this might have been on the students, imagine what it must have been like for the educators. Say, for example, that you are in charge of an obstetrics rotation. Will the students have had any exposure to internal medicine or surgery, key foundations for your discipline, so that you can teach more specialized material and skills, or will you be responsible for teaching your students the basics? As for preparing students for the next rotation—forget it. Each one will be heading off to a different subject. What, then, are your options? You could treat all the students as if they knew nothing. Some instructors are known to do that. You could try to build on what each student has learned already, different in each case, which would require extensive customization. You could simply teach what you considered important in your field, assuming that those students who get it are the smart one and those who don't are the dumb ones. But do any of these sound like a good way to train a doctor?

In short, when we looked at medical education from a process perspective, we saw no clarity of output, an unpredictable learning sequence, unreliable handoffs with no predictability in regard to what students know coming into a process step or what they will have to master before they move on, and lack of consistency in how training will occur within a rotation. We quickly realized that a disjointed approach virtually guarantees the problems so commonly attributed to medical education, such as excessive time and cost and lack of consistency and quality (the problems plaguing those Toyota competitors who haven't invested as much in process excellence as they might). The solution, though, is not more investment but a more holistic investment. If that existed, it would be possible to define acceptable and unacceptable progress along the way rather than evaluating students on effort, personality, and other impressions not directly related to professional performance. It would also be far easier to recognize sooner rather than later when students were struggling, so that a remedy might take minutes, hours, or days rather than weeks, months, or semesters.

MEDICAL EDUCATION AS A PROCESS WITH AN OUTPUT

I hope I have convinced you that there is much to be gained by looking at a wide range of activities—from seat assembly to medical school—through the process framework I have been using. Here is one more observation on the "process" of medical education.

Much of education, medical or otherwise, consists of training that is based on a schedule: A certain number of hours, days, weeks, or months is devoted to a topic, and then an evaluation is done to determine a grade. This is a "fixed input" and "variable output" approach. What is invested (time) is set; what is generated (skill) varies unpredictably and therefore requires subsequent inspection, sorting, and possible rejection and waste (see Figure 11-1). And, to borrow a phrase, a medical education is a mighty expensive thing to have to reject and waste.

For Toyota, training is a matter of "variable input" (time and coaching may vary) but "fixed output." (See Figure 11-2.) As with every other process, the output of any training—and of each stage of the training—is specified. Someone advances from one stage to the next only when he or she has passed the threshold. A well-specified training process with built-in tests will not deliver a half-trained person any more than a well-run assembly line will deliver a car with two wheels and half an engine. (Even if the line produced such a monster, it would not deliver it to anyone.)

Figure 11-1 Fixed inputs, variable outputs

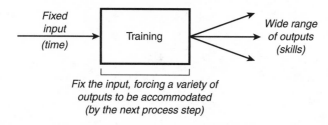

Fixed input (time)

Training

Wide range of outputs (skills)

Fix the input, forcing a variety of outputs to be accommodated (by the next process step)

Figure 11-2 Variable inputs, defined outputs

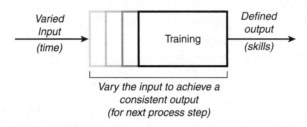

Looked at in this light, a problem with our medical education system is that its output is not very clearly specified—one can assume that an M.D. will know certain things, but there is much else that he or she may or may not know—and is certainly not specified in such a way as to fulfill many of the responsibilities of a practicing physician, inside or outside a hospital. And yet, there's no reason that the output of a medical education could not be much better specified and no reason why young doctors could not emerge ready, not only to apply their particular skills, but to take part in the much larger and more complex process of delivering medical care that is not only very good but absolutely safe. Probably cheaper, too.

CHAPTER 12

CONCLUSION

Why do some organizations outdistance the field while their peers and competitors struggle to keep up? The difference lies in the different approaches the leaders and the strugglers take to managing complex systems in which many people work collaboratively toward a common goal.

Most organizations are hindered by a structural problem: They manage their functions individually, not as steps in a well-integrated process. Each function does its job and somehow the whole thing comes together—except when it doesn't. At the same time, most organizations are also hindered by a dynamic problem: When problems crop up, many of them are treated—that is, ignored—as unavoidable noise. ("Ah, that darn thing never works." "Don't worry, we never get those on time.") This is a dynamic problem in that the organization is *not* dynamic; problems do not provoke change.

The leaders, which I have been characterizing as high-velocity organizations, have a different structural and dynamic approach. Though they invest heavily in the functional expertise they need in order to be world class, those functional specialties are always managed with an eye to their role in an overall process—delivering pills to a patient safely or delivering defect-free beds to customers or delivering well-trained new hires to an assembly line. But what separates the leaders from the followers even more is a dynamic difference. For the leaders, the daily chatter of imperfect systems is not unavoidable noise to be griped about or ignored; it is a stream of messages telling them where they can and must improve. These organizations know that they cannot conceptually design or plan their way to perfection, but they know that they can discover near-perfection by continually applying the four capabilities I have described all through this book.

What can great companies do to catch up to the market leaders and win the race? The experience of Bob Dallis, the automotive leader who restarted his career at Toyota, provides some clues.

Some months after Dallis had returned to the United States from Japan and begun his regular work, he had a chance to talk with a senior Japanese Toyota executive, who asked how his work was proceeding. Dallis explained that things were both good and bad. On the good side, he had greater facility in managing operations than he had ever had before. The bad news? When Dallis had been at a Big Three auto company, he had spent a lot of time learning the nuances of shop-floor process-management tools such as how to calculate the pitch of a *heijunka* box and how to determine the number of cards in a *kanban*-based pull system. Now things seemed a little too simple—just a systematic approach to designing and operating systems, a simple set of rules for problem solving and improvement, a clear way to share learning, and a well-defined role as a manager. Was he missing something?

"Bob," said the executive, "you have to understand that the Toyota Production System is much like golf." Not seeing the connection, Dallis protested, "But golf is very difficult." "No, it isn't," he was corrected. "It is a remarkably simple game." This debate about simple versus difficult continued until the executive asked Dallis to describe the last time he had played golf: what day, what time, what he wore, the route he took to get to the course, and so forth. Finally, he had walked and talked Dallis up to the first tee.

"And what did you do then?"

"Well, I played the hole."

"No, what did you *do*?" Dallis was asked again.

"Well, I took a ball from my bag, picked a driver, and hit it toward the hole."

"Did you get it in?"

"Of course not; it was par five."

"What did you do then, go home?"

"No! I found the ball and used a driver."

"Did you get it in?"

"No!"

"What next?"

"I found the ball and used a different club . . . and then a wedge . . . and then a putter."

You can see the pattern developing. This executive walked and talked Dallis through several holes shot by shot. Finally, he said, "See, it is a simple game. Take a ball, put it on the ground, hit it with a stick toward a hole, and keep repeating that until you are done." Dallis protested, "But it is really hard. There are traps and hazards, roughs and fast greens, in and out of bounds, obstacles, wind, and all sorts of other things." "But

Bob, aside from the ball, the club, and the hole, what is there?" Dallis tried to protest again until the executive gently interrupted and corrected him: "Bob, I said it was a simple game with simple rules. I never claimed it did not require a lot of practice."

On the topic of adhering to a simple rule, here is one more reflection:

Chapter 6 described the *jidoka* concept pioneered by the late Sakichi Toyoda. When a thread broke on a loom, the machine ought to stop and identify where the break had occurred so the operator wouldn't waste her time unwittingly doing pointless work. And in general, work should be designed with a built-in test that immediately tells the worker when and where a problem occurs (part of Capability 1), so as to unleash the creative dynamic of problem solving (Capability 2) and knowledge sharing (Capability 3).

The Toyoda family has a museum which, needless to say, contains many textile and automotive pieces. But of all the milestone products the company has created, the one chosen as the museum's centerpiece is a large loom designed and built by Sakichi Toyoda himself. It is right in the entrance atrium, and no matter what route you take through the museum, you cannot help but see it.

I remember being impressed at first by the loom's technical complexity. On most looms, the shuttle weaves back and forth, side to side, creating a sheet of fabric, but on this loom, the shuttle weaves in a circle, creating a cylinder of fabric. Still operating and in good repair, with fabric rising out of it like a serene plume of steam from a hot spring, it is aesthetically appealing as well as technologically fascinating.

Then I got around to reading the sign. This loom is one of a kind. Sakichi Toyoda never made a duplicate. Why not? Because he never figured out how to get the first one to stop when a thread broke.

In light of all the successes that Toyoda and his family had achieved, I was perplexed that the family would choose a failure—the founder's failure, no less—as the centerpiece of its museum. Finally, I came to recognize that the loom doesn't symbolize a failure; it represents a remarkable success. True, the machine itself is imperfect. But the very fact that there is only one of it perfectly embodies Sakichi Toyoda's commitment to *jidoka* and the commitment to *jidoka* he instilled in his company, a commitment that has lasted over generations. In his eyes, a machine, no matter how elegant, that would not warn its operator of an error could not be put to use. It was not reliable, and to pretend otherwise would be wrong. The many examples of self-correcting systems that we examined in this book, and the myriad others within Toyota and other high-velocity organizations, are fuller testimony to the value and continuity of that commitment.

Before we part, let's consider how to create an organization with a similar commitment. We've had many examples with Bob Dallis's mentors, Pratt & Whitney, Avenue A, Alcoa, the naval reactor program, and the medical practices in Chapter 11. High-velocity management is a skill and, like any other skill, it requires practice. Here is how to begin:

- Start small. Find a process or system that is reasonably tightly bounded so that the number of people learning together is relatively small. That way the chance for shared reflection will be relatively high. Think in terms of the local *jishuken*, discussed in Chapter 8, which were the necessary precursors for company and inter-company collaboration.

- Solve a problem that really matters. Don't pick an ancillary process about which no one cares, yourself included. When you start to score gains, you want people to sit up and take notice. Allegheny General Hospital went after central-line infections, West Penn Allegheny focused on operating-room delays, and Alcoa started with workplace risk.

- Don't think too much, but do a lot. That's where the real learning takes place. Despite all the golf videos and manuals available, no one ever mastered golf without hitting bucket after bucket of practice balls on the putting green and the driving range.

- Start with a small footprint but a long leg. Although you should start with a fairly small group and a fairly well-defined problem, as I said above, make sure that every layer of management between the shop floor (or its equivalent) and you is involved. After all, what you are trying to master is a fundamentally different set of roles and relationships, as made vivid in Chapter 10.

- Stay safe. Since you will certainly make errors as you learn, be sure that your experiment is safe and that it will not imperil your standing or put your organization at risk.

- Don't wait until you have enough free time. You never will. Budget time every day for designing a work process to see its problems, solving those problems, and sharing what you learn with others to whom the new insights may be useful, just like Gloria did at West Penn Allegheny.

Here is one last thought:

The title of Philip Crosby's seminal book says it all: *Quality Is Free.* Crosby, along with W. Edwards Deming and Joseph Juran, prophets of the quality movement, confronted conventional wisdom directly, uncompromisingly, and unapologetically. It was thought then that quality always has a cost. What you could get out of a system was limited by the money you had put into it. To get something more out of a system, you had to either spend more or give up something else. Crosby and the others showed that this belief was rooted in a perverse combination of arrogance and pessimism. It is arrogant to believe that anything we have created cannot be improved. It is pessimistic to believe that we are incapable of ever improving something that is flawed.

Deming, Juran, Crosby, Rickover, O'Neill, Toyoda, and all the others we have encountered in this book rejected that arrogant pessimism for a humble optimism. They were humble in recognizing that no matter what the investment of time, effort, and resources, what we create is riddled with imperfections. Their optimism was that no matter how flawed, with an energetic, open-minded commitment to discovery, we can always do better.

We ignore the truth of their message at our own peril. When individuals, groups, organizations, and societies fall back on that conventional wisdom, the dominant question is no longer *how*—how can something be done better?—but *what*—what must we sacrifice to get what we need? The language of trade-offs is found everywhere in political debates. In an otherwise affluent society, we have 40 million people who lack medical coverage, those who do have it must pay a crippling cost, and even for those who are not set back by the cost, the care may turn out to cause harm. In the language of trade-offs, we are faced with a decision: Do we provide more care to more people at great expense, or do we deny care because the additional burden is not affordable? The doctors, nurses, pharmacists, and hospital administrators we've met in this book have already shown that the language of trade-offs is a cop-out.

This is also true in the world of manufacturing. The idea that cars can be safe, reliable, high-performing, and tailored to a multitude of customer needs once seemed fantastic. Now it is the norm, the least one would expect of a car. Does it seem fantastic to think that we could live comfortably while still leaving a lighter footprint on the natural world? Of course we can. We just haven't quite figured out how. Yet.

The same thing is true wherever else we look. We do not need conceptual, hypothetical prognostication to say that we can do better. The empirical evidence is already available and irrefutable. Certain organizations already do much more with much less than their peers and competitors can conceive. It's not magic. What they have done, you can do.

It just takes practice.

REFERENCES

Abegglen, James C.; and Stalk, George, Jr. *Kaisha: The Japanese Corporation*, Basic Books, 1985.

Adams, D. "Student Debt Helps Drive Students into Specialty Matches," *American Medical News*, 46:10-2, 2003.

Adler, P. S.; Goldoftas, B., and Levine, D. I. "Ergonomics, Employee Involvement, and the Toyota Production System: A Case Study of NUMMI's 1993 Model Introduction," *Industrial & Labor Relations Review*, 50:3, page 416.

Adler, P. S.; Goldoftas, B.; and Levine, D. I. "Flexibility versus Efficiency? A Case Study of Model Changeovers in the Toyota Production System," *Organization Science* 10-1, January–February 1999, pages 43–68.

Argyris, Chris. *On Organizational Learning*, 2nd ed., Blackwell Publishing, 1999.

Argyris, Chris; and Schön, Donald. *Organizational Learning*, Addison-Wesley, 1978.

Armstrong, Elizabeth G.; Mackey, Marie; and Spear, Steven J. "Medical Education as a Process Managment Problem," *Academic Medicine* 79:8, August 2004, pages 721–728.

Aston, Adam; and Helm, Burt (with Michael Arndt and Amy Barrett). "The Race against Climate Change," *BusinessWeek*, December 12, 2005, pages 58–66.

Barnard, Chester. *The Functions of the Executive*, Harvard University Press, 1968.

Bates, David W. "Unexpected Hypoglycemia in a Critically Ill Patient," *Annals of Internal Medicine* 137, 2002, pages 110–116.

Bates, D. W.; Boyle, D. L.; Vander Vliet, M. B.; Schneider, J.; and Leape, L. "Relationship between Medication Errors and Adverse Drug Effects," *Journal of General Internal Medicine* 10, 1995, pages 199–205.

Berenholtz, S. M.; Pronovost, P. J.; Lipsett, P. A.; et al. "Eliminating Catheter-Related Bloodstream Infections in the Intensive Care Unit," *Critical Care Medicine* 32:10, October 2004, pages 2014–2020.

Berriel-Cass, D.; Adkins, F. W.; Jones, P.; and Fakih, M. G. "Eliminating Noso-comial Infections at Ascension Health," *Joint Commission Journal on Quality and Patient Safety* 32:11, November 2006, pages 612–620.

Bloom, S. W. "Structure and Ideology in Medical Education: An Analysis of Resistance to Change," *Journal of Health and Social Behavior* 29:4, December 1988, pages 294–306.

Bowen, H. Kent. "Chrysler and BMW: Tritec Engine Joint Venture," Harvard Business School Case 600-004.

Bowen, H. Kent; and Purrington, Courtney. "Pratt & Whitney: Engineering Standard Work," Harvard Business School Case 604-013, 2003.

Burns, James MacGregor. *Leadership*, Harper & Row, 1978.

Butler, Kerry; Mollo, Paul; Gale, Jane L.; Rapp, D. A. "Eliminating Adverse Drug Events at Ascension Health," *Joint Commission Journal on Quality and Patient Safety* 33:9, September 2007, pages 527–536.

Chandler, Alfred DuPont, Jr. *The Visible Hand*, Belknap Press of Harvard University Press, 1977.

Chassin, Mark R.; and Becher, Elise C. "The Wrong Patient," *Annals of Internal Medicine* 136, 2002, pages 826–833.

Christensen, Clayton M.; King, Steven; Verlinden, Matt; and Yang, Woodward. "The New Economics of Semiconductor Manufacturing," *IEEE Spectrum* 45:5, May 2008, pages 24–29.

Chu, Kenneth C.; Tarone, Robert E.; Kessler, Larry G.; Ries, Lynn A. G.; Hankey, Benjamin F.; Miller, Banj A.; and Edwards, Brenda K. "Recent Trends in U.S. Breast Cancer Incidence, Survival, and Mortality Rates," *Journal of the National Cancer Institute* 88, 1996, page 21.

Clark, Kim B.; and Margolis, Joshua D. "Workplace Safety at Alcoa (A)," Harvard Business School Case 692-040, 1991, revised 2000.

Cleary, Paul D. "A Hospitalization from Hell: A Patient's Perspective on Quality," *Annals of Internal Medicine* 138, 2003, pages 33–39.

Convis, Gary. "Toyota: Changes and Challenges," presentation, President, Toyota Motor Manufacturing Kentucky, Inc., August 8, 2001. In *The Managment Briefing Seminars*, Grand Traverse Resort and Spa, Traverse City, Michigan.

Crawford, John W.; and Krahn, Steven L. "The Naval Nuclear Propulsion Program: A Brief Case Study in Institutional Constancy," *Public Administration Review* 58(2), March-April 1998.

Crosby, Philip B. *Quality Is Free: The Art of Making Quality Certain*, McGraw-Hill, 1979.

Cusumano, Michael A. *The Japanese Automobile Industry: Technology and Management at Nissan and Toyota*, Harvard University Press, 1989.

Cusumano, Michael A. "Manufacturing Innovation: Lessons from the Japanese Auto Industry," *Sloan Management Review*, Fall 1988.

Deming, W. Edwards. *Out of the Crisis*, MIT Center for Advanced Engineering Study, 1986.

Deming, W. Edwards. *Quality, Productivity, and Competitive Position*, MIT Press, 1982.

Dertouzos, Michael L.; et al. *Made in America: Regaining the Productive Edge*, MIT Press, 1989.

Diamond, Jared. *Guns, Germs, and Steel*, W. W. Norton, 1997.

Duncan, Francis. *Rickover and the Nuclear Navy: The Discipline of Technology*, Naval Institute Press, 1990.

Duncan, Francis. *Rickover: The Struggle for Excellence*, Naval Institute Press, 2001.

Duncan, K. D. "Preventing Pressure Ulcers: The Goal Is Zero," *Joint Commission Journal on Quality and Patient Safety* 33:10, October 2007, pages 605–610.

Enarson, C., and Burg, F. D. "An Overview of Reform Initiatives in Medical Education, 1906 through 1992." *Journal of the American Medical Association* 268:9, 1992, pages 1141–1143.

Ewing, Hella; Bruder, Greg; Baroco, Paul; Hill, M.; Sparkman, L. P. "Eliminating Perioperative Adverse Events at Ascension Health," *Joint Commission Journal on Quality and Patient Safety* 33:5, May 2007, pages 256–266.

Fayol, Henri. *General and Industrial Management*, Pitman, 1949.

Federico, F. "Preventing Harm from High-Alert Medications." *Joint Commission Journal on Quality and Patient Safety* 33:9, September 2007, pages 537–542.

Finocchio, L. J.; Bailiff, M. A.; Grant, R. W.; and O'Neil, E. H. "Professional Competencies in the Changing Health Care System: Physicians' Views on the Importance and Adequacy of Formal Training in Medical School," *Academic Medicine* 70:11, 1995, page 1023.

Fisher, Anne. "American's Most Admired Companies," *Fortune* 157:5, March 17, 2008.

Fishman, Charles. "No Satisfaction at Toyota," *Fast Company* 111, 2007, page 82.

Fitzgerald, J.; Kanter, G.; and Benjamin, E. "Case Study: Preventing Surgical Complications at Baystate Medical Center," *Joint Commission Journal on Quality and Patient Safety* 33:11, November 2007, pages 666–671.

Furman, Cathie; and Caplan, Robert. "Applying the Toyota Production System: Using a Patient Safety Alert System to Reduce Error," *Joint Commission Journal on Quality and Patient Safety*, 33:7, July 2007, pages 376–386.

Garvin, David A. "Quality on the Line," *Harvard Business Review* 61, September-October 1983, pages 64–75.

Gibbons, W.; Shanks, H. T.; Kleinhelter, P.; and Jones, P. "Eliminating Facility-Acquired Pressure Ulcers at Ascension Health." *Joint Commission Journal on Quality and Patient Safety* 32:9, September 2006, pages 488–496.

Godwin, Robert, ed. *Columbia Accident Investigation Board Report*, Vol. 1, Apogee Books, 2003.

Graber, D. R.; Bellack, J. P.; Musham, C.; and O'Neil, E. H. "Academic Deans' Views on Curriculum Content in Medical Schools." *Academic Medicine* 62:11, 1998, pages 911–918.

Griffin, F. A. "Reducing Methicillin-Resistant Staphylococcus aureus (MRSA) Infections," *Joint Commission Journal on Quality and Patient Safety* 33:12, December 2007, pages 726–731.

Griffin, F. A. "Reducing Surgical Complications," *Joint Commission Journal on Quality and Patient Safety* 33:11, November 2007, pages 660–665.

Harwood, Williams. "Filming of Fuel Tank Roam Loss Saved *Discovery* from Big Hit," Spaceflight Now, available online at http://216.92.110.5/shuttle/sts114/050708Challock.

Hayes, Robert H.; and Wheelwright, Steven C. *Restoring Our Competitive Edge*, John Wiley, 1984.

Hayes, Robert H.; Wheelwright, Steven C.; and Clark, Kim B. *Dynamic Manufacturing: Creating the Learning Organization*, Free Press, 1988.

Hendrich, A.; Tersigni, A.R.; Jeffcoat, S.; Barnett, C.J.; Brideau, L.P.; Pryor, D. "The Journey to Zero at Ascension Health: Lessons Learned and Leadership Perspectives," *Joint Commission Journal on Quality and Patient Safety* 33:12, December 2007, pages 739–749.

Hippell, Eric von. "'Sticky Information' and the Locus of Problem Solving: Implications for Innovation," *Management Science* 40:4, April 1994, pages 429–439.

Hippell, Eric von; and Tyrie, Marcie J. "How Learning by Doing Is Done: Problem Identification in Novel Process Equipment," *Research Policy* 24:1, January 1995, pages 1–12.

Hoffer-Gittell, Jody. "Paradox of Coordination and Control," *California Management Review*, Spring 2000.

Hoffer-Gittell, Jody. *The Southwest Airlines Way*, McGraw-Hill, 2003.

Holman, Richard L. "World Wire," *The Wall Street Journal*, February 10, 1997, page A14.

Hua, Vanessa. "Auto Plant Takes to the Air: Alternative to Locked-Out Ports Is Extremely Expensive," *San Francisco Chronicle*, October 8, 2002, page B1.

Jaikumar, Ramachandran; and Bohn, Roger. "A Dynamic Approach to Operations Management: An Alternative to Static Optimization," *International Journal of Production Economics* 27, 1992, pages 265–282.

Jatoi, Ismael; and Miller, Anthony B. "Why Is Breast Cancer Mortality Declining?" *The Lancet Oncology* 4, 2003, pages 251–254.

Johnson, Chalmers A. *MITI and the Japanese Miracle: The Growth of Industrial Policy, 1925–1975*, Stanford University Press, 1982.

Juran, Joseph; and Gryna, Frank M., Jr. *Quality Planning and Analysis*, McGraw-Hill, 1980.

Knight, Malcolm; Loyazo, Norman; and Villanueva, Delano. "The Peace Dividend: Military Spending Cuts and Economic Growth," *World Bank Policy Research*, February 1996, Working Paper No. 1577.

Kohn, Linda T.; Corrigan, Janet M.; and Donaldson, Molla S. (editors). *To Err Is Human: Building a Safer Health System*, National Academy Press, 2000.

Koretz, Gene. "Toting Up the Peace Dividend: Has Military Spending Hit Bottom?" *BusinessWeek*, December 14, 1998, page 26.

Krafcik, John. F. "Triumph of the Lean Production System," *Sloan Management Review* 30:1, 1988.

Lancaster, A.D.; Ayers, A.; Belbot, B.; et al. "Preventing Falls and Eliminating Injury at Ascension Health," *Joint Commission Journal on Quality and Patient Safety* 33:7, July 2007, pages 367–375.

Langdale, L. A.; Schaad, D.; Wipf, J.; Marshall, S.; Vontver, L.; and Scott, C. S. "Preparing Graduates for the First Year of Residency: Are Medical Schools Meeting the Need?" *Academic Medicine* 78:1, January 2003, pages 39–41.

Langewiesche, William. "Columbia's Last Flight: The Inside Story of the Investigation—and the Catastrophe It Laid Bare," *Atlantic Monthly* 292, November 2003, Part 4, pages 58–88.

Leachman, Robert C. "Competitive Semiconductor Manufacturing: Final Report on Findings from Benchmarking Eight-Inch, sub-350nm Wafer Fabrication Lines," Competitive Semiconductor Manufacturing Program, March 31, 2002. Available from http://www.microlab.berkeley.edu/csm.

Leachman, Robert C.; and Hodges, David A. "Competitive Semiconductor Manufacturing: Program Update." Engineering Systems Research Center, University of California, Berkeley, 2007. Available from http://www.microlab.berkeley.edu/csm/.

LeMaster, K. M. "Reducing Incidence and Prevalence of Hospital-Acquired Pressure Ulcers at Genesis Medical Center," *Joint Commission Journal on Quality and Patient Safety* 33:10, October 2007, pages 611–616.

Leonard, Dorothy A.; and Rayport, Jeffrey F. "Spark Information through Empathic Design," *Harvard Business Review* 75:6, November 1997, pages 102–113.

Leonard-Barton, Dorothy; and Swapp, Walter C. *Deep Smarts: How to Cultivate and Transfer Enduring Business Wisdom*, Harvard Business Press, 2005.

Lesar, T. S.; Anderson, E. R.; Fields, J.; et al. "The VHA New England Medication Error," *Journal on Quality and Patient Safety* 33:2, February 2007, pages 73–82.

Lieberman, Marvin B.; and Dhawan, Rajeev. "Assessing the Resource Base of Japanese and U.S. Auto Producers: A Stochastic Frontier Production Function Approach," *Management Science* 51:7, July 2005, pages 1060–1075.

Lieberman, Marvin B.; Lau, Lawrence J.; and Williams, Mark. "Firm-Level Productivity and Management Influence: A Comparison of U.S. and Japanese Automobile Producers." *Management Science* 36:10, October 1990, pages 1193–1215.

Liker, Jeffrey K. *The Toyota Way: 14 Management Principles from the World's Greatest Manufacturer*, McGraw-Hill, 2004.

Ludmerer, K. *Time to Heal: American Medical Education from the Turn of the Century to the Era of Managed Care*, Oxford University Press, 1999.

MacDuffie, John Paul. "The Road to Root Cause: Shop-Floor Problem-Solving at Three Auto Assembly Plants," *Management Science* 43:4, April 1997.

Macher, Jeffrey T.; and Mowery, David C. "'Managing' Learning by Doing: An Empirical Study in Semiconductor Manufacturing." *Journal of Product Innovation Management* 20:5, 2003, pages 391–410.

Mann, K. "Thinking about Learning: Implications for Principle-Based Professional Education," *Journal of Continuing Education in the Health Professions* 22:2, 2002, pages 69–76.

Mattingly, Jack D. *Elements of Propulsion: Gas Turbines and Rockets*, AIAA, 2006, Chapter 1.

May, Matthew E. *The Elegant Solution: Toyota's Formula for Mastering Innovation*, Free Press, 2007. Foreword by Kevin Roberts.

Mazza, F.; Kitchens, J.; Kerr, S.; Markovich, A.; Best, M.; Sparkman, L. P. "Eliminating Birth Trauma at Ascension Health," *Joint Commission Journal on Quality and Patient Safety* 33:1, January 2007, pages 15–24.

McCannon, C. J.; Hackbarth, A. D.; and Griffin, F. A. "Miles to Go: An Introduction to the 5 Million Lives Campaign." *Joint Commission Journal on Quality and Patient Safety* 33:8, August 2007, pages 477–484.

Meisel, S.; Phelps, P.; and Meisel, M. "Case Study: Reducing Narcotic Oversedation across an Integrated Health System," *Joint Commission Journal on Quality and Patient Safety* 33:9, September 2007, pages 543–548.

Mintzberg, Henry. *The Nature of Managerial Work*. Harper & Row, 1973.

Nakamoto, Michiyo. "Toyota Fire HIts Japan Output," *Financial Times*, February 7, 1997, page 22.

NASA Glenn Research Center, "Beginner's Guide to Propulsion," document available online at http://www.grc.nasa.gov/WWW/K-12/airplant/bgp.html.

NASA Glenn Research Center, "Types of Gas Turbines," document available online at http://www.grc.nasa.gov/WWW/K-12/airpolane/trbtyp.html.

NASA Office of Safety and Mission Assurance, Review and Assessment Division. "Observations and Opportunities: Standards System and Waiver Processes: Alcoa Corporation Corporate Center, October 22, 2004.

NASA Office of Safety and Mission Assurance, Review and Assessment Division. "Observations and Opportunities: Standards System and Waiver Processes: Bath Iron Works, a General Dynamics Company," October 2004.

NNBE Benchmarking Team: NASA Office of Safety and Mission Assurance and NAVSEA 92Q Submarine Safety and Quality Assurance Division. *NASA/Navy Benchmarking Exchange (NNBE) Volume I: Navy Submarine Program Safety Assurance*, Interim Report, December 20, 2002.

NNBE Benchmarking Team: NASA Office of Safety and Mission Assurance, NAVSEA 08 Naval Reactors, and NAVSEA 07Q Submarine Safety and Quality Assurance Division. *NASA/Navy Benchmarking Exchange (NNBE) Volume II: Naval Nuclear Submarine Safety Assurance*, Progress Report, July 15, 2003.

NNBE Benchmarking Team: NASA Office of Safety and Mission Assurance and NAVSEA 07Q Submarine Safety and Quality Assurance Division. *NASA/Navy Benchmarking Exchange (NNBE) Volume III: Ongoing NNBE Activities and Software Subgroup Report I*. Progress Report, October 22, 2004.

Nikitin, Aleksandr; Kudrik, Igor; and Nilsen, Thomas. "The Russian Northern Fleet: Sources of Radioactive Contamination," Bellona Foundation, Report 2, 1996.

Nishiguchi, Toshihiro; and Beaudet, Alexandre. "The Toyota Group and the Aisin Fire." *Sloan Management Review* 40:1, Fall 1998, pages 49–59.

Nutter, D.; and Whitcomb, M. *The AAMC Project on the Clinical Education of Medical Students*, Association of American Medical Colleges, 2002.

Ohno, Taiichi. *Toyota Production System: Beyond Large-Scale Production*, Productivity Press, 1988.

O'Reilly, Charles. "New United Motor Manufacturing Inc.," Stanford Graduate School of Business Case Study HR-11, December 2, 1998.

O'Rourke, Ronald. *Navy Nuclear-Powered Surface Ships: Background, Issues, and Options for Congress*. Congressional Research Service Report for Congress, June 13, 2007.

Perrow, Charles. *Normal Accidents: Living with High Risk Technologies*, Basic Books, 1984; Princeton University Press, 1999.

Peterson, L. R.; Hacek, D. M.; and Robicsek, A. "Case Study: An MRSA Intervention at Evanston Northwestern Healthcare," *Joint Commission Journal on Quality and Patient Safety* 33:12, December 2007, pages 732–738.

Peto, Richard; Boreham, Jillian; Clarke, Mike; Davies, Christina; and Beral, Valerie. "UK and USA Breast Cancer Deaths Down 25% in Year 2000 at Ages 20–69 Years," *The Lancet* 355:9217, May 20, 2000, page 1822f.

Pittet, D.; Tarara, D.; and Wenzel, R. P. "Nosocomial Bloodstream Infection in Critically Ill Patients: Excess Length of Stay, Extra Costs, and Attributable Mortality," *Journal of the American Medical Association* 271:20, May 25, 1994.

Porter, Michael E. "What Is Strategy?" *Harvard Business Review* 74:6, 1996, pages 61–80.

Pratt, D. D.; and Collins, J. B. "Reconsidering 'Good Teaching' across the Continuum of Medical Education," *Journal of Continuing Education in the Health Profession* 21:2, 2001, pages 70–81.

Prestowitz, Clyde V. *Trading Places: How We Allowed Japan to Take the Lead*, Basic Books, 1988.

Pryor, D. B.; Tochin, S. F.; Hendrich, A.; et al. "The Clinical Transformation of Ascension Health: Eliminating All Preventable Injuries and Deaths." *Joint*

Commission Journal on Quality and Patient Safety 32:6, June 2006, pages 299–308.

Reason, James T. *Human Error*, Cambridge University Press, 1990.

Reason, James T. *Managing the Risks of Organizational Accidents*, Ashgate, UK, 1997.

Reitman, Valerie. "Toyota Factories in Japan Grind to a Halt," *The Wall Street Journal*, February 4, 1997, page A14.

Reitman, Valerie. "Toyota Sees Output Recovery by Friday, but Many Parts Suppliers Are Hurting," *The Wall Street Journal*, February 5, 1997.

Reitman, Valerie. "To the Rescue: Toyota's Fast Rebound after Fire at Supplier Shows Why It Is Tough—Its Affiliates, Going All Out, Built an Unfamiliar Part within a Matter of Days—Like Amish Barn-Raising," *The Wall Street Journal*, May 8, 1997, page A1.

Revans, Reg. *Action Learning*, Blond & Briggs, 1974.

Reynolds, Craig W. "Flocks, Herds, and Schools: A Distributed Behavioral Model," *Computer Graphics* 21:4, 1987, pages 25–34.

Rockwell, Theodore. *The Rickover Effect: How One Man Made a Difference*, Naval Institute Press, 1992.

Rolls-Royce, *The Jet Engine—A Complete Overview of the Modern Gas Turbine*, Key Publishing, n.d.

Rose, J. S.; Thomas, C. S.; Tersigni, A.; et al. "A Leadership Framework for Culture Change in Health Care." *Joint Commission Journal on Quality and Patient Safety* 32:8, August 2006, pages 433–442.

Saint, S. "Prevention of Intravascular Catheter-Related Infection." In *Making Health Care Safer: A Critical Analysis of Patient Safety Practices*, AHRQ Evidence Report Number 43, July 20, 2001.

Scott, Gregory K. *IMVP New Product Development Series: The Chrysler Corporation*, Massachusetts Institue of Technology, International Motor Vehicle Program, 1994.

Senge, Peter. *The Fifth Discipline: The Art and Practice of the Learning Organization*, Doubleday, 1990.

Shannon, R. P.; Frndak, D.; Grunden, N.; Lloyd, J. C.; Herbert, C.; Patel, B.; Cummins, D.; Shannon, A. H.; O'Neill, P. H.; Spear, S. J. "Using Real-Time Problem Solving to Eliminate Central Line Infections," *Joint Commission Journal on Quality and Patient Safety* 32:9, September 2006, pages 479–487.

Soufir, L.; Timsit, J. F.; Mahe, C.; Carlet, J.; Regnier, B.; and Chevret, S. "Attributable Morbidity and Mortality of Catheter-Related Septicemia in Critically Ill Patients: A Matched, Risk-Adjusted Cohort Study," *Infection Control and Hospital Epidemiology* 20, 1999, pages 396–401.

Southwest Airlines Annual Report, 2007.

Spear, Steven J. "The Essence of Just in Time," *Productivity, Planning, and Control* 13:8, 2002, pages 754–767.

Spear, Steven J. "Fixing Health Care from the Inside: Teaching Residents to Heal Broken Delivery Processes as They Heal Sick Patients," *Academic Medicine* 81:10, 2006, pages S144–S149.

Spear, Steven J. "Fixing Healthcare from the Inside, Today," *Harvard Business Review* 83:9, September 2005.

Spear, Steven J. "Jack Smith (B): Becoming a Toyota Manager (I)." Harvard Business School Case 604-059, 2004.

Spear, Steven J. "Jack Smith (C): Becoming a Toyota Manager (II)." Harvard Business School Case 604-060, 2004.

Spear, Steven J. "Learning to Lead at Toyota," *Harvard Business Review* 82:5, May 2004.

Spear, Steven J. "Workplace Safety at Alcoa (B)," Harvard Business School Case 600-068, 1999.

Spear, Steven J.; and Berwick, Donald M. "A New Design for Healthcare Delivery," *Boston Globe*, November 23, 2007.

Spear, Steven J.; and Bowen, H. Kent. "Decoding the DNA of the Toyota Production System," *Harvard Business Review* 77:5, September-October 1999, pages 96–108.

Spear, Steven J.; and Purrington, Courtney. "Jack Smith (A): Career Launch at Toyota," Harvard Business School Case 604-057, 2004.

Spear, Steven J.; and Schmidhofer, Mark. "Ambiguity and Workarounds as Contributors to Medical Error," *Annals of Internal Medicine* 142:8, April 19, 2005, pages 627–630.

Statement of Admiral F. L. "Skip" Bowman, U.S. Navy Director, Naval Nuclear Propulsion Program, before the House Science Committee, October 29, 2003.

Stevenson, Howard H.; Cruikshank, Jeffrey L.; Moldoveanu, Mihnea. *Do Lunch or Be Lunch: The Power of Predictability in Creating Your Future*, Harvard Business School Press, 1997.

Stewart, Thomas A.; and Raman, Anand P. "Lessons from Toyota's Long Drive: An Interview with Katsuaki Watanabe," *Harvard Business Review* 85:4, July–August 2007.

Sullivan, Rear Admiral Paul E., U.S. Navy Deputy Commander for Ship Design, Integration, and Engineering, Naval Seas Command, Statement before the House Science Committee on the SUBSAFE program, October 29, 2003.

Taylor, Frederick Winslow. *The Principles of Scientific Management*, Harper & Row, 1911.

Tolchin, S.; Brush, R.; Lange, P.; et al. "Eliminating Preventable Death at Ascension Health," *Joint Commission Journal on Quality and Patient Safety* 33:3, March 2007, pages 145–154.

Tosteson, D. C.; Aldenstein, S J.; and Carver, S.T. *New Pathways to Medical Education at Harvard Medical School*, Harvard University Press, 1994.

Toyota: United States Operations, company brochure, viewable online at http://www.toyota.com/about/our_business/operations/USOperations_FINAL.pdf.

Tucker, Anita; and Edmondson, Amy. "Why Hospitals Don't Learn from Failures: Organizational and Psychological Dynamics That Inhibit System Change," *California Management Review* 45:2, Winter 2003, page 55.

Tucker, Anita; and Spear, Steven J. "Operational Failures and Interruptions in Hospital Nursing," Health Services Research 41:3, 2006, pages 643–662.

United States Embassy, Japan. *Fact Sheet on U.S. Nuclear Powered Warship Safety.* Available from http://www.tokyo.usembassy.gov/e/p/tp-20060417-72.html.

Varian, Hal. "Economic Scene: Rising Productivity Is a Good Thing, Right? Tell That to the Newly Unemployed," *New York Times*, October 23, 2003.

Vaughn, Diane. *The Challenger Launch Decision.* University of Chicago Press, 1996.

Ward, A.; Liker, J. K.; Cristiano, J. J.; and Sobek, D. K. "The Second Toyota Paradox." *Sloan Management Review* 28:4, August 1995, page 129.

Ward, Elizabeth M.; Thun, Michael J.; Hannan, Lindsay M; and Jemal, Ahmedin. "Interpreting Cancer Trends," *Annals of the New York Academy of Sciences* 1076, 2006, pages 29–53.

Weinberger, S.; and Whitcomb, M. "The Clinical Education of Medical Students: Report on Millennium Competencies I & II." Carl J. Shapiro Institute for Education and Research, Harvard Medical School, and Beth Israel Deaconess Medical Center.

Whitcomb, M. E. "From the Editor: The General Professional Education of the Physician: Is Four Years Enough Time?" *Academic Medicine*, 2002.

Womack, J. P.; Jones, D. T.; and Roos, D. *The Machine That Changed the World*, Rawson Associates, 1990.

World Bank Group. *Pollution Prevention and Abatement Handbook*, July 1998.

NOTES

Chapter 1

Page 4: ***All this has led to staggering profitability ... Toyota's market capitalization ... was greater than that of GM, Ford, and Daimler-Chrysler combined.*** Thomas A. Stewart and Anand P. Raman, "Lessons from Toyota's
Long Drive," *Harvard Business Review* 85:7, 8, July-August 2007, page 74.

Page 5: ***This is not so, however, with Southwest ... this airline has generated
annual profit for more than 30 years in a row.*** Southwest Airlines Annual
Report, 2007.

Page 6: ***How has this been possible? According to my colleague, Jody Hoffer-
Gittell ...*** Jody Hoffer-Gittell, *The Southwest Airlines Way: Using the Power
of Relationships to Achieve High Performance*, McGraw-Hill, 2003; Jody
Hoffer-Gittell, "Paradox of Coordination and Contol," *California Management Review*, Spring 2000.

Page 6: ***Manufacturing integrated circuits ... can be brutally competitive.
According to the Competitive Semiconductor Manufacturing Program ...
there are significant disparities ... notably, the speed with which those
levels are achieved (... ramp-up time).*** Robert C. Leachman and David
A. Hodges, "Competitive Semiconductor Manufacturing: Program
Update," Engineering Systems Research Center, University of California,
Berkeley, available online from http://microlab.berkeley.edu/csm/; Robert
C. Leachman, "Competitive Semiconductor Manufacturing: Final Report
on Findings from Benchmarking Eight-inch, sub-350nm Wafer Fabrication
Lines," March 31, 2002; Jeffrey T. Macher and David C. Mowery, "'Managing': Learning by Doing: An Empirical Study in Semiconductor Manu-
facturing," *The Journal of Product Innovation Management* 20, 2003, pages
391–410.

Pages 6–7: ***Manufacturing circuits ... Christensen, Verlinden, King, and Yang
in their article ...*** Clayton M. Christensen, Matt Verlinden, Steven King,

and Woodward Yang, "The New Economics of Semiconductor Manufacturing," *IEEE Spectrum* 45:5, May 2008, pages 24–29.

Page 7: ***Not all rabbits are running for profit . . . The Institute of Medicine estimated that up to 98,000 of the 33 million Americans who are hospitalized each year die because something went wrong in the management of their care.*** Linda T. Kohn, Janet M. Corrigan, and Molla S. Donaldson, "To Err Is Human: Building a Safer Health System," Committee on Quality Health Care in America, National Academy Press, 2000.

Page 8: [Top] ***Other studies estimate that . . . an even greater number are injured or infected in the course of receiving care.*** Steven J. Spear, "Fixing Healthcare from the Inside, Today," *Harvard Business Review* 83:9, September 2005.

Page 8: ***Other studies estimate that an equal number die as a result of an infection.*** Richard Shannon, D. Frndek, N. Frunden, et al. "Using Real-Time Problem Solving to Eliminate Central Line Infections," *Joint Commission Journal on Quality and Patient Safety* 32:9, 2006, pages 479–487.

Page 9: ***Initially, this phenomenon was explained in terms of economic conflict . . . Books such as* MITI and the Japanese Miracle *(1982) . . .*** Chalmers A. Johnson, *MITI and the Japanese Miracle : The Growth of Industrial Policy, 1925–1975*, Stanford University Press, 1982; Clyde V. Prestowitz, *Trading Places: How We Allowed Japan to Take the Lead*, Basic Books, 1988.

Page 10: ***Arriving at MIT as a graduate student in the late 1980s was fortuitous . . . Books such as* Kaisha *. . .*** James C. Abegglen and George Stalk, Jr., *Kaisha, the Japanese Corporation*, Basic Books,1985; Michael L. Dertouzos, et al., *Made In America : Regaining the Productive Edge*, MIT Press, 1989.

Page 11: ***Researchers such as David Garvin documented differences in productivity among similar plants and found discrepancies of tenfold and even a hundredfold in quality.*** David A. Garvin, "Quality on the Line," *Harvard Business Review* 61:5, September–October 1983, pages 65f.

Page 11: ***Researchers such as . . . John Krafcik documented extraordinary differences in productivity between mass manufacturers and lean manufacturers in the auto industry.*** John F. Krafcik, "Triumph of the Lean Production System," *Sloan Management Review*, Fall 1988, pages 41–52.

Page 11: ***Researchers such as . . . Michael Cusumano provided a historical account of Toyota's rise to ascendancy.*** Michael A. Cusumano, "Manufacturing Innovation: Lessons from the Japanese Automobile Industry," *Sloan Management Review*, Fall 1988, pages 29–39.

Page 11: ***Researchers such as . . . James Womack, Dan Roos, and Dan Jones . . . in their landmark book* The Machine That Changed the World.** James P. Womack, Daniel T. Jones, and Daniel Roos, *The Machine That Changed the World*, Rawson Associates, 1990.

Page 11: ***Researchers such as . . . John Paul MacDuffie revealed some of the details of the powerful problem-solving mechanisms these manufacturers***

employed. John P. MacDuffie, "The Road to 'Root Cause': Shop-Floor Problem-Solving at Three Auto Assembly Plants," *Management Science* 43:4, April 1997, pages 479–502.

Pages 11–12: **Bob Hayes and Steve Wheelwright . . . put aside their focus on strategic decisions as the means toward Restoring Our Competitive Edge.** Robert H. Hayes and Steven C. Wheelwright, *Restoring Our Competitive Edge*, John Wiley, 1984.

Page 11–12. **Bob Hayes and Steve Wheelwright, with coauthor Kim Clark, put aside their focus . . . in order to achieve world-beating Dynamic Manufacturing.** Robert H. Hayes, Steven C. Wheelwright, and Kim B. Clark, *Dynamic Manufacturing: Creating the Learning Organization*, Free Press, 1988.

Page 15: **The difference between Toyota and its competitors . . . If everyone benchmarks the leader by imitating how work is done at a particular time and place, no one can do any better than the leader and everyone will look and act the same, commoditizing their sector and guaranteeing that no one will enjoy an advantage.** Michael Porter, "What Is Strategy?" *Harvard Business Review* 74:6, November–December 1996, pages 61f.

Page 17: [Line 6] **As Kent Bowen and I pointed out . . .** Steven J. Spear and H. Kent Bowen, "Decoding the DNA of the Toyota Production System," *Harvard Business Review* 77:5, September–October 1999, pages 96f.

Page 23: **However, it is not that they want . . . not a case of perverse Taylorism . . .** Frederick Winslow Taylor, *The Principles of Scientific Management*, Harper & Row, 1911.

Page 27: [Line 8] **Eric von Hippel and his coauthors have demonstrated the importance of learning in context. Because there are so many circumstantial factors that cannot be codified, problem solving and learning must occur when and where problems are experienced . . .** Eric von Hippel, "'Sticky Information' and the Locus of Problem Solving: Implications for Innovation," *Management Science* 40:4, April 1994, pages 429–439; Eric von Hippel and Marcie J. Tyrie, "How Learning by Doing Is Done: Problem Identification in Novel Process Equipment," *Research Policy* 24:1, January 1995, pages 1–12.

Page 27: **My late colleague Jai Jaikumar had "information perishability" as one of his axioms of information.** Ramachandran Jaikumar and Roger Bohn, "A Dynamic Approach to Operations Management: An Alternative to Static Optimization," *International Journal of Production Economics* 27, 1992, pages 265–282.

Chapter 2

Page 35: [Toward end of first paragraph] **For larger systems, bureaucratic coordination served the purpose of ensuring that the pieces acted in concert with each other.** See, for example, Alfred DuPont Chandler, Jr., *The Visible Hand*, Belknap Press, 1977.

Page 39: *A major upgrade of a car model can require hundreds of years of engineering effort.* A. Ward, J. K. Liker, J. J. Cristiano, and D. K. Sobek. "The Second Toyota Paradox: How Delaying Decisions Can Make Better Cars Faster," *Sloan Management Review* 36:3, 1995, pages 43–61.

Page 39: *A major upgrade of a car model . . . has engineering costs of tens of millions of dollars and total costs in the hundreds of millions.* H. Kent Bowen, "Chrysler and BMW: Tritec Engine Joint Venture." Harvard Business School Case 600-004, 2003.

Page 40: *Today the likelihood of successful treatment has increased dramatically.* Richard Peto, Jillian Boreham, Mike Clarke, Cristina Davies, and Valerie Beral, "UK and USA Breast Cancer Deaths Down 25% in Year 2000 at Ages 20–69 Years," *The Lancet* 355:9217, May 20, 2000, pages 1822f.

Page 40: *Today the likelihood . . . Death rates from all cancers fell in the United States ... building on improvements over the preceding decades with similar trends in other industrialized nations.* Elizabeth M. Ward, Michael J. Thun, Lindsay M. Hannan, and Ahmedin Jemal. "Interpreting Cancer Trends," *Annals of the New York Academy of Sciences* 1076, 2006, pages 29–53.

Page 40: *As for localized breast cancer specifically, the survival rate according to the American Cancer Society . . .* American Cancer Society, *Cancer Facts and Figures*, 2000 and 2007.

Page 40: *As for localized breast cancer specifically . . . The decrease in mortality was due to improved detection and better treatment.* Kenneth C. Chu, Robert E. Tarone, Larry G. Kessler, Lynn A. G. Ries, Benjamin F. Hankey, Banj A. Miller, and Brenda K. Edwards. "Recent Trends in U.S. Breast Cancer Incidence, Survival, and Mortality Rates," *Journal of the National Cancer Institute* 88, 1996, page 21.

Pages 40–41: *However, it wasn't just a single scientific breakthrough . . . There have been "substantial advances in the treatment of breast cancer . . ."* Ismael Jatoi and Anthony B. Miller, "Why Is Breast Cancer Mortality Declining?" *The Lancet Oncology* 4, 2003, pages 251–254.

Chapter 3

Pages 46–47: *In the wake of the Three Mile Island crisis . . . Yale professor Charles Perrow was struck by what had not gone wrong.* Charles Perrow, *Normal Accidents: Living with High Risk Technologies*, Basic Books, 1984; Princeton University Press, 1999.

Page 48: *Perrow is not alone in his prognosis. Jim Reason . . . emphasizes the point that "organizational accidents" don't occur because of a single, dramatic misstep.* James T. Reason, *Managing the Risks of Organizational Accidents*, Ashgate, UK, 1997.

Page 50: *And yet modern medicine has become a terrible disappointment . . . The Institute of Medicine has published studies that estimate the number*

of patients who lose their lives to medical error. Linda T. Kohn, Janet M. Corrigan, and Molla S. Donaldson, *To Err Is Human: Building a Safer Health System*, National Academy Press, 2000.

Page 51: *The variety of things that could go wrong was both shocking and fascinating.* Paul D. Cleary, "A Hospitalization from Hell: A Patient's Perspective on Quality," *Annals of Internal Medicine* 138, 2003; pages 33–39; Mark R. Chassin and Elise C. Becher, "The Wrong Patient," *Annals of Internal Medicine* 136, 2002, pages 826–833.

Page 51: *The variety of things that could go wrong . . . My friend and colleague, Dr. Mark Schmidhofer, and I began to wonder what these cases had in common. We found out that the answer was "plenty."* Steven J. Spear and Mark Schmidhofer, "Ambiguity and Workarounds as Contributors to Medical Error," *Annals of Internal Medicine* 142:8, April 19, 2005, pages 627–630.

Page 51: *Let's look at a case in which skilled and dedicated workers . . . Their failure to do so killed a patient.* David W. Bates, "Unexpected Hypoglycemia in a Critically Ill Patient," *Annals of Internal Medicine* 137, 2002, pages 110–116.

Page 53: *The investigation was drawing blanks until . . . Nursing is a hectic job with constant bursts of short-duration tasks and care for one patient inextricably intertwined with that of others.* Anita L. Tucker and Steven J. Spear, "Operational Failures and Interruptions in Hospital Nursing," *Health Services Research* 41:3, 2006, pages 643–662.

Page 55: *Yet here was Mrs. Grant's nurse . . . this kind of carefulness is not really what we are wired for.* James T. Reason, *Human Error*, Cambridge University Press, 1990.

Page 56: *But if that process was booby-trapped . . . David Bates . . . has done extensive research on the frequency of medication administration errors.* D. W. Bates, D. L. Boyle, M. B. Vander Vliet, J. Schneider, and L. Leape, "Relationship between Medication Errors and Adverse Drug Effects," *Journal of General Internal Medicine* 10, 1995, pages 199–205.

Page 57: *For example, my colleague, Anita Tucker, made detailed minute-by-minute observations of nurses and found that they confronted some sort of operational failure.* Anita Tucker and Amy Edmondson, "Why Hospitals Don't Learn from Failures: Organizational and Psychological Dynamics That Inhibit System Change." *California Management Review* 45:2, Winter 2003, page 55.

Page 58: *What killed Mrs. Grant? . . . Diane Vaughn calls this the normalization of deviance.* Diane Vaughn, *The Challenger Launch Decision*, University of Chicago Press, 1996.

Page 60: *On January 16, 2003, the space shuttle* Columbia *. . .* All quotes in this section (pages 60–71) are from Robert Godwin, ed., *Columbia Accident Investigation Board Report*, Vol. 1. Apogee Books, 2003. The other source of information for the material in this section is: William Langewiesche, "Columbia's Last Flight: The Inside Story of the Investigation—and the Catastrophe It Laid Bare." *Atlantic Monthly*, November 2003.

Page 64: ***The breach in the RCC panel . . . one estimate placed the size of the breach at 140 square inches.*** Dimensions from CAIB report and William Harwood, "Timing of Fuel Tank Foam Loss Saved Discovery from Big Hit," *Spaceflight Now*, July 28, 2005, available online at http://216.92.110.5/shuttle/sts114/050728hallock/.

Chapter 4

Page 92: ***When Alcoans got hurt or had close calls . . . Idiosyncratic confluences and coincidences of people, processes, products, places, and circumstances could create a hazardous situation where none had been known to exist. This was a seminal insight.*** The concept that discoveries have to be made *in situ* because information is "sticky" in that it is impossible to understand and represent conditions away from a work site has been explored by many researchers, including the MIT professor Eric von Hippel and his colleagues. See, for instance, Eric von Hippel and Marcie Tyrie, "How Learning Is Done: Problem Identification in Novel Process Equipment." *Research Policy* 24, 1995, pages 1–12. Dorothy A. Leonard has explored how the implicit nature of information requires that it be accessed in its most familiar situation before it can be transported and used productively elsewhere. See Dorothy A. Leonard and Jeffrey F. Rayport, "Spark Information through Empathic Design," *Harvard Business Review* 75:6, November 1997, pages 102–113; Dorothy Leonard-Barton and Walter C. Swapp, *Deep Smarts: How to Cultivate and Transfer Enduring Business Wisdom*, Harvard Business School Press, 2005.

Page 100: ***In most organizations, middle managers play an essential but bureaucratic role . . . These middle-management roles make it possible . . . to allocate resources and coordinate activities, as has been documented by Alfred Chandler and other business historians.*** Alfred DuPont Chandler, Jr., *The Visible Hand*, Belknap Press, 1977.

Page 100: ***In most organizations . . . Alcoa was not content with . . . the model of scientific management championed by Frederick Winslow Taylor in which the "brains" of the organization developed optimal procedures for the "brawns" to employ.*** That earlier model is outlined in Frederick Winslow Taylor, *The Principles of Scientific Management*, Harper & Row, 1911.

Page 103–104: ***Alcoa's engineered products plant in Cressona, Pennsylvania increased productivity on two lines by 87 percent . . . It managed any process it was using and thereby improved its performance by numerous measures simultaneously.*** Alcoa, *Annual Report*, 2003.

Page 104: ***In a similar fashion, Alcoa's Davenport, Iowa, plant addressed increased demand through better process design . . . inventory was*** *reduced by $1 million; and 19 improvements in environment, health, and safety were carried out.* Alcoa, *Annual Report*, 2005.

Page 104: *Alcoa's continued focus on improving its processes ... recognition as one of "the best-practice leaders in cutting their gas emissions."* Adam Aston and Burt Helm, with Michael Arndt and Amy Barrett, "The Race Against Climate Change," *BusinessWeek*, December 12, 2005, pages 58–66.

Page 106: [Line 10] *Short of that, as one of my professors pointed out, you are depending on despotism to get things done.* See, for instance, Howard H. Stevenson, Jeffrey L. Cruikshank, Mihnea C. Moldoveanu, *Do Lunch or Be Lunch: The Power of Predictability in Creating Your Future*, Harvard Business School Press, 1997.

Page 108: *There is another piece to my picture ... British thermal unit efficiency, costs of production, industry capacity, and effects on supply and demand.* "Alcoa's O'Neill Takes Long-Term, Free Market View," *Metals Week* 70, March 22, 1999, page 12.

Chapter 5

Page 110: *The U.S. Navy has launched more than 200 atomic-powered ships ... As of 2006, those ships collectively have had more than 5,700 reactor-years of operation and have "steamed" well over 134 million miles.* From "Fact Sheet on U.S. Nuclear-Powered Warship Safety," Embassy of the United States, Japan Web page at http://tokyo.usembassy.gov/e/p/tp-20060417-72.html.

Page 111: *Under fire or not, life for submarines was difficult ... Their cruising range was limited by the amount of fuel they could carry; once it was gone, they had to stop to refuel at sea or in port.* Ronald O'Rourke, *Navy Nuclear-Powered Surface Ships: Background, Issues, and Options for Congress*, Congressional Research Service Report for Congress, June 13, 2007, page 3.

Page 116: *Furthermore, Rickover was intimidating ... Theodore Rockwell ... wrote in his memoirs about a call between the two of them, conducted over the single undersea phone cable.* Accounts taken from Theodore Rockwell, *The Rickover Effect: How One Man Made a Difference*, Naval Institute Press, 1992.

Page 117: *It can't just be Rickover ... NR developed what one of its chroniclers, Francis Duncan, called "the discipline of engineering."* Francis Duncan, *Rickover and the Nuclear Navy: The Discipline of Technology*, Naval Institute Press, 1990.

Pages 124–125: *In the case of Three Mile Island (TMI) commercial reactor ... Even administrative or training problems can result in a report and provide learning opportunities for those in the program.* NNBE Benchmarking Team: NASA Office of Safety and Mission Assurance, NAVSEA 08 Naval Reactors, and NAVSEA 07Q Submarine Safety and Quality Assurance Division, *NASA/Navy Benchmarking Exchange (NNBE) Volume II: Naval*

Nuclear Submarine Safety Assurance, Progress Report, July 15, 2003, page 32. (In subsequent notes, this report will be referred to as NNBE-II.)

Page 125: ***During a General Accounting Office (GAO) review of the NR program in 1991, the GAO team reviewed over 1,700 of these reports out of a total of 12,000 generated . . .*** NNBE-II, page 29.

Page 126: ***NR requires that events of even lower significance be evaluated by the operating activity . . . part of a key process to determine the health of the activity's self-assessment capability.*** NNBE-II, page 29.

Pages 126–127: ***This was not just paperwork . . . The NASA benchmarking team pointed out that during Rickover's tenure and that of his several successors, each report "identifies the necessary action to prevent a recurrence."*** NNBE-II, page 29.

Page 128: [First new paragraph] ***The discipline of technology means that the organization must adapt . . . the match between the product and its use, and intense analysis of the present and anticipated future conditions of operation.*** Francis Duncan, *Rickover and the Nuclear Navy: The Discipline of Technology*, Naval Institute Press, 1990.

Page 130: ***The NASA benchmarking study stated this as follows: "Recommendations are prepared independently . . . to be documented in the recommendation with a discussion of the logic for not implementing them.*** NNBE-II, page 23.

Page 131–132: ***John Crawford . . .and Steven Krahn . . . described the organization-wide benefits of turning local discovery into systemic discovery: "This disciplined, formal engineering approach . . . allows focus to be placed on truly important areas, while ensuring that routine work gets done completely.*** John W. Crawford and Steven L. Krahn, "The Nuclear Propulsion Program: A Brief Case Study in Institutional Constancy," *Public Administration Review* 58:2, March–April 1998.

Page 132: ***The NASA benchmarking team likewise noted . . . this tool has contributed to a program philosophy that underscores the smaller problems in an effort to prevent significant ones.*** NNBE-II, page 29.

Page 133: ***Certainly Rickover was in the position and of the temperament to do all these.*** Theodore Rockwell, *The Rickover Effect: How One Man Made a Difference*, Naval Institute Press, 1992.

Page 134: ***. . . this one silver-haired guy who kept asking simple, basic questions . . . "I guess I'm not the only dummy in the class."*** Theodore Rockwell, *The Rickover Effect*, page 18.

Pages 134–135: ***Rickover was committed not only to his own learning but to others' learning . . . "calmly accepting mistakes and errors when honestly acknowledged, and giving each man as much responsibility as he could handle."*** Francis Duncan, *Rickover and the Nuclear Navy*, page 10.

Pages 135 (bottom)–136: ***Over the next several weeks, Rickover followed up with the candidate, who had both slimmed down and was accepted***

into the program. Francis Duncan, *Rickover and the Nuclear Navy*, page 247.

Page 136: *Selection into the NR program . . . "water chemistry control, radiological control, and reactor protection and safety."* Francis Duncan, *Rickover and the Nuclear Navy*, page 239.

Page 136: *Additional training followed . . . This approach was repeated again for additional progressions in rank and responsibility.* Francis Duncan, *Rickover and the Nuclear Navy*, page 253.

Page 137: *To be categorized as "close" to Rickover needs explanation . . . a driving passion of Rickover's life.* Theodore Rockwell, *The Rickover Effect*, page xiii.

Page 137: *Rickover's leadership . . . "to command—someone else would take care of the ship."* Francis Duncan, *Rickover and the Nuclear Navy*, page 261.

Page 140: *Prompted by that catastrophe . . . the nonnuclear portions of the submarine (responsible for submergence, flood prevention, control, and recovery) as disciplined and rigorous as the NR approach.* Statement of Rear Admiral Paul E. Sullivan, U.S. Navy Deputy Commander for Ship Design, Integration, and Engineering Naval Sea Systems Command before the House Science Committee on the SUBSAFE Program, October 29, 2003.

Page 140: *Pratt & Whitney.* This historic review of Pratt & Whitney's new product design management is based on H. Kent Bowen and Courtney Purrington, Harvard Business School Case 604-013, July 2003, plus more recent interviews with Pratt & Whitney and United Technology employees.

Page 142: [Line 4] . . . *The advantages of this approach include fuel efficiency and quieter operation.* See Jack D. Mattingly, *Elements of Propulsion: Gas Turbines and Rockets*, AIAA, 2006, chapter 1; also NASA Glenn Research Center document available at http://www.gvc.nasa.gov/WWW/K-12/airplane/bgp.html; and Rolls-Royce, *The Jet Engine—A Complete Overview of the Modern Gas Turbine*, Key Publishing, n.d.

Pages 142–143: *In its early years, Pratt had enough time and money . . . One engineer explained . . . his boss would check his work, have him fix the problems, and check his work again. When it was deemed sufficient, it went to the next boss for checking.* Account taken from H. Kent Bowen and Courtney Purrington, "Pratt and Whitney: Engineering Standard Work," Harvard Business School Case 604-013, July 2003.

Page 143: *But as times changed . . . Not only did military spending decrease with the end of the Cold War . . .* See, for instance, Gene Koretz, "Toting Up the Peace Dividend: Has Military Spending Hit Bottom?" *BusinessWeek*, December 14, 1998, page 26; and Malcolm Knight, Norman Loyazo, and Delano Villanueva, "The Peace Dividend: Military Spending Cuts and Economic Growth," *World Bank Policy Research*, February 1996. Working Paper No. 1577.

Page 146: *Paul Adams . . . explained to me . . .: "First we had to make sure we had the handoffs down . . . clarity as to situations in which those tools worked and the situations in which they didn't."* Based on telephone conversations between the author and Paul Adams.

Chapter 6

Page 155: *Toyota is undoubtedly one of these high-velocity organizations . . . racing ahead to become the world's most successful automaker, with the "healthiest profits in the industry."* Anne Fisher, "America's Most Admired Companies," *Fortune* 157:5, March 17, 2008, page 65.

Pages 155–156: *Toyota is undoubtedly . . . As Fortune wrote when putting Toyota on its 2007 list of the most admired companies: "You may recall that 25 years ago . . . The Prius is today as de rigueur in Hollywood as the hydrocarbon-swilling hummer used to be.* Anne Fisher, "America's Most Admired Companies," *Fortune* 157:5, March 17, 2008, page 65.

Pages 156: *And there's no doubt that Toyota's success is largely attributable to its "velocity of discovery" . . . Marvin Lieberman and his coauthors . . . found that Toyota outstripped its competitors on improvements in manufacturing labor productivity . . . and this process of discovery kept going decade after decade.* Marvin B. Lieberman, Laurence J. Lau, and Mark D. Williams, "Firm-Level Productivity and Management Influence: A Comparison of U.S. and Japanese Automobile Producers," *Management Science* 36:10, October 1990, pages 1193–1215.

Pages 156–157: *And there's no doubt that Toyota's success . . . In a separate study, Lieberman and Dhawan found that . . . "lagging firms have converged only slowly . . . while stronger firms like Toyota have made continual advances . . .* Marvin B. Lieberman and Rajeev Dhawan, "Assessing the Resource Base of Japanese and U.S. Auto Producers: A Stochastic Frontier Production Function Approach," *Management Science* 51:7, July 2005, pages 1060–1075.

Page 157: *Toyota's advances . . . come from myriad specific improvements . . . Taichi Ohno became frustrated that it took stamping press operators two to three hours for a setup . . . By the 1950s, setups consistently took less than an hour; and in the 1960s they were often down to three minutes.* Taichi Ohno, *Toyota Production System: Beyond Large-Scale Production*, Productivity Press, 1988. English translation of the Japanese original.

Pages 157–158: *Charles Fishman . . . reports on a process of incessant discovery in Toyotas's paint shops . . . One of the three booths was shut down and dismantled because it was no longer needed, which in turn freed up space in the shop.* Charles Fishman, "No Satisfaction at Toyota," *Fast Company* 111, 2007, page 82.

Page 158: *We have already seen that not all . . . By 1991, Lexus was introducing new models to round out its offerings, and by 1992, it was outselling*

Mercedes and BMW in the United States. Jeffrey K. Liker, *The Toyota Way: 14 Management Principles from the World's Greatest Manufacturer,* McGraw-Hill, 2004; Matthew E. May, *The Elegant Solution: Toyota's Formula for Mastering Innovation,* foreword by Kevin Roberts, Free Press, 2007.

Page 182: *Aisin, a first-tier supplier . . . What did Aisin do to achieve this enviable combination of variety, cost, and short lead time?* A version of this account appeared in Steven J. Spear, "The Essence of Just in Time: Embedding Diagnostic Tests in Work-Systems to Achieve Operational Excellence," *Productivity Planning and Control* 13:8, 2002, pages 754–767.

Page 190: *And this is not an isolated example. Paul Adler and his coauthors studied a series of new model introductions at Toyota's NUMMI joint venture with General Motors in California.* P.S. Adler, B. Goldoftas, and D. I. Levine, "Flexibility versus Efficiency? A Case Study of Model Changeovers in the Toyota Production System." *Organization Science,* 1999.

Chapter 7

Page 206: *I had the privilege of interviewing members of Mr. Ito's quality circle at Aisin . . . For 1994, then, the goal was to reduce rejects on Line 1, increase productivity by reducing idle time, and "produce a workforce in which new techniques can be learned and applied."* From the author's interviews with Ito and his team.

Pages 216–218: *Example: Teaching Others to Generate Knowledge While Solving Problems.* The account following this heading is based on one that appeared in Steven J. Spear and H. Kent Bowen, "Decoding the DNA of the Toyota Production System," *Harvard Business Review* 77:5, September-October 1999, pages 96–108.

Chapter 8

Page 225: *Jared Diamond asks a provocative question in* Guns, Germs, and Steel: *"Why did Eurasians conquer, displace, or decimate Native Americans, Australians, and Africans, instead of the reverse?"* Jared Diamond, *Guns, Germs, and Steel,* W. W. Norton, 1997.

Pages 226–227: *What did this mean in practical terms? When the Spanish conquistador Pizarro faced off with the Incan king Atahualpa . . . [the Spanish] had only 168 "ragtag" soldiers "in unfamiliar terrain . . . and far beyond the reach of timely reinforcements" . . . Atahualpa . . . commanded an army estimated at 80,000.* Jared Diamond, *Guns, Germs, and Steel,* page 68.

Page 234: *Furthermore, in "1982, when GM closed the plant and laid off the workforce, more than 6,000 grievances remained backlogged in the system."* Paul S. Adler, Barbara Goldoftas, and David I. Levine,

"Ergonomics, Employee Involvement, and the Toyota Production System: A Case Study of NUMMI's 1993 Model Introduction," *Industrial & Labor Relations Review* 50:3, page 416.

Page 234: ***Furthermore in "1982" . . . "Frontline managers were known to carry weapons for personal protection."*** Charles O'Reilly, "New United Motor Manufacturing, Inc." Stanford Graduate School of Business Case Study HR-11, December 2, 1998.

Page 234: ***However, in a seemingly overnight transformation, NUMMI scored remarkable successes. The MIT graduate student and researcher, John Krafcik . . . introduced the term* lean manufacturing *into the lexicon.*** John F. Krafcik, "Triumph of the Lean Production System," *Sloan Management Review*, 1988.

Page 241: ***Capturing knowledge so that it could be shared was hardly a trivial exercise. The GPC created 3,000 "visual manuals" . . . Each one took about 200 labor-hours to create, for a total of some 300 work-years.*** A rough estimate is that 200 hours per manual × 3,000 manuals = 600,000 hours. If a work-year is approximately 2,000 hours, this equals 300 work-years of investment.

Page 246: ***Reflecting on the progress of the North American Production Support Center, Latondra Newton stated: "Toyota needed to create a way to help people . . . But we also had to invent some things . . . we had to develop our own approaches to training and training the trainers.*** From the author's interviews and correspondence.

Page 247: ***. . . Although Toyota plants were doing work similar to that of their competitors . . . Some years later, researchers at the University of Michigan identified a second Toyota paradox.*** Allen Ward, Jeffery K. Liker, John J. Cristiano, and Durward K. Sobek II; "The Second Toyota Paradox: How Delaying Decisions Can Make Better Cars Faster," *Sloan Management Review* 28:4, August 1995, page 129.

Page 247: ***As for the nature of this second paradox . . . LH referred to an underbody and chasis that would be common to a series of . . . automobiles, including the Chrysler Concorde, New Yorker, and LHS, the Dodge Intrepid, and the Eagle Vision.*** For a detailed discussion of new product development at Chrysler in the 1990s, see Gregory K. Scott, *IMVP New Product Development Series: The Chrysler Corporation*, Massachusetts Institute of Technology, International Motor Vehicle Program, 1994 (http://www.IMVP.mit.edu/papers/94/Imvp053a.pdf). All the quotes in this paragraph are from this source.

Pages 247–248: ***As for the nature of this second paradox . . . According to MIT graduate student and researcher Gregory Scott, the LH . . . was the "first major fruit" of a new approach to new product development.*** See Gregory K. Scott, *IMVP New Product Development Series: The Chrysler Corporation*, available online as previously cited.

Pages 254–255: *The lessons-learned book told the stylist which curvature radii could be manufactured and which could not . . . The "second paradox" researchers explained: "Lessons-learned books describe the current company capability . . . a very detailed definition of what can be done from each functional area's viewpoint . . . [New paragraph] The Michigan authors went on to emphasize . . . "Each deviation from the lessons-learned books . . . may develop a new technology or process advance to make the design feasible, and then revise the lessons-learned book.* This refers to Ward, Liker, et al., "The Second Toyota Paradox," *Sloan Management Review* 28:4, August 1995, page 129.

Chapter 9

Page 263: *It is an understandable view that leaders are responsible for setting objectives, allocating resources for the pursuit of those objectives, and establishing an emotional tone for the organizations they lead, including establishing the right combination of incentives to achieve objectives.* Chester Barnard, *The Functions of the Executive*, Harvard University Press, 1968; Henri Fayol, *General and Industrial Management*, Pitman, 1949; James MacGregor Burns, *Leadership*, Harper & Row, 1978; Henry Mintzberg, *The Nature of Managerial Work*, Harper & Row, 1973.

Pages 264 and following: *Learning to Lead at Toyota: Bob Dallis was an accomplished auto-manufacturing manager who made a huge career shift . . .* This entire section is based on Steven J. Spear, "Learning to Lead at Toyota," *Harvard Business Review* 82:5, May 2004.

Page 278: [Line 11] *Dating back to Frederick Winslow Taylor and before,* Frederick Winslow Taylor, T*he Principles of Scientific Management,*Harper & Row, 1911.

Page 293: *Convis has addressed this point: "I remember when Mr. Higashi . . . That's the only way to understand the issues."* "Toyota: Changes and Challenges," presented by Gary Convis, President, Toyota Motor Manufacturing Kentucky, Inc., August 8, 2001, in *The Management Briefing Seminars*, Grand Traverse Resort and Spa, Traverse City, Michigan.

Chapter 10

Page 295: *On Tuesday, February 4, 1997,* **The Wall Street Journal** *reported the following . . .* Valerie Reitman, "Toyota Factories in Japan Grind to a Halt," *The Wall Street Journal*, February 4, 1997, page A14.

Page 296: *The Journal estimated that a shutdown could cost Toyota . . . An expert quoted by the* **Financial Times** *predicted the following . . .* Michiyo Nakamoto, "Toyota Fire Hits Japan Output," *Financial Times*, February 7, 1997, page 22.

Page 297: [Line 2] *By the next day, the Journal ran a story that was headlined, "Toyota Sees Output Recovery by Friday, but Many Parts Suppliers*

Are Hurting" . . . Valerie Reitman, "Toyota Sees Output Recovery by Friday, but Many Parts Suppliers Are Hurting," *The Wall Street Journal*, February 5, 1997.

Page 297: *TOKYO—Toyota Motor Corp. expects to resume "near normal" production by Friday at 20 Japanese assembly plants idled after a fire destroyed a supplier's factory last weekend.* . . . Valerie Reitman, "Toyota Sees Output Recovery by Friday, but Many Parts Suppliers Are Hurting," *The Wall Street Journal*, February 5, 1997.

Page 298: *Observers eager to read accounts of profuse corporate apologies . . . Buried in news summaries . . .was the following brief item: "Toyota Resumes Most Production."* . . . Richard L. Holman, "World Wire," *The Wall Street Journal*, February 10, 1997, page A14.

Pages 298–299: *How could the company have rebounded so quickly? . . . a hint appeared in the Journal: "By the following Thursday . . ."* Valerie Reitman, "To the Rescue: Toyota's Fast Rebound after Fire at Supplier Shows Why It Is Tough—Its Affiliates, Going All Out, Built an Unfamiliar Part Within a Matter of Days—Like an Amish Barn-Raising," *The Wall Street Journal*, May 8, 1997, page A1.

Page 300: [Line 10] *In an in-depth study published a year after the fire, Toshihiro Nisiguchi and Alexandre Beaudet found that recovery from the fire was achieved . . . with "very little direct control from Toyota."* Toshihiro Nishiguchi and Alexandre Beaudet, "The Toyota Group and the Aisin Fire," *Sloan Management Review* 40:1, Fall 1998, pages 49–59.

Page 300: *These accounts suggest another possible explanation . . . Nishiguchi and Beaudet agreed that the recovery had been accomplished without "haggling over issues of technical proprietary rights or financial compensation."* Nishiguchi and Beaudet, "The Toyota Group and the Aisin Fire."

Pages 301–302: *Software designers, whose systems have to be dynamic . . . Craig Reynolds set out to create a program that imitated bird flocking . . . Those simple rules worked well and scaled reliably. They were the backbone for the computer-generated animation of bats swarming in a* **Batman** *movie and the stampede in* **The Lion King.** Craig W. Reynolds, "Flocks, Herds, and Schools: A Distributed Behavioral Model," *Computer Graphics* 21:4, 1987, pages 25–34.

Page 304: *In other words, the first task . . . Kayaba, another supplier, parceled out responsibility to three of its suppliers on the basis of equipment availability and appropriateness (the largest had approximately 100 employees, and the smallest only 6), helping them ramp up but doing no P-valve production in its own plant.* Nishiguchi and Beaudet, page 52.

Pages 304–305: *Regardless of where production responsibility landed . . . Brother . . . had to "cobble together a P-valve production line by adapting computerized milling equipment that usually makes sewing machine and typewriter parts."* Valerie Reitman, *The Wall Street Journal*, May 8, 1997.

Page 305: *We've seen that high-velocity organizations are set apart . . . Denso not only shared . . . but "also modified Aisin's design drawings and process instructions to make them more appropriate for machining centers.* Nishiguchi and Beaudet, page 54.

Page 309: *After the Aisin fire, . . . that is exactly the situation that confronted Toyota when 29 ports on America's West Coast were shut down from September 29 to October 8, 2002, due to labor-management conflict.* Hal Varian, "Economic Scene; Rising Productivity Is a Good Thing, Right? Tell That to the Newly Unemployed, *The New York Times*, October 23, 2003; Steven Greenhouse, "Labor Lockout at West's Ports Roils Business," *The New York Times*, October 1, 2002.

Page 309: *After the Aisin fire, . . . Some of the cargo ships were too big to pass through the Panama Canal.* Steven Greenhouse, "Five Questions for David J. Olson: If Longshoremen Strike, Which Businesses Will Suffer?" *The New York Times*, September 8, 2002.

Page 310: *A decade earlier . . . A disruption in shipments from Japan would affect North American body shops, engine production, and final assembly as well as many suppliers that used foreign-sourced materials.* Toyota: United States Operations, company brochure, available at http://www.toyota.com/about/our_business/operations/USOperations_FINAL.pdf.

Page 311: [Line 9] *Materials manufactured but not yet loaded could be diverted, but materials already at sea had to be replaced.* Vanessa Hua, "Auto Plant Takes to the Air, Alternative to Locked-Out Ports Is Extremely Expensive," *The San Francisco Chronicle*, October 8, 2002, page B1.

Chapter 11

Page 328: *patient falls are 86 percent lower, and birth injury rates are nearly three-quarters lower.* See the following articles, arranged in chronological order:

D. B. Pryor et al. "The Clinical Transformation of Ascension Health: Eliminating All Preventable Injuries and Deaths," *Joint Commission Journal on Quality and Patient Safety* 32:6, June 2006, pages 299–308.

J. S. Rose, et al., "A Leadership Framework for Culture Change in Health Care," *Joint Commission Journal on Quality and Patient Safety* 32:8, August 2006, pages 433–442.

W. Gibbons, H. T. Shanks, P. Kleinhelter, and P. Jones, "Eliminating Facility-Acquired Pressure Ulcers at Ascension Health," *Joint Commission Journal on Quality and Patient Safety* 32:9, September 2006, pages 488–496.

D. Berriel-Cass, F. W. Adkins, P. Jones, and M. G. Fakih, "Eliminating Nosocomial Infections at Ascension Health," *Joint Commission Journal on Quality and Patient Safety* 32:11, November 2006, pages 612–620.

F. Mazza, et al., "Eliminating Birth Trauma at Ascension Health," *Joint Commission Journal on Quality and Patient Safety* 33:1, January 2007, page 15–24.

S. Tolchin, et al., "Eliminating Preventable Death at Ascension Health," *Joint Commission Journal on Quality and Patient Safety* 33:3, March 2007, pages 145–154.

H. Ewing, et al., "Eliminating Perioperative Adverse Events at Ascension Health," *Joint Commission Journal on Quality and Patient Safety* 33:5, May 2007, pages 256–266.

A. D. Lancaster, et al., "Preventing Falls and Eliminating Injury at Ascension Health," *Joint Commission Journal on Quality and Patient Safety* 33:7, July 2007, pages 367–375.

K. Butler, et al., "Eliminating Adverse Drug Events at Ascension Health," *Joint Commission Journal on Quality and Patient Safety* 33:9, September 2007, pages 527–536.

A. Hendrick, et al., "The Journey to Zero at Ascension Health: Lessons Learned and Leadership Perspectives," *Joint Commission Journal on Quality and Patient Safety* 33:12, December 2007, pages 739–749.

Page 328: ***The Mayo Clinic has reported a reduction of more than half in medical injuries at its hospitals.*** Steven J. Spear, Donald M. Berwick, "A New Design for Healthcare Delivery," *Boston Globe*, November 23, 2007.

Page 328: ***Hospitals that have participated in the Institute for Healthcare Improvement's 100,000 Lives Campaign . . . An estimate at 18 months into the program was that more than 120,000 avoidable deaths hadn't occurred.*** See the following:

"Hospital Initiative to Cut Errors Finds About 122,300 Lives Saved," *The Wall Street Journal*, quoting an Associated Press report.

C. J. McCannon, A. D. Hackbarth, and F. A. Griffin, "Miles to Go: An Introduction to the 5 Million Lives Campaign," *Joint Commission Journal on Quality and Patient Safety* 33:8, August 2007, pages 477–484.

S. Meisel, P. Phelps, and M. Meisel, "Case Study: Reducing Narcotic Oversedation Across an Integrated Health System," *Joint Commission Journal on Quality and Patient Safety* 33:9, September 2007, pages 543–548.

F. Federico, "Preventing Harm from High-Alert Medications," *Joint Commission Journal on Quality and Patient Safety* 33:9, September 2007, pages 537–542.

K. D. Duncan, "Preventing Pressure Ulcers: The Goal Is Zero," *Joint Commission Journal on Quality and Patient Safety* 33:10, October 2007, pages 605–610.

K. M. LeMaster, "Reducing Incidence and Prevalence of Hospital-Acquired Pressure Ulcers at Genesis Medical Center," *Joint Commis-*

sion Journal on Quality and Patient Safety 33:10, October 2007, pages 611–616.

J. Fitzgerald, G. Kanter, and E. Benjamin, "Case Study: Preventing Surgical Complications at Baystate Medical Center," *Joint Commission Journal on Quality and Patient Safety* 33:11, November 2007, pages 666–671.

F. A. Griffin, "Reducing Surgical Complications," *Joint Commission Journal on Quality and Patient Safety* 33:11, November 2007, pages 660–665.

L. R. Peterson, D. M. Hacek, and A. Robicsek, "Case Study: An MRSA Intervention at Evanston Northwestern Healthcare," *Joint Commission Journal on Quality and Patient Safety* 33:12, December 2007, pages 732–738.

F. A. Griffin, "Reducing Methicillin-Resistant Staphylococcus aureus (MRSA) Infections," *Joint Commission Journal on Quality and Patient Safety* 33:12, December 2007, pages 726–731.

Page 335: ***The medical staff at Allegheny General Hospital (AGH) focused on the problem . . . Allegheny General Hospital: Providing Better Care for Sick Patients*** This account is based on Richard P. Shannon, Diane Frndak, Naida Grunden, Jon C. Lloyd, Cheryl Herbert, Bhavin Patel, Daniel Cummins, Alexander H. Shannon, Paul H. O'Neill, Steven J. Spear, "Using Real-Time Problem Solving to Eliminate Central Line Infections," *Joint Commission Journal on Quality and Patient Safety* 32:9 September 2006, pages 479–487.

Page 335: ***These infections add $3,700 to $29,000 to the cost of care for patients who become ill . . .***

Tamara D. Pittet and R. P. Wenzel, "Nosocomial Bloodstream Infection in Critically Ill Patients: Excess Length of Stay, Extra Costs, and Attributable Mortality," *JAMA* 271, 1994, pages 1598–1601.

S. Saint, "Prevention of Intravascular Catheter-Related Infection," Chapter 16 of *Making Health Care Safer: A Critical Analysis of Patient Safety Practices*, AHRQ Evidence Report, Number 43, July 20, 2001.

S. M. Berenholtz, P. J. Pronovost, P. A. Lipsett, et al., "Eliminating Catheter-Related Bloodstream Infections in the Intensive Care Unit," *Critical Care Medicine* 32, 2004, pages 2014–2020.

L. Soufir, J. F. Timsit, C. Mahe, J. Carlet, B. Regnier, and S. Chevret. "Attributable Morbidity and Mortality of Catheter-Related Septicemia in Critically Ill Patients: A Matched, Risk-Adjusted Cohort Study, *Infection Control Hospital Epidemiology* 20:6, 1999, pages 396–401.

Page 349: ***Remember my friend Mark Schmidhofer . . . As a process it has been criticized for its cost, its length, and the mismatch between what medical students are taught and what new doctors need to know.*** D. Adams, "Student Debt Helps Drive Students into Specialty Matches," *American Medical News* 46, 2003, pages 10–12.

Page 350: ***When we looked at medical education reform proposals . . . expanding the curriculum with courses such as medical ethics . . .*** S. W. Bloom, "Structure and Ideology in Medical Education: An Analysis of Resistance to Change," *Journal of Health and Social Behavior* 29, 1988, pages 294–306.

Page 350: ***When we looked at medical education reform . . . some reformers think a medical education should last even longer.*** M. E. Whitcomb, "From the Editor: The General Professional Education of the Physician: Is Four Years Enough Time? *Academic Medicine* 77, 2002, page 846; D. Nutter, M. Whitcomb, "The AAMC Project on the Clinical Education of Medical Students." *Association of American Medical Colleges*, 2002; S. Weinberger and M. Whitcomb, "The Clinical Education of Medical Students: Report on Millennium Competencies I & II, *Association of American Medical Colleges*, 2001.

Chapter 12

Page 363: ***Here is one last thought: The title of Philip Crosby's seminal book says it all:*** Quality is Free. ***Crosby, along with W. Edwards Deming and Joseph Juran . . .*** Philip B. Crosby, *Quality Is Free: The Art of Making Quality Certain*, McGraw-Hill, 1979; W. Edwards Deming, *Quality, Productivity, and Competitive Position*, MIT Press, 1982; W. Edwards Deming, *Out of the Crisis*, MIT Center for Advanced Engineering Study, 1986; Joseph Juran and Frank M. Gryna, Jr., *Quality Planning and Analysis*, McGraw-Hill, 1980.

INDEX

About the Author

Steven J. Spear, four-time winner of the Shingo Prize and recipient of the McKinsey Award, is a senior lecturer at MIT and former assistant professor at the Harvard Business School. A senior fellow at the Institute for Healthcare Improvement, he is the author of numerous articles appearing in academic and trade publications, including the *Harvard Business Review* and *The New York Times*.